Second Edition

Confidence in Public Speaking

Paul Edward Nelson
Ohio University, Athens

Judy Cornelia Pearson
Ohio University, Athens

wcb
Wm. C. Brown Publishers
Dubuque, Iowa

Book Team
Judith A. Clayton Senior Developmental Editor
Lynne Niznik Assistant Developmental Editor
Vickie Blosch Production Editor
Kevin Pruessner Designer
Mavis M. Oeth Permissions Editor
Shirley M. Charley Visual Research Editor

wcb
group

Wm. C. Brown Chairman of the Board
Mark C. Falb President and Chief Executive Officer

wcb

Wm. C. Brown Publishers, College Division
Lawrence E. Cremer President
James L. Romig Vice-President, Product Development
David Wm. Smith Vice-President, Marketing
David A. Corona Vice-President, Production and Design
E. F. Jogerst Vice-President, Cost Analyst
Marcia H. Stout Marketing Manager
Linda M. Galarowicz Director of Marketing Research
William A. Moss Production Editorial Manager
Marilyn A. Phelps Manager of Design
Mary M. Heller Visual Research Manager

For our children:

Dana Jergen
Christopher John
Christopher James
Kathryn Cornelia
Benjamin Joseph
Rebekah Kristina

Contents

7 Language in Your Speech 136

8 Delivery and Visual Aids 160

9 Informative Speaking 192

10 Persuasive Speaking 222

11 Informative and Evaluative Listening 258

Preface

This newly revised second edition of *Confidence in Public Speaking* has been written for students in their first college course in public speaking. As its title implies, the text attempts to increase students' confidence as public speakers through an understanding of concepts and practice in actually preparing and delivering public speeches. To reduce anxiety, students begin with brief performances based on easy-to-master skills and then progress to increasingly complex performances that build on the skills previously learned and applied.

Experienced instructors will find that they can easily supplement this book with their own past lessons. Inexperienced teachers and graduate teaching assistants will find that the text and the instructor's manual will provide them with the guidance they may need.

Confidence in Public Speaking takes student interests into account and is written so that concepts are relatively easy to understand and apply. Public speaking terms and concepts are set in boldface type and are defined in context and in a vocabulary section at the end of each chapter. Other pedagogical aids invite immediate application of these concepts.

Organization

Confidence in Public Speaking is based on the assumptions that students learn best in small, palatable increments that can be mastered with relative ease, and that effective learning proceeds from the simple to the complex. Thus concepts and applications move from the shorter and simpler to the longer and more complex.

Chapter 1, An Introduction to Public Speaking, provides an overview of public speaking by presenting a conceptual foundation for all that follows. The student discovers the communication process and how it applies to public speaking.

Chapter 2, You as a Public Speaker, examines the student as a speaker, the relationship between self-concept and confidence, and the concept of source credibility as it functions in public speaking. Chapter 3, Analyzing Your Audience, examines demographic, knowledge, interest, and attitude information that is useful to the public speaker. The chapter reveals both formal and informal ways of gathering these four kinds of information about an audience.

Chapter 4, Speech Preparation: Selecting a Topic and Stating Your Purpose, provides techniques for discovering topics and purposes appropriate to both speaker and audience. Chapter 5, Finding, Evaluating, and Organizing Support Material, offers suggestions and techniques on gathering information from interviews and written resources, taking notes on that information, and organizing a speech according to any of six patterns of organization, each with examples from student papers. Chapter 6, Introducing and Concluding Your Speech, focuses on the functions and components of introductions and conclusions. Chapter 7, Language in Your Speech, reveals eight ways speakers can use definitions in their speeches, four ways they can achieve literacy, and five ways they can improve their descriptive powers.

Chapter 8, Delivery and Visual Aids, concentrates on vocal and bodily aspects of delivery and on the potentials and problems of using various visual aids. Chapter 9, Informative Speaking, surveys the purposes, rhetorical principles, and learning principles of informative speeches. Chapter 10, Persuasive Speaking, discusses the purposes, principles, and strategies of persuasive speaking. The last chapter, chapter 11, Informative and Evaluative Listening, provides useful suggestions on how to listen to and evaluate public speeches. Some teachers may wish to assign this chapter early in the course.

Special Features *Confidence* is filled with pedagogical aids to enhance student learning. Most chapters include a content outline, behavioral objectives, application exercises, checklists, application assignments, vocabulary lists, and numerous illustrations.

Forty-six application exercises, which appear after concepts, are introduced and explained, allowing students to immediately apply what they have learned.

Seven checklists provide an opportunity for students to check their own progress in meeting chapter objectives. For example, the checklists for source credibility for the informative speech and the persuasive speech give students a means of specifically measuring whether they have applied the credibility suggestions of the text to their speeches.

Eighteen application assignments, which appear near the ends of the chapters, include both oral and written assignments. These assignments are organized incrementally, so that students can learn to master the skills in a way that both reduces speaking anxiety and improves confidence. The series begins with the simplest of ice-breaking performances, in which students reveal information about themselves, and proceeds incrementally to the more complex persuasive speeches of reasons, opposition, and action.

The text ends with a series of eleven appendices, containing student examples of all the speeches and papers assigned except the initial self-introduction. These speeches and papers are not drawn from professional speakers or from *Vital Speeches;* instead, they are actual student speeches that meet the application assignments.

Instructor's Manual

Confidence in Public Speaking is accompanied by an *Instructor's Manual* that includes additional instructions, objectives, and procedures for the speech performances and written assignments in the text; answers to appropriate application exercises; and 36 additional activities. The examination questions include 33 essay questions with answers, 139 true-false questions, and 128 multiple-choice questions. The manual helps the instructor adapt the large number of performances and exercises to fit either a quarter or a semester program.

The Authors

Paul Nelson earned his Ph.D. in Speech and Dramatic Art at the University of Minnesota. He was the basic course director and director of the Honors College at the University of Missouri, served as chair of the Speech Department at Iowa State University, and is now Dean of the College of Communication at Ohio University.

Judy Pearson earned her Ph.D. in Speech Communication at Indiana University. She served as basic course director at Indiana University-Purdue University at Fort Wayne, at Bradley University, and at Iowa State University. She is an Associate Professor in the School of Interpersonal Communication at Ohio University.

We (Paul Edward Nelson and Judy Cornelia Pearson) are a husband-and-wife writing team from Ohio University in Athens, Ohio. We have co-authored two editions of *Confidence in Public Speaking* and another text, *Understanding and Sharing: An Introduction to Speech Communication,* because we enjoy teaching and because we want to share what we have learned about speech communication with others. We also have six children, who provide an incentive for writing these books, which we hope you find useful for your students.

We regard ourselves first and foremost as teachers and enjoy teaching introductory speech courses. We team teach the introductory communication course in Ohio University's School of Interpersonal Communication. Both of us were privileged to win the Central States Speech Association's Outstanding Young Teacher Award.

Together we have had thirty years of experience teaching the basic speech course, and *Confidence in Public Speaking* is part of our effort to share with you and your students the ideas we have learned.

Acknowledgments *Confidence in Public Speaking* is truly a team effort. Our students have given fine speeches and written good papers, which we have used as examples in this book. Our publisher, editors, and reviewers helped us to minimize errors and emphasize strengths. Southeastern Ohio, with its scenic Appalachian foothills, provided a beautiful setting for writing a book.

We give special thanks to our professors at the University of Minnesota and Indiana University, to our colleagues in the Midwest Basic Course Directors' Conference, who share our affection for speech fundamentals, to our highly supportive colleagues at Ohio University, and to our children—for whom the phrase "I have to work on the book" has become a frequent plea. JoAnn Lipsey, Ann Stanley, and Brenda Jones helped proofread the manuscript. The people at Wm. C. Brown Publishers—especially our editor, Judith A. Clayton—have earned our grateful appreciation, as have those faculty members from other colleges and universities who evaluated our work at several stages of development. They include

Lawrence W. Hugenberg; Youngstown State University
Stanford P. Gwin; University of Southern Mississippi
Tom Jenness; University of Idaho, Moscow
Phoebe P. Hollis; University of Nebraska, Omaha
John H. Sloan; Memphis State University
Doris Newburger; Borough of Manhattan Community College

Finally, we hope that you will find *Confidence in Public Speaking* to be a book that works well for you.

Paul Edward Nelson
Judy Cornelia Pearson

Confidence in Public Speaking

Chapter 1

Objectives

After you have completed chapter 1, you should be able to answer the following questions:
  1. What is the difference between students' attitudes toward a public speaking course before and after they take the course?
  2. What are four reasons why you should learn to give public speeches?
  3. What point of view toward learning to give public speeches is expressed in this book?
  4. What are the ten steps in learning the public speaking process?
  5. What are the main components of the public speaking process?
  6. What is unique about the classroom public speaking situation?

An Introduction to Public Speaking

Speech is civilization itself. The word, even the most contradictory word, preserves contact—it is silence which isolates.

Thomas Mann

How do you feel about being a student in a public speaking course? Do you approach the course with enthusiasm because you have good ideas you want to share with others? Or are you taking the course because it is required? Do you welcome the chance to give a speech in front of an audience, or can you think of a hundred other things you would rather do? Whether you welcome public speaking with enthusiasm or approach it with reluctance, you may be comforted to know that a fear of public speaking is widespread and that it can be overcome.

Introduction

More people are afraid of public speaking than they are of heights, water, airplanes, or crowds. The *Bruskin Report* states that Americans' number one fear is public speaking.[1] Most of your fellow students share the same anxiety. Fortunately, nearly everyone in this course will take steps toward overcoming that emotion, because fear springs from a wariness of the unknown. If you have not given many speeches before, or if you have not had previous positive experiences, you are likely to feel some anxiety about giving public speeches. Do you remember how uncomfortable you were the first time you went on a date and knew you were about to encounter your first kiss? How comfortable were you the first time you drove a car? You learned to overcome many of your anxieties through experience. That fact is as true of public speaking as it is of kissing or driving.

At one university, students who had graduated from the business department were asked several years after graduation which courses they found to be most valuable. One might expect business students to value most highly the courses they took in accounting, business law, insurance, or marketing. Instead, the graduates said the courses they took in English and speech—courses in written and spoken communication—were of most value after graduation.[2] You, too, will probably find that the speech course you approached with reluctance turns out to be a course that serves you well both in and out of school.

Why Should You Learn to Give Public Speeches?

Why should you approach this public speaking course with an open-minded willingness to learn? What are you supposed to gain from learning how to select topics, or from preparing and delivering speeches? Keep in mind that public speaking is a useful skill that can improve your personal competence, social development, and professional growth.

Public Speaking Is a Useful Skill

As a student of public speaking, you learn communication skills which you can use in many areas. Not only do teachers speak to students, lawyers to juries, and the clergy to congregations, but sales managers address sales personnel, supervisors address subordinates, and workers address fellow workers. One of the reasons students go to college is to learn skills that will improve their chances of success. Success in most pursuits depends on effective communication skills.

Even people who choose careers that do not seem to demand public speaking skills may eventually learn and use them. One of the authors spent four summers teaching union workers how to give public speeches. These workers had jobs that did not seem to require public speaking. They were boot and shoe makers, assembly line workers, seam welders, and steel workers. However, all of them had been elected officers of their unions and found themselves having to speak frequently to hundreds of union members. None of them had completed college, none of them had taken a course in public speaking, but all of them spent their vacation at a university learning how to give speeches. The union workers found public speaking to be a useful skill.

An Introduction to Public Speaking

You can increase your personal competence by learning how to give public speeches. **Competence** is the quantity and quality of things you can do. If you can draw the plans for a house, do the plumbing, electrical work, and the building, you are much more competent than the person who only knows how to install a light switch. Similarly, the person who can communicate well with individuals, lead a group in solving a problem or making a decision, or address an audience

Public Speaking
Can Increase Your
Personal
Competence

is more competent than the person who can communicate only on a one-to-one basis. When your employer says, "You did such a fine job that I want you to tell others how you did it," you do not want to say, "Sorry, I can't talk in front of a group."

Increasing your personal competence has implications that go far beyond job performance: it can increase your feelings of self-worth. If you cannot see yourself delivering a public speech, then that role will be difficult for you. However, if you learn how to deliver a public speech, you will have the satisfaction of conquering a common fear and will be able to deliver speeches whenever you want to. Learning to speak publicly, like going on a diet or stopping smoking or climbing mountains, increases your feelings of self-worth.

Public Speaking Can Help Your Social Development

Your skill in public speaking is a mark of social maturity. You learned how to communicate in small steps over a long period of time. First, you learned how to communicate with your parents to get food, sleep, and other physical comforts. As you grew older and went to school, you learned how to communicate with your peers. Now, much later, you are learning how to build on this capacity to interact with an increasingly larger audience by giving public speeches to a class. This skill may give you the courage to speak out more frequently in your classes, to run for a position in student government, or to accept a job that includes speaking to others.

Your skill in public speaking can give you special status in many ways. Recently the authors attended a class reunion. Few in the class had attended college or had any public speaking experience. The person selected to be master of ceremonies was someone who was unafraid of public speaking. He was accorded special social status by his classmates because he could do the job with confidence.

Public Speaking Can Help Your Professional Growth

Whatever you choose as an occupation, you will find that in most jobs communicating with an audience will be necessary for success. The lineworker typically does not have to give speeches or even talk in small groups, but if that person advances to supervisor, he or she must communicate with subordinates. Office workers may not have to address groups, but their managers do. The president of a large company has to address a board of directors, stockholders, employees, reporters, and the public.

Success in almost any occupation increases the necessity for communication. Some of this communication involves public speaking. The football player who never dreamed he would be a public speaker is asked to speak at athletic banquets. A graduate student in speech finds himself tutoring the center on the Vikings football team because he needs advice on public speaking. Even the stereotypical scientist who works alone in her lab finds that success in the lab means invitations to deliver papers at professional meetings. Similarly, the student elected president of the student body, chairperson of the business club, or leader of a group finds that public speaking accompanies professional success.

Some of the communication involved in professional work occurs in a small group context or with just one other person. Nonetheless, a course in public speaking can serve you well in these situations, too. Public speaking skills transfer to other communication situations. Your ability to demonstrate your credibility, to analyze an audience, to state your purpose, to organize your ideas, to introduce and conclude your remarks, to select appropriate language, and to use your body and voice effectively—these can all be as important in small-group communication as they are in public speaking.

Our original question was, "Why should you learn how to give public speeches?" The answer is that public speaking is a useful skill that can improve your personal competence, help your social development, and enhance your professional growth. In the next section you will discover the point of view toward public speaking that we emphasize in this book.

A Point of View on Public Speaking

Since you are a student in public speaking, you have a right to know the authors' point of view toward the subject. In stating it, we recognize that a course in public speaking involves a three-way interaction among textbook, teacher, and student. Each part may have alternative views that are as valid as the ones you find here. The three words that summarize our approach in this text are *confidence, understanding,* and *practice.*

Confidence

Confidence means that you have trust in yourself or that you have a feeling of assurance or certainty about yourself. Public speaking is intimately linked to confidence. Confidence is learned over time through repeated positive experiences. You might "lack confidence" to give a public speech because you have not given many speeches before, but after you have prepared and delivered several, your confidence will increase.

From our point of view you can gain confidence in the public speaking class if you, as a student, are given the maximum opportunity to deliver many speeches, some short and some relatively long, in front of an audience. We encourage the idea of learning the skills in increments, one or several at a time, during many speaking experiences. All complex skills are learned this way. The master electrician starts off as an apprentice who begins by running after wires and tools, not by wiring a house. The skilled surgeon begins by dissecting frogs and fetal pigs in freshman biology, studies the human body in medical school, and only much later performs operations. Public speaking is a complex skill that requires an ability to select appropriate topics; to interview and conduct library research; to organize materials; to inform through illustration, example, and demonstration; and to persuade through argument, evidence, and emotion. It is unlikely that a first course in public speaking can be anything more than an introduction to this complex skill. In fact, you could spend a lifetime developing it.

As you deliver speeches in class, there are some ways you can help increase confidence in yourself and others. The guiding principle is that speakers need to be told in many ways the things they are doing well. One of the authors has the

class applaud every speech. This is one way to reward a speaker, but it does not specify exactly what, if anything, the speaker did well. You can let your classmates know what they did well by telling them after their speech, either in or out of class. In addition, in your speech, you can mention other students' speeches in a complimentary way. You can imitate a strategy which a classmate used successfully. If you tell other people what they did well, they may do the same thing for you, and all will benefit.

An Introduction to Public Speaking

You gain confidence, then, over time, with repeated positive experiences and encouragement from instructors and fellow students. You can also gain confidence by avoiding those things your audience does not like in your presentations. Your teacher may orally critique the speeches of the day and suggest improvements; or students and teacher may offer written critiques. Applause, written compliments, and suggestions for improvement will increase your confidence with each speaking experience.

A second aspect of the authors' point of view is that public speaking as a skill depends on your understanding of the public speaking process. Do you know how to find all the current information on your topic? Do you know how to analyze an audience so that you can be reasonably sure one argument is a better one to use than another? Do you know how to support an argument with evidence and which evidence is most acceptable to this particular audience? These are just a few of the many skills you need in preparing a speech. To give you an overview of these and other public speaking skills, complete checklist 1. **Understanding**

_____ 1. Have you brainstormed for ideas you can use in your speech?

_____ 2. Have you selected a topic from those ideas that can be narrowed to the time limit and that is appropriate to your audience?

_____ 3. Have you analyzed the audience so your topic, message, and organization will be appropriate to that audience?

_____ 4. Have you researched and interviewed for information and ideas you can use in your speech?

_____ 5. Have you developed the content of a speech by selecting appropriate information and arguments?

_____ 6. Have you composed an introduction that gains attention, introduces the topic, builds credibility, and relates your topic to you and your audience?

_____ 7. Have you organized a speech in a pattern appropriate to the topic and the audience?

_____ 8. Have you developed a conclusion that summarizes, synthesizes, inspires, or invites action?

_____ 9. Have you practiced a speech alone or in front of others so you can deliver it with a minimum of attention to notes?

_____ 10. Have you examined and analyzed written and oral comments to determine effective and ineffective aspects of a speech?

Checklist 1: Overview of Skills in Public Speaking

These ten skills are discussed in this text. They may seem forbidding on first reading, but you will have the entire term to develop them. You may find that you already have some of these skills and need only polish them. In any case, you will be given a great deal of information about each skill, and you will have the opportunity to practice all of them in your public speaking class.

Reprinted by permission. © 1979 NEA, Inc.

Practice

The third element of the authors' point of view is that public speaking cannot be learned entirely from a book. A book can greatly improve your understanding, but it cannot give you confidence or teach you the skills of public speaking that you can develop through practice. Reading about public speaking is like reading the ten commandments: they are easy to read—the ideas are within human understanding—but they are very difficult to practice. For instance, a book can tell you about delivery: voice variety, gestures, movement, facial expression, vocalized pauses, and so on. However, will reading about it keep you from saying "Ahh" in your speech? No, learning to speak in public requires practice. The "Born Loser" has selected an unfortunate time to practice his speech; you may wish to consider more carefully where and when you practice.

To support the notion of practice, this text includes application exercises. Most take little time, but all are designed to help you put ideas into practice as you learn them. The exercises do not have to be completed in class; with the instructor's permission, you can do most of them on your own. Completing the exercises will help in both your speeches and exams, because all of us remember what we do longer than we remember what we read. As the old Chinese proverb states: "Tell me, I'll forget. Show me, I may remember. But involve me and I'll understand."

The application exercises will also reinforce your confidence. Some are best completed if you perform them. You will be able to perform the exercises and your speeches best if you have a roommate, wife or husband, father or mother, or friend who is willing to listen to you. You can increase your confidence by successfully completing the application exercises.

In brief, the authors firmly believe that students best learn to speak in public as they become confident, and that confidence is developed from positive reactions to what they do well and specific comments on those areas in which they need improvement; from an understanding of the process of public speaking—from brainstorming for ideas to examining the comments after a speech; and from practice, by completing the application exercises and delivering speeches in class. Finally, we believe that students can best learn—to be confident, to understand, and to practice—in increments, because complex skills are easiest to master in small, manageable steps.

One of the reviewers who evaluated the first edition of *Confidence in Public Speaking* summarized the approach well:

> The authors' basic approach, that confidence can be gained through doing incremental speech assignments, is psychologically sound and actually *does work* with the insecure speech student. I have observed initially fearful pupils end the semester with a healthy attitude of enthusiasm and with a sense of achievement. Because the first assignment is ungraded and each succeeding task is given incremental value, the student is encouraged to build toward expertise. The grading process is used as a yardstick to measure growth rather than as a punitive device. Oral positive comments and applause are valuable for encouragement, and written negative and positive criticisms as positive reinforcement for change and improvement. I heartily endorse the use of written feedback by the teacher and student peers. The authors wisely realize that support helps the psyche but that knowledge is developed by understanding the course content.

Next we turn to the components of the public speaking process.

Components of the Public Speaking Process

The public speech is a message a speaker delivers to an audience in a particular situation. A message is predominantly **verbal**, unless the "speaker" is a mime, but some of it is **nonverbal** as well. A message is conveyed by facial expression; gesture; volume, variety, and tone of voice; pauses and silence; as well as by words, and sounds that are not words. The words can be familiar or unfamiliar, monosyllabic or polysyllabic, formal or informal. A **message,** then, is a blend of these verbal and nonverbal components that is meaningful to an audience. In public speaking, the message is preconceived, intentional, and purposeful.

Components of the Public Speaking Process

1. The message
2. The speaker
3. The audience
4. The situation

The Message

The public speaker should be aware that an audience actually receives numerous messages during a speech. Some of these messages are verbal—composed of words; others are non-verbal. Anything your behavior conveys, from the time you rise to give your speech until you sit down afterward, may constitute a message to your audience. For instance, suppose you were up until 2 A.M. studying for an exam. You are ready for your speech, but you just finished taking an exam in the last hour and your head is still spinning from the five questions you didn't even have time to answer. When your speech teacher calls on you after four other speeches have been given, you are slow to respond. You proceed to the front of the room. Once there you take longer than usual to find your note cards. During your speech you lack your usual vibrancy and dynamism. You finish with relief and hurry back to your seat. One message received by the audience might be an almost unanimous one: "The speaker certainly didn't want to give that speech." That would be an example of an unintentional message.

Public speaking messages should be intentional. That is, the speaker should be conscious of every word and movement, aware of the consequences, and relatively sure of the audience's probable response. In the hypothetical situation described, you, the speaker, may have intended to convey a message about U.S. foreign policy. Instead, the main message projected was that you didn't want to give the speech.

Public speaking messages are preconceived. They can be memorized or delivered from a manuscript—in the latter case the speaker reads every word. Although Mark Twain is reported to have said that it usually takes more than three weeks to prepare a good impromptu speech, impromptu actually means without prior preparation. Usually the public speech is delivered extemporaneously, which means that considerable preparation went into the speech even though it is supposed to sound spontaneous and fresh. Whether a public speech is memorized, read from a manuscript, or given extemporaneously, it is preconceived or preplanned.

Public speaking messages are purposeful. The two most common purposes of public speeches are to inform and to persuade. Often both purposes are involved in a single speech. When the president of the United States addresses the nation on television, he is often trying to inform us of some national problem and to persuade us to embrace his position on it. Even a comedian's patter can be considered public speaking because it is intentional, preconceived, and purposeful. Indeed, comedians are among the most skillful speakers in anticipating audience responses.

The Speaker

The **source** of the message in the public speaking process is the speaker. He or she is responsible for conveying the message. The speaker is the focus of attention to such a degree that he or she is usually the only one facing all the other people in the room. Interaction with the audience is limited, the only exchange occurring in a question and answer period, if one exists.

In the classroom the speaker is usually a fellow student. This situation reduces some of the mystery about the speaker—the credibility that an "outsider" sometimes commands. Still, a classroom speaker may speak with authority by virtue of research, experience, talent, or age. A student speaker is also generally heard more than once, so he or she can build on what was said before. The individual who has given several good preliminary speeches may be remembered as a good speaker for later speeches. A kind of halo effect occurs. The student who gives high quality speeches from the beginning gets high grades from the teacher and fellow students, which inspires the speaker to continue to give good speeches.

The third component of the public speaking process is the audience. The number of persons in the audience can range from very few to thousands; in the classroom they usually number from fifteen to fifty. Even though there is little verbal exchange or interaction with an audience (unless there is a question and answer period), the audience still provides valuable feedback.

The Audience

Feedback refers to verbal and nonverbal cues from which a speaker can infer audience response. For instance, a speaker may hear people laugh at her joke, see people frown at a repulsive example, or watch people drift into daydreams as their attention wanders. Smiles, gasps, groans, and applause are all audience feedback. The feedback that you receive from an audience will cause you to adjust your speech. For instance, if an audience appears confused, you might add examples to clarify your point. If audience members are bored, you may want to delete sections of your speech. As we shall demonstrate in chapter 3, the effective public speaker is well aware of cues from his or her audience and adapts to them. An example of feedback is provided in Herb's response to Dagwood.

Members of the classroom audience have one characteristic that makes them unusual. With the exception of the instructor, they are all students. They may also have other common characteristics. They may be similar in age, from the same geographical area, from families of similar income level, or predominantly

Catholic, Jewish, or Protestant. The single characteristic that causes the student audience to be a highly sympathetic one for you is that they, too, must give speeches to the same group. Finally, the classroom audience is unusual because one person, the teacher, is in the audience grading the speech.

The Situation

The particular public speaking **situation** can make a big difference to the public speaker—how the speaker decides on the appropriate topics, or the words that can and cannot be used, and even how much to say about the issues involved. A topic that is appropriate in a large inner-city community college may be quite inappropriate in a small rural four-year college.

More specifically, in a classroom situation, time is limited, the speakers and audience are students, several speakers may have to speak one directly after another, and questions and comments may be invited. This situation is one in which you are expected to give extemporaneous speeches to inform and to persuade, and you are being evaluated as a speaker.

Compared to most public speaking situations, the classroom situation is controlled. It is a place to learn how to give public speeches in a positive atmosphere. The class is given to help students learn public speaking skills. The instructor is employed for that purpose. The audience consists entirely of fellow students who are there to learn the same ideas. A classroom speaker might not receive the same empathy from an outside audience that he or she might from a classroom audience. The classroom is a safe place to give speeches. You cannot lose your job, forfeit a commission, or be sued as you might if you were facing employers, buyers, or a group antagonistic to your topic. Instead, you can make mistakes, experiment, and learn without dire consequences.

The Process

Perhaps you are wondering why this section is called "components of the public speaking **process**." The word *process* underlines the dynamic nature of public speaking—the fact that the speech is an active force in people's minds from the topic's inception in the speaker's mind until the last person forgets it. The word *process* highlights the idea that public speaking is an interrelated art that functions through the interplay among speaker, audience, and situation. These three components are not autonomous; none can function alone. There is no speaker without an audience, and both speaker and audience appear in a context called the situation.

Overview of Increments

The point of view expressed in this text is that public speaking consists of gaining confidence, understanding the process of public speaking, and practicing speeches. To gain confidence and understanding you can learn the skills in gradual increments by completing the application exercises as you come to them. In other words, you need to master some skills before you can master others. The following overview gives the main topics to be covered in the remainder of the text.

Increments Used in the Text

1. Source credibility
2. Audience analysis
3. Appropriateness of topics
4. Organization of information
5. Functions of introduction and conclusion of speech
6. Language in speeches
7. Delivery
8. Purposes of speeches
9. Listening and evaluation

Chapter 2 begins the process by exploring those skills you can develop to project yourself as a competent, trustworthy, and dynamic speaker. Chapter 3 focuses on audience analysis skills: developing questions to ask the audience, drawing inferences from questionnaires and observation, and adapting to the audience. Chapter 4 concentrates on finding an appropriate topic for speaker and audience and stating a speech purpose so that the results can be assessed. Chapter 5 helps you select support materials for your speech by means of personal experience, interviews, and printed materials. It also suggests ways to locate and organize your information. Chapter 6 reveals the functions that the introduction and conclusion of a speech fulfill. Chapter 7 discusses the language in your speech: the particular characteristics of spoken language, methods of sharing meanings, ways to achieve literacy in oral discourse, and methods of improving your descriptive powers.

After you have analyzed the audience, selected a topic, and composed the introduction, body, and conclusion in appropriate language, chapter 8 offers you ways of improving your delivery and your use of visual aids. Chapters 9 and 10 focus on two of the most common speech purposes—to inform and to persuade. The last chapter, chapter 11, considers some methods of informative and evaluative listening, so that you can become as skilled at comprehending and critically listening as you are at delivering speeches to an audience. The appendixes include samples of student speeches to illustrate the assignments that appear throughout the book.

Preparing a Speech before You Are Ready

Many speech professors have their students give a brief speech very early in the course. Sometimes the teacher will ask students to introduce themselves (see the exercise at the end of the chapter); at other times the teacher will ask students to reveal what is unique about themselves, to relate an interesting experience from their home life or work, or to interview and introduce another person in the class. In any case, the first speech can come before you are ready. The following

suggestions are designed to help you with that first speaking experience in your public speaking class. You may or may not be able to accomplish all the suggestions listed here, but some of them may be useful in your first experience.

1. Try to speak conversationally, but loud enough for everyone to hear.
2. Try to speak at a relaxed pace, because fellow students are often encouraged to write down information gleaned in this first speech.
3. Try to focus on a few aspects of the topic that will be of most interest to your audience, instead of consuming lots of time telling everything you know about it.
4. See if you can cast your speech in the form of a story, a narrative that will address the topic and be memorable to the audience.
5. Help the audience to get acquainted with you, your name, and the kind of person you are, by means of the information that you impart. You can help, for example, by writing your name on the board, pronouncing it carefully, and repeating it for the audience.
6. If you have a few minutes to get ready, write down a few key words to remind yourself what you intend to cover, so that you will not be nervous about forgetting. Perhaps these few suggestions will assist you in your first classroom speech. The remainder of this book is designed to help you with slightly longer and more complex speeches.

Conclusion   Public speaking is a useful skill which can improve your personal competence, help your social development, and enhance your professional growth. To learn the skills of public speaking, you should develop self-confidence by understanding the ideas and practicing the skills that are explained throughout the text. You must understand that public speaking is a communication process in which message, speaker, and audience interact in a particular situation. You can enrich your life by learning how to develop and deliver speeches yourself, as well as by learning how to listen in order to gain information and to evaluate the speeches of others. You will move toward that goal by reading chapter 2.

16   An Introduction to Public Speaking

In order to learn the names of your classmates and something about them (1) write on the board those items that members of the class wish to know about one another—name, major, year in school, hometown, hobbies, marital status, and so on; (2) have the class introduce themselves according to the items on the board; and (3) have each speaker give the first name of the person who came before him or her. (Number 3 is optional, because it is easier to do if the class can assemble in a circle and move systematically around it from speaker to speaker.) Classmates should take notes on the information as a first step in audience analysis. In later speeches, the more you know about the audience the better you will be able to inform and persuade.

feedback Verbal and nonverbal indications from the audience that let the speaker know the audience's response; includes frowns, quizzical looks, raised eyebrows (nonverbal cues), or questions after the speech (verbal cues).

message All that you convey to your audience from the time you rise to speak until you sit down; in public speaking the message should be intentional, preconceived, and purposeful.

nonverbal message What you communicate to your audience through gestures, movement, voice variety, eye contact, pauses, silence, clothing, words, and sounds that are not words.

situation The circumstances or context in which public speaking occurs. The classroom public speaking situation is characterized by strict time limits, particular kinds of speeches, and a specific type of delivery in front of a student audience.

source In public speaking, another name for the speaker—the person who communicates the message to the audience.

verbal message What you convey to your audience through your words, the primary means of conveying information in public speaking.

1. "What Are Americans Afraid of?" *The Bruskin Report,* 1973, No. 53.
2. Barbara A. Magill, Roger P. Murphy, and Lilian O. Feinberg, "Industrial Administration Survey Shows Need for Communication Study," *American Business Communication Association Bulletin,* 38 (1975), 31–33.

Chapter 2

Objectives

After you have completed chapter 2, you should be able to answer the following questions:

1. How does your self-perception relate to you as a public speaker?
2. How is the idea that attitudes follow behavior linked to your development as a public speaker?
3. What is the relationship between source credibility and earning the right to speak?
4. What are four dimensions of source credibility?

When you have completed chapter 2, you should have practiced skills in

1. Describing your own perceptions of yourself;
2. Relating yourself to topics appropriate for you;
3. Determining ways to communicate your competence;
4. Discerning what will help you gain your audience's trust;
5. Discovering values that you share with the audience;
6. Interviewing another person for information; and
7. Introducing another person to improve his or her credibility.

Application Exercises

1. Your self-perception.
2. Who you are; what you can speak about.
3. Signaling your competence.
4. The tokens of trust.
5. Coorientation: the roots of commonality.

You as a
Public Speaker

Speech is human, silence is divine, yet also brutish
and dead; therefore we must learn both acts.

Thomas Carlyle

In your public speaking class, you will be the source of messages. How you see   **Introduction**
yourself, your **self-perception,** is very important in determining how you will be
viewed as a source. Your self-perception, or self-concept, is composed of two parts:
your self-image and your self-esteem. Your self-image is how you view yourself—
as a student, as a speaker, and as a person. Your self-esteem is how you feel about
your self-image—whether you see yourself, for example, as interesting, successful, or happy. Do you view yourself as bright, witty, ambitious, and analytical?

19

Your behavior as a public speaker will be influenced by how you perceive yourself—by the self-image and self-esteem that you hold. For instance, if you view yourself as highly confident, you will probably behave that way in front of an audience; if you feel you lack confidence, you will probably convey that feeling to the audience.

As you learn to give public speeches, you may change the way you see yourself. As you gain experience in delivering speeches, you may discover that you are a person who can successfully deliver an effective speech. People who think well of themselves seem to have an easier time giving speeches than those who do not. One of the purposes of a course in public speaking is to help you perceive yourself positively as a public speaker. This can make a big difference in the classroom and an even bigger change in your life.

One key to changing your self-perception is to recognize that, in many cases, your attitudes follow your behavior.[1] You have to eat black bread (behavior) before you can develop positive attitudes toward black bread. You have to dance (behavior) before you can develop a positive attitude toward dancing. You do not have to wait until you gain a positive attitude about yourself to start behaving as if you had that attitude. Instead, if you behave in a certain manner, your attitudes will change to account for the behavior. You have to act like a confident public speaker before you can develop positive attitudes about *being* a confident speaker.

One of the authors had a student who was having difficulty as a public speaker. In class this student exhibited many signs of shyness. She smiled too quickly and too long, spoke softly, and stood as far away from the audience as possible. Her classmates, in their comments on her speech, wrote statements like: "Don't be afraid of us; we're your friends"; "Doesn't speak loudly enough to hear"; "Hides in her notes. Seems afraid to look at us."

In her next speech this student was determined to overcome her shyness, which had resulted in ineffective speeches and low grades. She practiced her speech five times in an empty classroom. She practiced speaking with greater volume and intensity. She walked right up to the front row to show her new assertiveness. She even practiced behaving righteously indignant by pretending that the audience was not taking her seriously.

After this preparation, she gave her most effective speech. Her teacher and her classmates told her so. She was behaving more boldly than her self-perception would ordinarily permit, but her actions depicted her true feelings about the topic more than they had before. Attitudes followed behavior: she felt better about the speech than about any other she had delivered. The experience modified her self-perception because she began to see herself as a person who could give an effective speech. Her success increased her feelings of self-confidence.

Learning to become assertive is related to self-perception, as is learning to be less dominant. A student who was an experienced contest speaker gave every speech as if he were delivering a formal oration. From his experience and point of view, speaking in that manner was consistent with his self-perception. But,

You as a Public Speaker

standing behind a podium, speaking in formal language, and assuming a strong, dominant relationship with an audience is not appropriate for all topics, purposes, and audiences. His classmates thought he seemed a bit lofty, condescending, and domineering. They also thought he had an excellent speaking voice, great self-confidence, and good organization.

Both of these students were limited by their self-perceptions: one could not see herself as assertive; the other could not see himself as anything but assertive. They saw themselves as being only one kind of person. Similarly, some students are limited because they see themselves only as comedians, eternal optimists, debaters, intellectuals. A public speaker who hopes to address different audiences about a variety of topics needs to develop flexibility, so that he or she can approach audiences in ways that are appropriate for the topic, the audience, and the situation.

How the audience perceives you as a speaker comes under the heading of source credibility. In the next section we will explore this subject and suggest ways in which you can indicate to an audience why you have the right to speak to them about a particular topic.

Circle the following adjectives that best describe the way you perceive yourself. Underline the adjectives that best describe the way you think the audience will perceive you as a speaker. Complete the exercise in pencil so that you can repeat it at the end of the course and note any differences.

Application Exercise 1: Your Self-Perception

Assertive	Exciting	Experienced	Formal
Anxious	Gregarious	Humorous	Polite
Bold	Reserved	Talented	Handsome
Bashful	Shy	Thorough	Beautiful
Cautious	Open-minded	Scientific	Pretty
Colorful	Conservative	Caring	Bright
Daring	Extreme	Energetic	Fast
Analytical	Good-looking	Gracious	Slow
Effective	Average	Casual	Aggressive

The classical term for the influence of the source or speaker is *ethos*. The modern term for the same idea is **source credibility.** Do not confuse this term with the believability or credibility that a source of information such as a book or magazine holds. Source credibility refers to the speaker's credibility, independent of his or her material; the believability of the information you find will be considered in chapter 5. Working on your own self-concept is one means of improving your source credibility. Another way is to recognize and act on factors that audiences perceive to be important in evaluating a speaker. This chapter will focus

Source Credibility

on source credibility, defining the concept and identifying methods of improving your source credibility as a public speaker. In this examination you will explore four factors that determine credibility and how student speakers have applied them in classroom speeches.

What Is Source Credibility?

The idea that *who* speaks makes a difference is at least twenty-three centuries old. Aristotle said that a speaker's "character may almost be called the most effective means of persuasion he possesses."[2] In recent years this idea has been expanded by experimental studies that have attempted to determine exactly what an audience perceives in its evaluation of a speaker. The results of these studies provide a new perspective on you as a speaker.

To refine your source credibility, you need to know both what it is and what it is not. Source credibility is not something a speaker possesses like a suit of clothes, something that is positively impressive to every audience. Source credibility is not an inherent feature of a speaker; instead, it is born of the relationship between speaker and audience. The audience perceives a speaker at a particular time, in a particular place, on a particular occasion, and related to a particular topic. Source credibility is an evaluation, a judgment made by an audience about a speaker. Source credibility, then, is an audience's perception of a speaker. As a pair of researchers expressed the idea, "Credibility is in the eye of the beholder."[3]

Miss Peach by Mel Lazarus. Courtesy of Mel Lazarus and Field Newspaper Syndicate.

The implications of this perspective for you as a public speaker are that (a) you have to establish source credibility with every audience you face because it is not readily transferable and the audience's perceptions determine your credibility; (b) you may be more credible on some subjects than on others; and (c) you may be more credible in some situations than in others. As a classroom public speaker, you have to establish source credibility with your classmates. This chapter is designed to help you reach that goal.

An audience sees you as credible only if you or the person introducing you lets the audience know how you earned the right to speak to them about a certain topic. Your credibility springs from your own life, your experiences, your convictions, and your accomplishments. It comes from who and what you are.

Earning the Right to Speak

The "who you are" portion of your credibility rests on all of those characteristics over which you have no control. A female student might be able to say, "I am a woman. I am five feet one inch tall and I am twenty-three years old. I have lived my whole life in a world that seems designed for six-foot men. Today I am going to inform you and maybe even raise your consciousness about the problem of being a petite woman." Similarly, you would be using the "who you are" portion of your credibility to emphasize your parentage, race, geographical origins, family size, and so on.

The "what you are" part of your credibility rests on choices you have made. These characteristics of your life include the jobs you have held; the college and major you chose; the friends you select; the religion you practice; the hobbies, sports, and recreation in which you participate; and all other aspects of your life in which you are the one who makes the selection. In a classroom speech these characteristics might lead you to say, "I am a practical nurse working on my bachelor's degree." Such a statement might increase your credibility because it is a clear indication that you already have a career and some education. It also shows that you are surpassing the minimum necessary qualifications for your profession by working toward a college degree. Or suppose you say, "I spent four years in the Navy." This statement might increase your qualifications to speak on any number of topics relating to your experience in the military.

To increase your skill in developing source credibility, always describe your relevant qualifications in every speech you give. One common error student speakers make is that they forget to state the origins of their credibility for each speech because they told fellow students about themselves on the first day of class. Unfortunately, few people remember such information for very long. If being a Navy veteran is related to your topic and is likely to enhance your credibility, then you would be wise to remind the audience of it, even if they have heard it several times before. Also, you should listen carefully to other speakers to find out what they say about themselves that impresses you. See if you can learn from their methods of encouraging the audience to accept them as credible speakers.

Application Exercise 2: Who You Are; What You Can Speak About

List in the left-hand column some "I statements" that reveal who or what you are. Next to each—in the right-hand column—list some possible topics for which the "I statement" could be a credibility builder. An example is provided.

Who or What Statement
"I am the oldest of eight children in my family."

Possible Topics
For or against Birth Control; Population Problems; Family Communication; Advantages of a Large Family.

A Classroom Experience in Source Credibility

A vivid demonstration of how source credibility works came in a public speaking course taken by more than 770 students at a large university. The students were divided into 35 sections of 22 students each. Each section was invited to select its best speaker. After several run-off contests, the three finalists were asked to deliver their speeches to all 770 students and a guest judge. One of the finalists was a twenty-year-old woman, who delivered a speech on what it is like to be a handicapped university student. (She was confined to a wheelchair after an auto accident that injured her spine and left her paralyzed below the waist.) She told how able-bodied students walk far around students in wheelchairs, how most students avert their eyes when they approach a fellow student in a wheelchair, and how people struggle to avoid mentioning a person's handicap when they speak to an obviously handicapped person.

The second and third speakers were both black men. One spoke on black power; the other spoke on his experience as a black on a predominantly white campus. The reactions of fellow students to the black men were very similar to the reactions to the handicapped woman: avoidance, averted eyes, and a reluctance to talk. The most interesting point about these three winners, however, was that they clearly had earned the right to speak on the topics they chose.

Source credibility is based on an audience's perceptions of a speaker. A speaker earns it by showing the audience why he or she should be regarded as credible. As an old saying goes, "Before you express yourself, you need a self worth expressing."

What does an audience perceive that makes them believe a speaker is credible? If credibility is based on individual judgments by the audience, then what is the basis of those judgments? What will your classmates be observing to make their decisions about your credibility? Four of the most important dimensions of source credibility are competence, trustworthiness, dynamism, and coorientation.[4]

Four Dimensions of Source Credibility

Dimensions of Source Credibility

1. Competence
2. Trustworthiness
3. Dynamism
4. Coorientation

Competence

The first dimension of source credibility is **competence**. The audience sees a competent speaker as someone who is qualified, trained, skilled, experienced, authoritative, reliable, or knowledgeable about the subject he or she is discussing. Few speakers possess all of these qualities, but even one or two might be sufficient to gain positive audience perception. For instance, the audience perceives the highly skilled machinist, who displays her metal work in the speech, "Artistic Possibilities through Modern Technology," to be credible on that subject, as much as the Biblical scholar who demonstrates his ability to interpret scripture.

Your competence as a speaker is signaled by what you convey to the audience through—among other things—your words, your visual aids, and even your air of authority on the subject. How can you build something into your speech that will help the audience see and understand the basis for your authority? What experience have you had that is related to the subject of your speech? What special training or knowledge do you have? How can you suggest to your audience that you have earned the right to speak about this subject? The most obvious way, of course, is to tell the audience the basis for your authority or expertise. However, the creative speaker can think of dozens of ways to hint, suggest, imply, and indirectly indicate competence without being so explicit, condescending, or arrogant.

For example, the single thing that most impressed one audience about a speaker's credibility was something he did throughout his speech. It was not a direct statement saying "I am intelligent," but it implied the same thing: every time the speaker made a point, he supported it with evidence from written sources. Many speakers do that. However, this speaker quoted every written source, including long passages, from memory. Few speakers do that. He then cited the source by author, title, and page number. Sometimes, just to underline his point, he even mentioned that the quoted passage was "toward the bottom of page 59." No notes; direct quotes from memory; specific books, authors, and pages—the speaker was signaling his competence to the audience.

What can you do as a speaker to signal your competence? Watch how others do it. Observe your classmates. Listen to politicians, professors, television personalities, and note how they do it. Then consider this list of specific possibilities that have been used in classroom speeches.

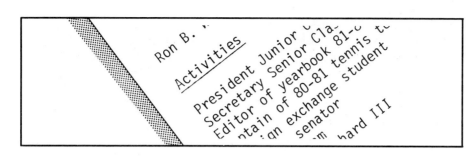

Figure 2.1 Your experience can signal competence.

"I've finally found that special someone — me!"

1. Reveal your experiences with the topic: "I spent four years fighting fires in our national forests."
2. Disclose your convictions related to the topic: "I am the only Christian Scientist in this class, so today I will explain to you some of my beliefs."
3. Use sources of information that are not commonly known: "According to *Daedalus,* a publication of the National Academy of Arts and Sciences. . . ."

4. Wear clothing, makeup, or jewelry, or carry objects like a calculator, stethoscope, or binoculars to signal your relationship to the topic. A student in biochemistry wore a white lab coat to class to speak about a topic in her field.

5. Secure information from live sources, either by phone or in person, to show that you go further than the library for information.

6. Deliver the entire speech without notes, even though you are not required to memorize it.

7. Master a videotape, recorder, or an opaque or overhead projector, and use audio or visual aids to vividly illustrate your points.

8. Use live models to illustrate your point. A student speaking on violence in college football brought a 6′ 9″ lineman to stand with him during the speech.

9. Mention experiences or relationships that are relevant to the topic: "Last summer when I was in Russia . . ." or "As I said to my uncle, who is president of this university. . . ."

10. Demonstrate your talents. A student giving a speech on wildlife accompanied her speech with ten large, color drawings of the animals she discussed. She had rendered the drawings herself.

An imaginative speaker can think of more than these ten ways to help an audience perceive competence. Try it yourself by completing the application exercise here.

Application Exercise 3: Signaling Your Competence

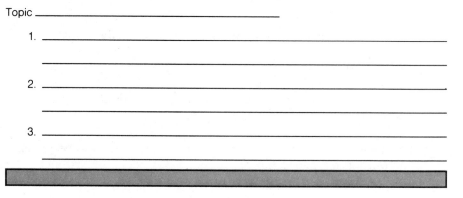

Write down a topic and then list three things you could do to signal your competence on it. For example, under the topic "U.S. Relations With Panama," you might state, "(1) My interest in Panama began with my stay there as an army brat when my father was in the Army Corps of Engineers; (2) I have taken two political science courses and two history courses that covered political and historical points about Panama; and (3) I plan to go back to Panama after I get my civil engineering degree."

Topic _____

1. _____

_____

2. _____

_____

3. _____

_____

Trustworthiness, the second dimension of source credibility, is a measure of how the audience finds the speaker—how honest, fair, sincere, and honorable. As with the other dimensions of source credibility, these qualities are earned. You probably judge another person's honesty by both his or her past behavior and your present views on integrity. In public speaking class your classmates will evaluate your trustworthiness by what they see you do in class or what they see or hear about you outside. What can you do in your speech to help the audience perceive the trustworthiness of your public presentations?

Trust is usually a feeling that another person respects you and cares enough about your welfare to behave as admirably behind your back as he or she does to your face. One professor surprised his students by asking each of them to give his or her term paper to someone else in the class. Then he asked each member of the class to take the other student's paper and look up every footnote, examine every quotation, and verify every page number. About a week later, when the class had accomplished their task, the professor found that there were a few incorrect page numbers and that a number of words from direct quotations had been altered or deleted.

One student had made up at least one source because he could not find it anywhere else. Some of his page numbers did not lead to the information cited. Some of his quotations were taken out of context in such a way that the author seemingly said the opposite in the paper of what was said in the source. In scholarship there is an article of trust that says sources must be cited accurately. Making up sources is taboo. Citing incorrect page numbers is a serious misdemeanor. Taking quotations out of context to distort the original meaning is the equivalent of a felony. Students usually are trusted in their writing, but in this case that trust was violated. No one could examine this student's writing again without at least wondering if he had cheated.

Trust is a certain predictability that others will behave in ways that respect our individual welfare. But how does this show itself in public speaking? Visiting speakers come fully armed with credentials, advance publicity, and sometimes outstanding reputations in their fields. Their known background helps an audience to decide whether they are to be trusted. In the classroom the audience decides more quickly, and with less evidence, whether the speaker is trustworthy, fair, and sincere. It is important to discuss what helps you decide when a person is trustworthy. No research study has a good answer for this question.

For the authors, some signs of trust are looking the listener in the eye, citing sources accurately and consistently, speaking with a steady, strong voice at a moderate rate, dressing appropriately, moving purposefully and gesturing with determination, leaning toward the listener, and saying things that the listener believes to be true or verifiable.

These cues may not be the same as yours. In some cultures, looking away from a person is a sign of trust, while looking one in the eye is an aggressive threat. Some people view a person with a strong voice and purposeful gestures as a possible huckster. You have to decide the cues that signal trust to you and your classmates. Then you have to learn how to use them as a public speaking tool.

Application Exercise 4: The Tokens of Trust

List below four cues that help you trust a speaker (e.g., she states that she has helped other people in my circumstances) and four cues that make you distrust a speaker (e.g., she uses too many words that I have never heard before). If you have a chance, compare notes. You may find that the very cues that help you trust a speaker make another person distrust the speaker.

Tokens of Trust
1.

2.

3.

4.

Tokens of Distrust
1.

2.

3.

4.

A third dimension of source credibility is **dynamism.** This term refers to the boldness, energy, activity, strength, and assertiveness of the speaker. Audiences apparently value behavior that can be described in this manner. Perhaps when we consider the opposites—meek, passive, tired, weak, and retiring—we can see why audiences favor the more dynamic features in a speaker.

Dynamism

What signs of dynamism can you provide as a speaker? One is purposeful movement: walking, pointing, and gesturing. A popular lecturer, Leo Buscaglia, works so intently as he speaks that he is constantly mopping his brow. Another sign of dynamism is vocal variety and rate. The speaker who can roar, purr, speed up, and slow down is providing signs of activity and energy. The kinds of words you choose also can signal dynamism. Colorful words, vivid verbs, forceful adverbs and adjectives all signal strength and assertiveness. To state, "I don't know, he looks sort of ordinary to me," is meek and bland, while to say, "He had an everyday face, undistinguished by handsomeness or notable flaws, but his slightly tilted head and his attentive eyes made people want to disclose their secrets to him," is more dynamic. The first statement reveals so little that it is lacking in dynamism; the second, with its specific, concrete descriptors, brings some life to this seemingly ordinary person.

A person whose face never changes expression does not appear to be dynamic, but the person who can frown, smile, and show surprise does. The person who stands like a wooden soldier throughout a speech with hands glued to his sides does not appear dynamic, but a person who shakes his fists and pounds on the lectern does. The dynamic person, as you will see in the example that follows, exudes power.

A certain fraternity once violated certain rules by sponsoring a big drinking spree one weekend. The members were a bit uneasy because on Monday night the dean of students was invited to the house for dinner. They were relieved when he showed up apparently unconcerned and unaware of their transgression. The balding, elderly gentleman with rimless glasses and a happy face sat smoking cigars with his hosts before dinner. After a pleasant meal he was invited as the guest to say a few words. He rose and said, "Gentlemen, I know what happened here this weekend, and I want you to know if it ever happens again I will close the doors of this damned fraternity," whereupon he snatched up his hat and walked calmly out of the fraternity house. That was a dynamic speech.

The fourth dimension of source credibility is **coorientation.** This term refers to the shared values, beliefs, attitudes, and interests of speaker and audience. Voluntary audiences are drawn to speakers whose ideology is similar to their own. Quite often these speakers articulate their ideas and beliefs better than members of the audience could themselves. In the classroom a speaker can establish coorientation with an audience by revealing the many ways in which he or she shares their approach to life, in terms of the issues, the information being presented, or the persuasive proposition. Thus we use the word coorientation, a shared vision of audience and speaker.

Coorientation

Coorientation is generally the most important dimension of source credibility. Without it, competence, trustworthiness, and dynamism may count for nothing. In the classroom, coorientation is partly subsumed by the commonality of the situation. Because all members of the audience (except the teacher) are students, they share common concerns (about tuition, housing, relations with the campus community, and so on). Still, audiences appreciate being reminded of their common ground with the speaker. Even to start a speech with "Fellow Students" or "Fellow Americans" is to emphasize coorientation between speaker and audience.

An effective speaker spells out the roots of commonality throughout a speech. One married student, who lived in a tin shack the university called "married student housing," pointed out that though his house was not pretty, he and his wife had about five times as much room as most of the audience had in a three-person dormitory room. He noted that his roomy quarters cost only $60.00 per month, considerably less than the other students were paying for their cramped space. He had a kitchen. Did they? And so on. He was working on the common value they placed on living space, conserving funds, and conveniences. His speech was a clever exercise in establishing coorientation and then pointing out the differences in their situations.

To help you consider values you may share with your audience, complete this exercise. First, indicate the approximate number of people who fit the categories listed. In the second column, identify one or two cues that suggest the particular descriptor. Finally, compare your answers with others in the class and determine the accuracy of your hunches. Discuss some of the discrepancies that occur.

Application Exercise 5: Coorientation: The Roots of Commonality

Descriptor	Estimated Number of Students	Cues That Suggest This Trait	Actual Number of Students
Scholarly	8	Study before class	6
Republicans			
Poor			
Religious			
Dependent			
Ambitious			
Democrats			
Nonreligious			
Liberal			
Independent			
Lazy			
Attractive			
Wealthy			
Conservative			
Modest			
Honest			
Apolitical			
Dishonest			
Middle-class			
Immodest			

As a beginning student reading about the four dimensions of source credibility, you might feel that establishing such credibility is beyond your capability. However, you do not have to meet the expectations of all of the dimensions. For example, many highly credible speakers exhibit little dynamism. Professors have been repeatedly criticized on this point. Their special strength is their knowledge. In this chapter, however, you have begun to learn how to project competence, dynamism, trustworthiness, and coorientation so that your audience will perceive you as a credible source on the topics that you choose.

Checklist 2 summarizes the content of this chapter. Before you give a speech, use the list to help guide you toward greater credibility as a public speaker.

Checklist 2: Guide for Increasing Credibility in Public Speaking

_____ 1. Have you selected a topic about which you are involved, so that you can be perceived as sincere, responsible, reputable, and trustworthy?

_____ 2. Have you considered the competence dimension of source credibility by building into your speech cues that indicate your experience, training, skill, and expertise on the subject?

_____ 3. Have you considered the trustworthiness dimension of source credibility, by building trust through concern for your audience's welfare, objective consideration of their needs, friendly rapport, and responsible, honest handling of the speech content?

_____ 4. Have you selected a means of delivery and content that will help the audience see you as dynamic—energetic, strong, emphatic, and assertive?

_____ 5. Are you indicating in your speech one or more ideas, beliefs, attitudes, or characteristics that you hold in common with most of the people in your audience?

Conclusion

You have discovered in this chapter that self-perception, or how you see yourself, is related to how the audience perceives you. You also have learned that source credibility is based on how the audience regards you as a speaker. Source credibility influences the audience and helps them decide whether to believe you or to challenge your words. Your credibility is based on audience perceptions of your competence, trustworthiness, dynamism, and coorientation. You can learn to improve your credibility with an audience by showing them through your expertise and experience that you are competent; by showing them through consistency and example that you are trustworthy; by showing them through the enthusiasm and energy of your words and actions that you are dynamic; and by letting them know the experiential and ideological ties that bind you, the speaker, to them, your audience.

Source credibility is among the few factors that have a demonstrable effect on audience acceptance of the speaker and the message. It is, therefore, important for you to know what source credibility is and to practice those skills likely to enhance it. Source credibility is not a characteristic of a speaker; it is one feature of the speaker-audience relationship. In the next chapter, we turn to a more thorough examination of the other partner in this relationship: the audience.

Application Assignment

Introducing Another Person

Interview a classmate. Collect facts, stories, and observations about him or her that you can present to the class. Deliver this information to the class without reading it; use as much eye contact as possible. Your speech will be evaluated on the audience's interest in the information you selected; on your ability to use notes sparingly and to look at the audience and person being introduced as much as possible; on your ability to project (speak loudly enough); on your rate, or speed, and articulation; and on your ability to get the audience to consider the person you are introducing as a credible source on some subject. Appendix A gives examples of such a speech.

Vocabulary

competence A dimension of source credibility that focuses on the audience's perception of the speaker's expertise, knowledge, and background relating to the topic.

coorientation A dimension of source credibility that focuses on the audience's perception of the similarity of the speaker's ideas, beliefs, and experiences to their own.

dynamism A dimension of source credibility that focuses on the audience's perception of the speaker's energy and enthusiasm as expressed in movement, gestures, and vocal expression.

self-perception The way a speaker sees himself or herself, especially as a speaker.

source credibility The audience's perception of the speaker's dynamism, trustworthiness, competence, and coorientation. High source credibility means that the audience responds favorably to the speaker in some or all of these four areas.

trustworthiness A dimension of source credibility that focuses on the audience's perception of the speaker's honesty, sincerity, and consistency.

Endnotes

1. Daryl J. Bem, *Beliefs, Attitudes and Human Affairs* (Belmont, Ca.: Brooks/Cole, 1970) p. 3.
2. Aristotle, "Rhetoric," W. Rhys Roberts trans. in *The Basic Works of Aristotle,* Richard McKeon, ed. (New York: Random House, 1941), 1: 1356a, lines 12–14.
3. Ralph L. Rosnow and Edward J. Robinson, eds., *Experiments in Persuasion* (New York: Academic Press, 1967), p. 18.
4. Derived from a study by Christopher J. S. Tuppen, "Dimensions of Communicator Credibility: An Oblique Solution," *Speech Monographs* 41 (1974): 253–60.

Chapter 3

Outline

Introduction: Developing audience sensitivity.
  I. Four objectives of audience analysis.
    A. Demographic information: knowing your turf.
    B. Knowledge information: inquiring and questioning.
    C. Interest information: watching and listening.
    D. Attitude information: surveying your audience.
  II. Adapting your speech to your audience.
Conclusion: Summary of objectives for audience analysis.

Objectives

After you have completed chapter 3, you should be able to answer the following questions:
  1. What is audience analysis?
  2. What are four kinds of information that you should seek to increase your sensitivity to an audience?
  3. What are some informal ways of assessing an audience's characteristics, knowledge, interests, and attitudes?
  4. What are some more formal ways of assessing these same four kinds of information about an audience?
  5. How can you adapt your speeches to your particular audience?
When you have completed chapter 3, you should have practiced skills in
  1. Recognizing audience sensitivity;
  2. Drawing inferences from observing your audience;
  3. Gathering demographic information from your audience;
  4. Drawing inferences from demographic information;
  5. Determining your audience's knowledge;
  6. Determining your audience's interests and attitudes; and
  7. Delivering a brief speech in which you analyze your audience.

Application Exercises

  1. How do we analyze audiences?
  2. Who exhibits audience sensitivity?
  3. Drawing inferences from observation.
  4. Drawing inferences from demographics.
  5. What are your audience's interests?
  6. Audience attitude analysis.
  7. Observing adaptation to an audience.

36

Analyzing Your Audience

Oratory is the art of enchanting the soul, and
therefore he who would be an orator has to learn
the difference of human souls. . . .

Socrates

You stand up in front of the class to give your speech on the martial arts only **Introduction** to discover in the question-and-answer period that you are getting a number of difficult questions. Unknown to you, five members of your class have already earned higher belts in karate than you have.

You stand up in front of the class to give your speech on adopting children. The apparent disinterest of the class amazes you until you are reminded afterwards that no one in the class has children and no one happens to be adopted. The topic that was so close to you was highly distant from them.

In both instances you could have avoided a distressing situation by analyzing your audience.

Application Exercise 1: How Do We Analyze Audiences?

In the last chapter, in Application Exercise #5, you made some guesses about the characteristics of the audience to whom you are going to speak. Re-examine that exercise now. How did you make your judgments? What kind of information did you use? Did you observe your audience and make judgments? Did you go beyond your observations and draw inferences about audience members? Did you receive information about any audience members in other ways? Based on this experience, how would you go about receiving information about another audience? Suppose that you were assigned to give a speech to another section of the public speaking class at your university. What would you do to gain information about your audience? What assumptions would you make?

You may wish to compare your own ideas about how to gain information about an audience with some of your classmates. Pay particular attention to those suggestions made by people who were highly successful in guessing the characteristics of the individuals in your class. What cues did they use? What cues did they view as unimportant?

Audience analysis is an attempt to learn as much about the audience as possible so that you can achieve your purpose of informing or persuading them. You cannot inform a room full of people who already know, and you cannot persuade a room full of people who already believe. Similarly, you cannot interest people in something that is far removed from their present situation. But how do you find out what the audience already knows, believes, and is interested in? You find out by means of audience analysis.

Audience analysis can be as informal as observing that the class is nearly all male, and it can be as formal as using a battery of questionnaires to reveal class knowledge, interests, attitudes, beliefs, and values. In this chapter you will move from relatively simple and informal means of audience analysis to relatively complex and formal means. What you are working toward in this chapter is sensitivity to your audience.

Audience sensitivity is a speaker's ability to anticipate and respond to an audience. Highly skilled public speakers seem to know what to say to get the audience response they seek. The successful comedian in his monologue knows how to get a laugh a minute because he knows what will be funny to his audience. The skillful lawyer knows the jury well enough to select arguments that appeal to them. And the effective evangelist knows the songs, passages, and sermon themes that inspire a congregation. Audience sensitivity is a product of knowing an audience and of acting on that knowledge. Audience analysis is a step toward learning audience sensitivity.

A speaker who is sensitive to an audience observes some of the most subtle cues, as well as the more obvious ones. She notices that people are looking around the room instead of focusing on her. She observes that, while most of the audience is laughing at her jokes, a few people look upset or unhappy about the humor. She may notice that audience members are glancing at their watches, looking out the window, or staring at some information written on the chalkboard. Both nonverbal and verbal cues from the audience are processed by speakers who are sensitive to their audiences.

Audience analysis is also a means of accelerating the process of getting acquainted. If all the people in your audience are acquaintances, you already know a great deal about their interests, knowledge, and beliefs. If they are not, you have to devise methods of finding out these things.

Examine your own experience and try to specify the behavior of persons you believe to be sensitive or insensitive to audiences. Think of those who must regularly relate to audiences: political figures, movie stars, TV personalities, newspaper editors, professors, comedians, and so on. The main benefit of exploring sensitivity and insensitivity to audiences is that you can adopt the behavior of those individuals who exhibit audience sensitivity and avoid the behavior of those who demonstrate insensitivity.

Application Exercise 2: Who Exhibits Audience Sensitivity?

Four Objectives of Audience Analysis

We have stated that audience analysis is important in public speaking. This chapter is based on the assumption that any speech is a transaction between the speaker and the audience and that the transaction is more likely to be successful if the speaker and audience know as much as possible about each other. When the audience is voluntary, audience analysis is somewhat easier: the audience knows something about the speaker, and the speaker knows what kind of an audience he or she attracts. When the audience is captive, as it is in the classroom situation, audience analysis is more important because in early speeches the audience may not know very much about the speaker, and vice versa.

Objectives of Audience Analysis

1. Demographic information
2. Knowledge information
3. Interest information
4. Attitude information

Four kinds of information about the audience will be helpful to you: demographic, knowledge, interest, and attitude information. As you examine these four kinds of information, both informal and formal means of obtaining them will be explained. The press of time in the classroom may limit your inquiry to informal means only. However, more formal means, such as the use of questionnaires, are included here so that you may use them when you have the time and initiative.

An informal way of securing **demographic information** about your audience is to become a sharp observer. *Demographics* is the study of populations, and it literally means "characteristics of the people." What would you as a sharp observer note as the characteristics of your audience? Some of the most obvious are often overlooked by speakers. Consider the enthusiastic dressmaker who gives an informative speech on how to make an evening gown—to a predominantly male audience who yawn throughout. Consider a classroom audience of students having a serious struggle finding enough money for tuition—listening to a speech on the best restaurants in Europe. In both cases the speaker has made a serious error by overlooking obvious demographic characteristics.

What can you ask yourself about your audience to avoid such problems?

How many males and how many females are in your audience?
What races or ethnic groups are represented?
What ages are represented?

Other questions to ask yourself can be based on your knowledge of your college and the students who choose to go there:

Where are the members of your audience from?
Where do they live now?
How financially well off are they?
How bright and inquisitive are they?
What are the members of your audience majoring in?
Do they drive to school?
Do they belong to various organizations?

The first set of questions rests largely on your ability to see and to count; the second, on your knowledge about your college and your ability to draw **inferences** from that knowledge. These inferences are educated guesses about what the audience is like.

Demographic
Information:
Knowing Your
Turf

Application Exercise 3: Drawing Inferences from Observation

Given the observations listed below, what inferences would you draw about the audience's probable response to a speech on abortion, inflation, or gun control?

The audience responded very positively to an earlier informative speech on race relations.

The audience consists mainly of inner-city people with Italian, Greek, and Slavic names.

The audience consists of many married persons with families.

The audience members attend night school on earnings from daytime jobs in factories and businesses.

Most of the audience members come from large families.

This application exercise can provide practice in drawing inferences from observational data. Another practical method of doing the same application exercise is to use observations you have made about your own classmates.

This informal means of "eyeballing" the audience is a method that anyone can use. More formal methods of gathering demographic information yield more accurate information about characteristics that you can and cannot see. For instance, just by looking at your audience, you may find it difficult to discover the members' marital status, religion, income, and political affiliation. You can obtain this information by using a questionnaire like the one shown in figure 3.1.

Analyzing Your Audience

Figure 3.1
Demographic
questionnaire.

Demographic Questionnaire

Name (optional) _____

1. Age _____

2. Sex:

   Male _____   Female _____

3. Occupation _____

4. Religion _____

5. Marital Status _____

6. Race _____

7. Income _____

8. Year in school:

   Freshman _____ Sophomore _____ Junior _____ Senior _____

9. College or curriculum _____

10. Major _____ Minor _____

11. Grade point average _____

12. Campus organizations to which you belong:

    _____

    _____

13. How do you pay for your education? (check one or more)

    Savings _____ Summer work _____ Parents _____

    Scholarship _____ Financial Aid _____

14. To what off-campus organizations do you belong?

    _____

    _____

15. Your home town and state _____

The name of the respondent should be omitted from the questionnaire or made optional because even demographic questions can offend. (On most job applications, people are no longer required to answer questions about age, sex, religion, race, marital status, or income.) However, many people will answer such questions if they can remain anonymous or if the information is going to be compiled along with similar information from many others.

The kind of demographic questions you ask will depend in part on your topic. If you were to give an informative speech on "Three ways to save money on transportation," you might want to know how many students in your class own cars, bikes, mopeds, or motorcycles. You might want to know how many commute and how many walk to school. You might want to know how far they have to travel to campus, how much they spend on gas, and who pays their transportation costs.

To understand the kinds of information you can gather from demographic data, look at figure 3.2, which shows the results of a questionnaire for a class of twenty-two students. As you look at the items and the numbers, try to envision what this class would be like as an audience. What topics would be good choices for a speech? What topics should be avoided?

What can you infer about this class? Keep in mind that an inference is simply an educated guess, a conclusion that goes beyond the evidence. For instance, the results indicate that everyone in class is between eighteen and twenty-five years of age. That is a verifiable fact, not an inference. But if you infer that the people in class are likely to be interested in the cost of education, in the issue of required courses, and in the subject of grading, then you are making an inference. You are guessing, but your guesses are "educated" guesses.

Be cautious about inferences even though you have to make them to give a speech. There is always the possibility that your inference will be incorrect. For example, an audience tally of thirteen men and nine women might lead you to infer that more of the audience would be interested in automobiles than in cooking, but that inference could be incorrect. The presence of six Catholics in an audience might lead you to infer that a speech on birth control would not be welcome, but again you might be incorrect.

What are some other inferences that could be drawn from the results of our questionnaire? Most of the class are in social sciences and business; so the audience is more likely to be interested in people and money issues than in technology and literature. Many students are in campus and off-campus organizations related to religion; so they may be interested in religious issues. What inferences would you make about the information on marital status, race, year in school, and hometown?

Demographic information about your audience is necessary, but it is shaky at best unless you support it with information from your observations and with data on the interests and knowledge of your audience. Watch for patterns. The demographic information tells you that the members of your audience work at night

Figure 3.2
Demographic analysis.

Demographic Analysis

Age:
18 year olds: 5
19 year olds: 7
20 year olds: 7
21 year olds: 2
25 years old: 1

Gender:
Male: 13
Female: 9

Race:
Caucasian: 19
Black: 2
Hispanic: 1

Marital status:
Married: 2
Divorced: 1
Single: 19

Religion:
Protestant: 1
Catholic: 6
Jewish: 3
None: 2

Grew up in:
Small town: 8
Urban area: 4
Rural area: 10

Year in school:
Freshman: 5
Sophomore: 7
Junior: 7
Senior: 3

College or Curriculum:
Sciences: 3
Social Sciences: 8
Humanities: 3
Business: 8

Grade Point Averages:
4.0–3.5: 2
3.0–3.4: 8
2.5–2.9: 5
2.0–2.4: 6
1.5–1.9: 1

Campus Organizations:
Fraternities: 2
Sororities: 1
Student government: 9
Religious organizations: 12

Off-Campus Organizations:
National Rifle Association: 3
Recreation groups: 6
Church groups: 13

and on weekends to earn money. You infer that they are working their way through school and would, therefore, be interested in a speech on how to survive financially at this school. But does the way your classmates dress, talk, and act support your inference? Maybe working is just a social expectation, and the money goes for nonessentials. Watch for patterns; see if the demographic information is supported by other kinds of audience information.

THE FAMILY CIRCUS®   By Bil Keane

2-1

Copyright 1980
The Register and Tribune
Syndicate, Inc

"Mommy didn't think it was that funny when I
said it this afternoon. I had to
go to my room."

Application Exercise 4: Drawing Inferences from Demographics

What inferences would you make about an audience if the main feature revealed by the demographic analysis were any one of the following? What inferences would you draw if all five features described the same audience?

The audience is predominantly female, age nineteen to twenty-five.
The audience is predominantly Catholic.
Most members of the audience are humanities majors.
No one in the audience has a job.
Many in the audience are members of social groups like sororities.

On the basis of your inferences what topics would be appropriate for each audience? What might you observe to verify your inferences?

"Have you ever been skiing? If you haven't let me tell you about all the fun you're missing."

A second kind of information the public speaker seeks about the audience is **knowledge information.** How much does the audience already know about your topic? How much background do they need to understand your subject? What do you have to tell them before they know enough to be persuaded? As was the case with demographic knowledge, there are informal and formal ways to discover how much an audience knows. Since you will always use the informal means but may only occasionally use more formal methods, we will look first at some informal ways of determining audience knowledge.

The demographic information that you have about your audience will help you determine their knowledge as well. A student's major, for instance, allows you to make an educated guess, an inference, about that person's knowledge. The demographic information may indicate that some members of your audience are physical education majors and others are interested in outdoor sports, including hunting, fishing, and spectator sports. However, the demographic information alone does not reveal how much the audience knows about the topic of your informative speech on, for example, competitive skiing.

What is an informal means of discovering how much your audience knows about a particular topic? The answer is deceptively simple but effective. You will have some forewarning before you have to deliver a speech. Use that time to find out how much your classmates know about your topic by asking them. Ask them while you are waiting in the halls between classes, in the classroom before class begins, or after class. If your classmates know very little about competitive skiing,

you know that you will have to give them very basic information. If they have a general knowledge of the topic, you can plan to review basic information quickly and go on to more technical considerations.

A second means of learning how much your audience knows about a topic is more subtle. Keep your eyes and ears open. Do your fellow students talk about going on a ski trip? Do any of them wear tags on their jackets that indicate they have been to a ski area? Do any of them have ski racks on their cars? Watch and listen carefully, and you may well find out how much your audience knows about your topic.

A more formal way to discover how much an audience knows about a topic is to ask them written questions. This method works best if you make the questions very easy to answer in very little time. For example, suppose you have decided to deliver a speech on why jogging is unhealthy. You might ask them questions like these:

1. Are you a runner or a jogger?
2. Have you ever been a runner or a jogger?
3. Have you ever read an article about running or jogging?
4. Have you ever read a book about running or jogging?
5. Have you ever talked with anyone about why people should not run or jog?
6. Have you ever read any information against running or jogging?
7. Have you ever suffered any physical disabilities from running or jogging?
8. Are you familiar with the causes of heart trouble?
9. Do you know how often or how much you should exercise for optimum good health?
10. Do you have family or friends who are runners or joggers?

All of these questions can be answered in a couple of minutes with a "yes" or a "no." The answers should help you decide (a) how much background information you have to provide about the dangers of jogging, (b) how much—if any—resistance you will face in delivering a speech against jogging, and (c) how much the audience needs to know to understand your point of view. Whether you gather your information informally or formally, you can inform and persuade better if you know how much your audience knows about your topic.

Interest Information: Watching and Listening

Demographic and knowledge information are not the only kinds of information the effective speaker seeks from the audience. A third kind is **interest information.** Again, there are informal and formal ways to discover your audience's interests. Informal methods include inquiry, observation, and listening.

In the same way that you can informally discover your audience's knowledge about a topic, you can discover their interests by talking to them before and after class. You can also observe them carefully. How many members wear letter jackets, uniforms, shirts with the name of an employer, sorority pins, wedding bands,

Analyzing Your Audience

or campaign buttons? Currently, many students have their interests printed on their t-shirts: beer drinking, mountain climbing, skiing, sky diving, and motorcycle racing. One student had "I am single and sexy" printed across her chest.

In addition to talking and watching, you can listen. A speech course provides an excellent opportunity to discover audience interests because everyone in class reveals them in his or her speeches. What do the members of your class talk about? To which topics do most respond favorably? Attentive looks, impatience, fatigue, or questions can signal the audience's response to speaker and topic.

Assessing audience interests by the informal means of inquiry, observation, and listening may be the only methods that you can use. However, if you take a little more time and effort, you can use a more formal method of gathering interest information about your audience: write your own questions, make some copies, and have your classmates answer the questions before class begins or during class, with your teacher's permission. This method serves you as a speaker in two ways. First, your questions will arouse the class's interest in your proposed topic because they, too, will be curious about the answers. Second, answers to the questions will provide information you can use in informing or persuading the audience.

For example, suppose you are planning a speech on gun control. Questions like these would provide you with important information about the relationship between your audience and your topic.

1. I (do, do not) own a gun.
2. Someone in my family (does, does not) own a gun.
3. I (do, do not) approve of gun ownership for hunting and recreation.
4. I (do, do not) approve of gun ownership for personal protection.
5. I (agree, disagree) that all guns should be registered.
6. I (agree, disagree) that only handguns should be registered.
7. I (agree, disagree) that rifles and shotguns should be registered.
8. I (agree, disagree) that people should own guns only if they have been trained to use them.
9. I (do, do not) belong to the National Rifle Association.
10. I (do, do not) believe that gun offenders should be severely punished.

From the results of such a survey, you should uncover information about your audience's interests and beliefs and be able to make some inferences about their predispositions toward guns and gun control.

A questionnaire should not be used to determine your own position on an issue; you should already have a position. If your survey shows that most of your class-mates disagree, then your task is to inform them on the issue or to figure out how to persuade them to your point of view.

Application Exercise 5: What Are Your Audience's Interests?

List some topics that you might speak about that would be interesting to your classroom audience. Generate some questions that would be important to ask for each topic. You may use the questions on gun control as a model of some of the questions that can be asked. If time permits, and your instructor allows, determine the answers to the questions from your audience. Do the answers to the questions help define the audience's interest in the topic? Why or why not?

Attitude Information: Surveying Your Audience

A fourth way to analyze an audience is to gather **attitude information.** Before delivering a speech, you should try to find out the audience's attitude toward your topic. Demographic information may indicate that most of your classmates come from middle-class families. You may want to deliver a persuasive speech against welfare. But how do you know what attitudes the class holds on that issue? As with the other kinds of information, there are informal and formal ways to dis-cover an audience's attitudes about an issue.

One informal method is to examine the demographic information and observe the audience's membership in various groups. Do your classmates belong to po-litical parties? Do they see themselves as conservative or liberal? To know that members of your audience are conservative Republicans may tell you something about their attitudes on welfare, warfare, big business, unions, and a host of other issues. Do they belong to the National Rifle Association, the National Organization for Women, the Right to Life organization, Christian Crusade, or fraternal groups? Membership in any of these organizations may permit you to draw inferences.

As Daryl Bem points out in *Beliefs, Attitudes, and Human Affairs,* there is a certain predictability about a person's position on the issues:

> . . . My neighbor says that his major value is individual freedom and that therefore he is opposed to open-housing laws and to legislation which regulates the possession of firearms. I may disagree with his opinions, but I can appreciate the logic involved. Curiously, however, my freedom-loving neighbor also advocates stiffer penalties for the use of marijuana, feels that women belong in the home, and believes that consenting adults who engage in homosexual behavior should get long prison terms. Here the logic involved is less than clear, yet these opinions too seem strangely predictable. . . .[1]

You, too, may find that an attitude signaled by membership in an organization can help you infer other predictable attitudes.

A second informal means of assessing audience attitudes depends on your sensitivity. You may be quite accurate in assessing audience attitudes because of your knowledge about your school, your community, and your region. Ordinarily you do not have to ask the entire class if they believe in pre-marital sex, welfare, unionism, abortion, equal rights for women, big business, or the Democratic Party. You can make an educated guess, an inference, based on your own experience with the group.

Another important consideration in assessing audience attitudes is the strength or intensity of an attitude. Perhaps you know your audience well enough to infer that they are inactive and even apathetic about local, state, and national affairs. Perhaps you know that most are strong adherents of a certain religion. Your estimate of how strongly the audience feels about various issues can be instructive in determining what they need to know.

Finally, informal analysis of attitudes can include audience characteristics like ambition, intelligence, pride, motivation, aspirations, and open-mindedness. Are the members of your audience in school primarily to secure higher paying jobs when they graduate? Do they seem to be curious about things they do not know? Are they willing to listen to positions they do not embrace? These characteristics, like their organizational membership, their apparent position on the issues, and the strength or intensity of their beliefs can help you determine how to approach them in a speech.

More formal means of assessing audience attitudes can also be devised. Suppose you plan to deliver a speech against the ownership of pets. You might ask the audience to indicate their attitude and the strength of their attitude by choosing any of answers A through E for questions like those that follow.

A. Strongly Agree   D. Disagree
B. Agree   E. Strongly Disagree
C. Neutral

1. Dogs, cats, hamsters, and other four-legged furry pets are good for children and adults.
2. These animals should be restricted so that they are always under the owner's control.
3. More of these animals should be sterilized to prevent overpopulation in urban areas.
4. Laws that require dog owners to clean up after their own dogs are a good idea.
5. These animals should be restricted to rural areas only.
6. I am amused by people who care for their pets as if they were children.
7. I believe that people spend too much money on pet food and pet care.
8. I think that pets should be owned only by persons who can afford to feed and care for them.
9. I believe that raising a pet is a healthy activity for almost anyone.
10. I think that people in urban areas should be limited to small pets that never need to leave the confines of the home.

If the members of your audience like owning pets, you will have to approach them differently with your topic than if they already tend to agree that pets are a public problem. Your analysis of audience answers can provide you with important information that will determine what you say in your speech and how you say it.

You are delivering a persuasive speech to convince an audience that they should vote for a particular candidate for student government president. Your audience attitude analysis indicates the following:

Application Exercise 6: Audience Attitude Analysis

The majority of the members of the audience have a negative predisposition about student elections.
The majority do not believe that the student government does anything for students.
The majority have a positive attitude toward elections at the state and national levels.
Few people in the audience have ever exercised their right to vote.

What arguments would you use, what evidence would you use, and what reasons would you advocate to persuade this audience to vote for your candidate? What unusual strategies might work to persuade such an audience?

You have surveyed four kinds of information that can be useful in analyzing your audience: demographic, knowledge, interest, and attitude. You have examined both informal and formal means of gathering these four kinds of information. The results of this analysis are not a certain key to your success as a speaker, but they can help you greatly. Information gathering can help you to select topics, determine what the audience needs to know, decide how easily they can be persuaded, and look for the illustrations, arguments, and evidence that should be included in your public speeches. In short, audience analysis should help you to adapt to your audience.

Adapting Your Speech to Your Audience

We began this chapter with the concept of audience sensitivity, that particular quality of an effective speaker to anticipate audience responses. Audience sensitivity combines interpretation of audience feedback with **audience adaptation.** The four types of information discussed in the previous section make adaptation to an audience possible.

Recently, a student delivered an informative speech on how to raise an expensive breed of dog. The audience consisted mainly of middle-class sophomores who had considerable difficulty identifying with the topic. The topic was not, however, the main problem. One fault in the speech was that the speaker did not adapt to the audience. Another student in the same class delivered a speech on raising hackney ponies. He pointed out that he was raised in a poor section of New Haven, Connecticut. Mentioning that his father was an immigrant who never earned much money, even though he was fluent in six languages, and that his family was large, he told how he and his brothers pooled their resources to buy some good breeding stock. Ultimately, their venture brought income from both selling colts and winning prize money in contests. This speaker had selected a topic that the audience might have found as difficult to identify with as raising expensive show dogs. Both topics seem like upper-class preoccupations. But unlike the student who spoke about dogs, the student who spoke about hackney ponies had analyzed the audience carefully. By explaining why he was an unlikely breeder of expensive horses, he put himself on an equal footing with his audience. Even though he was not rich, this "city kid" demonstrated that he could raise expensive horses profitably.

Adapting to an audience also takes place *during* a speech. Have you ever watched the hosts on television talk shows? They try various kinds of humor—about events reported in the newspaper, about the president of the United States, about their guests. When something works (gets audience response), they tend to say more about that topic. When the topic "bombs," they drop it quickly or even make fun of themselves for bringing it up. They are adapting to their audience as they speak. Similarly, an effective speaker uses various propositions, arguments, and illustrations, notes the audience reaction, and expands on the points that elicit a response and passes over those that do not. This is all part of audience sensitivity.

"Change, please."

Application
Exercise 7:
Observing
Adaptation to
an Audience

Observe a lecturer, visiting dignitary, talk show host, or some other person who must relate to audiences outside the classroom. Before you observe the speaker, write a short paragraph on the information that he or she probably has available before the speech. For instance, does the speaker know the probable ages, genders, races, and other demographic features represented by most of the people in the audience? Does the part of the country in which he or she is speaking make a difference in deciding how to adapt the message? Does the time of day or evening of the speech make a difference? Does the speaker know the audience's knowledge level on the topic of the speech? Does he or she know if the audience is voluntary or captive (which may indicate a difference in interest level)? Does the speaker know what the audience's attitude is on the topic?

Next, observe the speaker and take notes on how the person adapts to the audience. Identify five demographic features of the audience and suggest how the speaker should adapt the speech in order to accommodate them. List how much knowledge the audience probably had about the topic and determine whether the speaker talked above, below, or at the knowledge level of the audience. Was the audience interested in the speaker's topic before the speech? Did the speaker increase or decrease that interest? How do you know? What was the audience's overall attitude about the topic? Were they in agreement with the speaker or did they disagree? Did the speaker handle the topic appropriately, given the attitude of the audience?

As you answer these questions consider some of the specific features of the speaker's adaptation. Did he or she make references to the audience, situation, or other circumstances early in the speech? Did he or she seem to be aware of the nonverbal and verbal cues offered by the audience during the speech? What did the speaker do in reaction to specific audience responses? How did you know that the speaker was interpreting feedback? What does the speaker do that you can do in your speeches?

Conclusion

In this chapter you have seen how to analyze an audience on the basis of four kinds of information: demographics, interest, knowledge, and attitude. You have also examined informal and formal ways of gathering this information and adapting to your audience. The object has been for you to become sensitive to your audience and thereby know what topics, arguments, illustrations, and information will be appropriate in your speeches.

As you begin to use the various methods of audience analysis when preparing your speeches, your confidence and effectiveness will increase.

With audience information in mind, we will turn next to the important task of selecting an appropriate topic.

Application Assignment

Assumptions Paper

Write your name at the top of your paper and list five assumptions about your class, based on formal or informal analysis of demographic, knowledge, interest, and attitude information. Each assumption must be an inference based on your knowledge of the class. Your five statements should include your assumption (inference) and the basis for that assumption. For example, one item might look like this:

1. *Assumption:* A majority of the individuals in my audience are interested in the subject of marriage.
   Basis: Nearly everyone is between nineteen and twenty-six years of age; only two classmates are married; at least three indicated that they are now going with someone that they intend to marry; and nearly all indicated that they intend to marry and have children in the future. The fact that few are married and the fact that nearly all intend to marry leads me to believe that this audience will be interested in the topic of marriage.

Assumptions Speech

In a two-minute speech, share with the audience one of your five assumptions that no one else has given. State your assumption and the basis for it and see if the class agrees that it is true of a majority of your classmates. In one class hour you can share between ten and twenty assumptions that may be used to justify future topics for informative and persuasive speeches.

Vocabulary

attitude information The audience's positive or negative judgments about a topic.

audience adaptation A speaker's attempts to adjust to an audience by strategically choosing everything from an appropriate topic to appropriate attire to effective arguments and evidence for that audience.

audience analysis A speaker's procedure of discovering demographic, knowledge, interest, and attitude information about an audience, relevant to the speaker's purpose.

audience sensitivity A speaker's ability to anticipate and respond to an audience; combines skills of audience analysis and feedback interpretation; connotes flexibility and ability to adjust to an audience.

demographic information Verifiable facts about an audience, including such characteristics as age, sex, occupation, and race.

inference A tentative assumption that goes beyond the verifiable facts about an audience; an educated guess based on limited evidence.

interest information The topics, arguments, and ideas that are most likely to hold the audience's attention.

knowledge information How much or how little an audience knows about a topic.

1. Daryl Bem, *Beliefs, Attitudes and Human Affairs* (Belmont, Ca.: Brooks/Cole, 1970), p. 4.

Endnote

Chapter 4

Objectives

After completing chapter 4, you should be able to answer the following questions:
1. What determines the appropriateness of your topic?
2. What is meant by topic involvement, speaker competence, topic interest, worthwhileness, significance, and timeliness?
3. What are the differences among general purpose, long-range goal, and immediate purpose?
4. What are the two most common general purposes?

When you have completed chapter 4, you should have practiced skills in
1. Brainstorming for topics;
2. Narrowing and limiting a particular topic;
3. Stating a general purpose, a long-range goal, and an immediate purpose for a particular topic;
4. Stating the purpose of one of your speeches behaviorally; and
5. Listing some of the more common behavioral purposes of informative and persuasive speeches.

Application Exercises

1. Brainstorming for topics.
2. Brainstorming by topic areas.
3. What you read in the newspaper.
4. What magazines you read.
5. Topic, purposes, and goal.

Speech Preparation: Selecting a Topic and Stating Your Purpose

In all matters, before beginning, a diligent preparation should be made.

Cicero

After you have analyzed your audience, you are ready to begin the actual preparation of your speech. The first step is to select a topic and state your purpose. Probably no task in speechmaking gives novice speakers so much trouble. You may spend as much as ninety percent of your total preparation time thinking about topics on which to speak. This is common for beginning speakers. Therefore, this chapter is designed to provide you with assistance in the task of selecting a topic and stating your purpose.

Introduction

GEE, IT'S AMAZING HOW YOU CAN GET RIGHT THROUGH RUSH HOUR TRAFFIC SO EASY, BUGS.

IT JUST TAKES A LITTLE CAREFUL PLANNING.

STUDENT DRIVER

DANGER HIGH EXPLOSIVES

Reprinted by permission of NEA. © 1980 Warner Bros., Inc.

Selecting a Topic for You and Your Audience

You may be fortunate enough to have many topics about which you want to speak. If you do not, however, there are some methods that can help you assess your own interests. By applying these methods, you, like everyone else, will find that you know more about or are more interested in some topics than others. Whether you are conscious of it or not, for many years you have probably been reading and paying more attention to some ideas than to others. The purpose of the next sections, on brainstorming and personal inventories, is to help you tap your own resources so that you can discover speech topics that are appropriate to you and your audience.

Brainstorming for Topics

One of the most effective ways of selecting a topic for a speech is known as **brainstorming,** a technique in which you list or name as many possible ideas as you can in a certain period of time. Among the guidelines suggested for effective brainstorming are (1) don't criticize any ideas; (2) no idea is too wild; (3) quantity is important; and (4) seize opportunities to improve or add to ideas.[1]

Application Exercise 1: Brainstorming for Topics

In order to discover the usefulness of brainstorming and to generate a number of possible topics, try this exercise. Take out a pencil and paper, check the time, and allow yourself exactly five minutes to write down as many topics as come to mind. The topics do not have to be stated as specific speech topics: they can be individual words, phrases, or sentences. The range in number of ideas written in this exercise varies from five or six to as many as thirty possible topics.

After you have written down all the topics you can in five minutes, write three more topics in the next three minutes. Most people find it difficult to write down any more ideas, but those who can generally find their best ideas come after they have brainstormed for a period of time.

After you have completed your list of topics, select five that are particularly interesting to you. Finally, from these five, select the one that has the best potential for a public speech. Keep in mind that you should already have or be able to find information about this topic and that you will have to adapt the topic to a specific audience.

60   Speech Preparation: Selecting a Topic and Stating Your Purpose

Some people find they have better luck with a limited form of brainstorming. After some general topic areas are suggested, they brainstorm ideas relating to the specific area. Suggested topic areas might include "Current economic issues in the news," "Current political issues in the news," "Current social issues in the news," "Current educational issues in the news." Similarly, you might brainstorm for ideas relating to these broad topic areas: "Movies," "Television," "Music," "Books." If you feel this limited form of brainstorming might be helpful in identifying a topic for your speech, try the following exercise.

Application Exercise 2: Brainstorming by Topic Areas

Take out paper and pencil and divide the paper into four to six sections. Write down one of the following topic areas at the top of each section.

Job experiences you have had
Places you have traveled
City, state, or area you are from
People who make you angry
Happy experiences you have had
Unusual experiences you have had
Personal experiences with crime
Your involvement in marriage, divorce, or other family matters
Experiences with members of other groups—the old, the young, other racial or ethnic groups
The effect of the drug culture on your life
Your relationship to local, state, or federal government
Your background in painting, music, sculpture, theater, dance, or other arts
Your feelings about grades, college education, sororities and fraternities, college requirements, student government, or alternatives to a college education
Your reactions to current radio, television, or film practices, policies, or programming
Recent Supreme Court decisions that affect you
Your personal and career goals

Spend approximately three to five minutes jotting down specific topics for each of the four to six topic areas you chose. Underline one topic in each area that is especially interesting to you. From these four to six underlined topics, select the one for which you have the most information or best access to information and which you can adapt to your specific audience.

Personal Inventories Identifying Your Interests

Another way to identify topics for the public speech is to complete personal inventories. Personal inventories are more structured than most brainstorming techniques, but they are similar to limited brainstorming because they require self-analysis and understanding. Again, like limited brainstorming, personal inventories require you to look at your own behavior for clues about what attracts and interests you.

Every time you decide to read something, you make choices. For example, you select particular kinds of magazines, perhaps news magazines, gardening publications, or sports magazines. When you read the newspaper, you probably do not read the entire paper. Instead, you may read the front page, the comic section, and the sports section. Someone else may read the wedding announcements, the obituaries, and the want ads. The choices you make about reading materials directly reflect your interests. People have different interests, and those interests are reflected in the sections of the newspaper they read. To discover your own interests in a systematic manner, complete the following exercise.

Application Exercise 3: What You Read in the Newspaper

Consider the newspaper you generally read and record which sections you read often ($+$), sometimes (0), rarely or never ($-$).

_____ Front Page News	_____ Letters to the Editor	_____ Home and Family
_____ Comics	_____ Obituaries	_____ Art and Music
_____ Sports	_____ Birth and Wedding Announcements	_____ Books
_____ Opinion Page	_____ Travel	_____ Radio, Television, and Theater

Similarly, individuals' interests are reflected in the magazines they normally read. Complete this exercise to discover your own interests. Consider the magazines you normally purchase or subscribe to and note which ones you read regularly ($+$), occasionally (0), rarely or never ($-$).

_____ News Magazines (for example, *Time, Newsweek, U.S. News & World Report*)
_____ Traditional Women's Magazines (for example, *Ladies Home Journal, Good House-keeping, Redbook*)
_____ Feminist Publications (*Working Woman, Ms., New Woman*)
_____ Political Publications (*Nation, New Republic, National Review*)
_____ Recreational Magazines (*Sports Illustrated, Skiing, RV Travel*)
_____ Hobby Magazines (*Popular Mechanics, The Workbasket*)
_____ Confession Magazines (*True Story, True Confessions, Modern Romances*)
_____ Religious Magazines (*Commonweal, The Watchtower, The Upper Room*)
_____ Sex Emphasis Magazines (*Playboy, Playgirl, Penthouse, Cosmopolitan*)
_____ Professional Journals (*Elementary English, Journal of Abnormal and Social Psychology, American Educational Research Journal*)

The newspaper sections and magazines you typically read give a rough indication of some of your own interests. Other indications of personal interests are hobbies or leisure time activities, organizations to which you belong, books you have read recently, television shows you watch frequently, and kinds of movies you most enjoy. Your choice of college, major, and elective courses also usually indicates your interests.

After you have completed some form of personal inventory, you can identify more clearly speech topics or subject areas that are most appropriate for you. From your study of audience analysis in chapter 3, you know your topic choice must also be appropriate to your particular audience. In addition, time limitations, the classroom setting, and the general assignment will affect the topic you select. With all these factors in mind, we turn now to a consideration of the appropriateness of the topic you have tentatively selected.

Appropriateness of the Topic

Topic appropriateness depends on three factors: the speaker, the audience, and the speech occasion. The speaker should be interested in the topic and have some competence in the subject matter of his or her speech. The topic should also be of interest and value to the audience. Finally, the topic should be significant, timely, and appropriately narrowed and limited to the speaking situation. Let us consider each of these factors in more depth.

DENNIS the MENACE

"YOU MUSTN'T TALK ABOUT OUR PRIVATE LIFE TO THE NEIGHBORS."

"I DIDN'T KNOW WE **HAD** ONE."

Questions to Consider in Topic Selection

"Is the topic interesting to me?"
"Is my audience interested?"
"Is my topic narrow enough?"
"What does my audience feel about this?"
"How much do I know about the subject?"

Appropriateness to the Speaker

In chapter 2, we explored the importance of the speaker in public speaking. In this chapter, we emphasize the importance of the speaker's interests and abilities in selecting a speech topic. As a speaker, you should have **topic involvement;** that is, the topic should be one that matters to you. An easy test of your involvement with the topic you have tentatively selected is to ask yourself this question: "Would I feel that an attack on my speech is in some way an attack on me?" For instance,

if you gave your speech on bartending as a career for women and someone attacked the speech, would you see the commentator's criticism as a personal affront? If such an attack on your speech would not make you feel very defensive, your topic probably does not mean very much to you, and you are not highly involved in it.

You should also have some **topic competence** or expertise on the topic you have selected. Do you devote time and energy to the particular topic? Involvement and competence generally are signaled when you put in a great deal of time and expend a great deal of energy on something. If you are involved in pursuing a career in medicine, psychology, or home economics, you will display your interest by committing time and energy to learning the subject matter and the skills that will lead to success in one of those careers.

Observing fellow students as they speak will probably reveal to you those who are involved in their topics and those who are not. Speakers who talk with more conviction, passion, and authority are more involved with their topics. They give many indications that they care about the subject. The person who has, by chance, selected a topic from a *Reader's Digest* article the night before the speech usually cannot convey the sense of involvement that is so important in public speaking. When the president talks on television about one of his favorite plans, when Ralph

Nader speaks on consumerism, and when your professor discusses his or her favorite subject, they usually show that they are involved, that the topic is important to them. You can display the same kind of involvement by choosing a topic that is part of you.

If you select a topic in which you are involved, you will probably know more about that subject than do many of your classmates. This personal knowledge is something students often forget to consider in their speeches. Speeches do not have to consist entirely of sources from a library. They may be better, in fact, if you can make contributions from your own experience.

Each of us has personal experiences and knowledge that can be developed into an effective speech. You might consider your hometown, state, or country and its unique features that you can share. Is there something unusual in your college education or in your career plans? Do you have goals and aspirations that differ from those of your classmates? When the authors consider the most memorable speeches they have heard over a number of years of teaching, they remember the speech in which a young woman asked for donations to cancer research after she had told the audience about her own mother's tragic death from the disease; the speech in which a woman who had seventeen children attempted to persuade the audience against abortion; the speech in which a black man told of prejudicial treatment at the university; the speech in which a handicapped woman told the audience what it was like to be a student confined to a wheelchair; and the speech by the Vietnam veteran who spoke against military involvement in Southeast Asia. You may not be able to find an aspect of yourself or your experience that is quite as dramatic as these, but you can strengthen your speech by taking advantage of personal experience and previous knowledge of the topic.

Appropriateness to the Audience

In chapter 3 we explored the importance of audience analysis and adaptation. When you are considering the appropriateness of your topic to the particular audience you will be addressing, you should strive for **topic interest** and **topic worthwhileness;** that is, the topic should be worth the time and attention the audience will be asked to devote to your speech. In order to adapt your topic to the audience, you should discover all you can about the audience that is relevant to your topic. From the information you gather and the inferences you are able to draw, you will be better able to decide how you should reconcile your topic with this audience.

Audience analysis can reveal the challenges you face in making the topic interesting to your audience. For instance, if you want to speak in favor of engineering as a career for women and your audience analysis indicates that a majority of your listeners are men majoring in engineering and women majoring in science, you should not necessarily conclude that the topic is inappropriate. Instead, you will have to adapt your persuasive message to a position that is more familiar to them. For example, you may initially make the audience less comfortable with their stereotyped career choices so they are "softened" for a position closer to the one you hold.

Speech Preparation: Selecting a Topic and Stating Your Purpose

"I would like to talk to you for a minute today about the causes of war, the history of war since 4280 B.C., the effects wars have on societies and finally, possible solutions to war."

When you are to give an informative speech, audience analysis might indicate that the audience already knows a great deal about your tentative subject. This might cause you to question whether the topic is worthwhile for that audience. At the least, you will have to adapt your topic by finding additional information they do not have on the subject. For example, if you want to deliver an informative speech on the latest domestic crisis, but your analysis of the audience indicates a high information level, you can adapt your topic by changing the perspective to an aspect of the subject on which they are not so well informed. You might consider discussing the background of the conflict, the background of the personalities and the issues, experts' speculation on future events, the possible consequences of the confrontation, or other related but less well-known matters. Audience analysis helps you adapt your topic to the particular audience and ensures that the topic will be worthwhile to them.

Appropriateness to the Occasion

Finally, the topic should be appropriate to the public speaking occasion. The topic should have **topic significance;** it should concern a major issue rather than a minor one. It also should have **topic timeliness;** that is, it should be current or relevant. **Topic narrowness** is also important to limit the amount or range of information presented.

In order to be significant, the topic need not focus on "beauty," "goodness," or "truth"; nor should it necessarily deal with world-shaking events. On the other hand, describing to an audience how you spent last Saturday night, what you ate for breakfast, or with whom you graduated from high school are probably not significant enough to warrant a public speech.

We can usually distinguish between highly significant topics and nonsignificant ones. However, the precise degree of significance is more difficult to determine and often depends on the particular public speaking situation, including the classroom setting, time of day, general assignment, and other speeches that have preceded yours.

For example, in preparing for your speech, you should recognize and acknowledge the speeches that have preceded yours. Students frequently express concern over choosing the same topic that another student has selected. Most teachers do not limit their students to topics that have not been used before in their classrooms, but you should be aware of changes you may need to make if someone else speaks on the same topic. Occasionally two students will speak on the same topic on the same day; sometimes one of these students will directly follow the other. When this occurs, you should recognize the importance of timeliness and adapt your speech accordingly. Do not apologize for your topic choice; instead, acknowledge that the class has been given valuable background information on the topic and try to expand on the information they already possess.

The topic should also be timely or relevant to current events. One of the authors recalls hearing an informative speech on a predicted revolution in a South American country. While the speech was generally appropriate for the speaker, the audience, and the occasion, it was not a successful speech because it was dated—the revolution had occurred well over a year before.

Finally, the topic should be appropriately narrowed and limited. If you believe that your tentative topic is too broad, you probably need to reduce it to more manageable proportions by making it more specific and less abstract. If, in brainstorming, you came up with the topic of overpopulation, and your personal inventory indicated that you have an interest in sociology and medicine, you might consider using this topic after you have narrowed it to more appropriate dimensions. You might limit the topic by making it increasingly specific and concrete, as in this sample:

Overpopulation
Overpopulation in developing nations
Overpopulation in India
Religion as a cause of overpopulation in India
The effect of the Hindu religion on overpopulation in India

This topic has now been limited enough for an eight- to ten-minute speech.

If you cannot narrow and limit your topic by making it more specific, you might take the broad topic category and try to think of as many particular smaller topics as you can that would fit under that heading:

Overpopulation
Historical overpopulation
Sociological effects of overpopulation
Control of overpopulation
Ethical considerations in the control of overpopulation
Effects of overpopulation on this campus
Overpopulation: Projections for the year 2000

This list could continue. All of the topics are related to overpopulation, and at least some topics would be adequately limited for an eight- to ten-minute speech. Either of these two methods can be used to reduce the broad topics resulting from brainstorming and personal inventories.

Now answer the questions in Checklist 3. If you cannot answer yes to all of them, you need to spend additional time on your choice of a topic before going on to state the purpose and goal of your speech. When you can answer all these questions in the affirmative, you are ready to proceed.

_____	1. Do you, as the speaker, have *involvement* with the topic?
_____	2. Do you, as the speaker, have *competence* in the topic area?
_____	3. Based on audience analyses, does this topic hold *interest* for your audience?
_____	4. Based on audience analyses, is the topic *worthwhile* to your audience?
_____	5. Is the topic *significant* in terms of the speech occasion?
_____	6. Is the topic *timely* in terms of the speech occasion?
_____	7. Have you appropriately *narrowed and limited* the topic for the occasion?

Checklist 3: Checklist for Topic Appropriateness

After you have selected a topic for your speech and considered its appropriateness to you, your audience, and the public speaking occasion, your next task is to write a statement of purpose. Your statement should encompass a general purpose, an ultimate goal, and an immediate purpose.

Stating the Purpose of Your Speech

The **general purpose** of your speech is the overall reaction you seek from your audience. Your general purpose may be to *inform*—to have your listeners achieve understanding, comprehension, or knowledge. In other words, you wish to achieve cognitive change in your audience. You want the audience to know more, to understand more. You may want your listeners to understand the causes of a disease, the uses of an instrument, the places where they can find something, types of trees, origins of language, the dangers of drugs, or historical reasons for overpopulation in India.

General Purpose: To Inform, to Persuade

Another general purpose of public speaking is to *persuade*. Persuasive speaking is a form of communication in which the speaker intentionally attempts to modify the listeners' behavior by changing perceptions, attitudes, beliefs, or values. The purpose of the persuasive speech is to alter the audience's cognitions (what they know), their affective domain (how they feel about what they know), and ultimately their behavior (how they act).

Other general purposes of speeches are to entertain, advocate, actuate, describe, and define. These general purposes, identified by various speech teachers, are only a few of the many general purposes of speeches that can be identified and categorized. They occur less frequently than speeches to inform or persuade. In fact, some of them form subsets of the two main general purposes. In this book we will concentrate on the speech to inform and the speech to persuade.

Ultimate Goal of Your Speech

The ultimate goal of your speech is the "end product" you have in mind for your audience. The ultimate goal is generally not realized in a single speech, but is accomplished over a long period of time with several persuasive or informative attempts. Your speech is only one bit of information or persuasion that will contribute toward this end product. For example, politicians running for political office have as their ultimate goal persuading the voters to elect them. In your daily interactions with your parents, you may be attempting to persuade them to perceive you as more responsible than they currently do. In a variety of ways—through your handling of your finances, through your care in using the family car, through your sensitivity to their feelings, and through your verbalizations—you wage a persuasive campaign. Your ultimate goal in a public speech may be to increase the sensitivity of your audience to sexist language, to have the audience stop drinking, to inform the audience of the role of the papacy in the Roman Catholic Church, or to persuade listeners to avoid aerosol sprays.

Immediate Purpose of Your Speech

The **immediate purpose** of your speech is linked to the general purpose and the ultimate goal. It is what you want your audience to know, to understand, or to do as an *immediate* result of your speech. It is the purpose of your one "bit" of information or persuasion. The audience has no doubt heard something about your topic before, and they are likely to hear something about it again. Your particular presentation is just one exposure in a series they are likely to have to that topic in a lifetime. Among your immediate purposes may be to have the audience learn the officer ranks in the U.S. Army, to have them distinguish between two similar butterflies, to make sure they can recall the name of a candidate for city council, or to tell their children that they love them.

The more specific your purpose, the easier it is to determine whether you have accomplished it. The only way we know that cognitive, affective, or behavioral change has occurred is to observe or measure behavior. A history teacher cannot tell if a student knows a chronology of events unless the student can list the order of events on paper or in an oral statement. The politician running for re-election cannot tell if her constituents are persuaded that she has a good record unless they vote for her in the election. Stating the purpose of your speech in behavioral terms increases the likelihood of determining effectiveness.

Some behavioral purposes of informative speeches include getting an audience to *recognize* differences or similarities between or among objects, persons, or events; to *compare* items; to *define* words, objects, or concepts; and to *state* what they will know as a result of your speech. For example, an informative speaker might say, "The immediate purpose of my speech is to have the audience remember at least three of the four reasons I cite for purchasing their food at a discount market"; "The immediate purpose of my speech is to teach the audience to distinguish between a clerk-typist and a secretary"; "The immediate purpose of my speech is to enable the audience to recognize edible mushrooms." In each case the purpose is stated in such a way that the speaker can determine whether it has been accomplished.

Behavioral Objectives

To read more about the topic
To sign this letter
To complain to officials
To tell others
To listen to other speakers on the topic
To join a group
To vote
To eat
To answer my questions
To state my main arguments

Among the behavioral purposes of persuasive speeches are getting an audience to *accept* or *reject* an idea; *approve* or *disapprove* of a plan; *agree* or *disagree* with a suggestion; *favor* or *oppose* a person, object, or concept; *buy* or *stop buying* a product; and *vote* or *not vote* in a prescribed manner. For instance, a persuasive speaker might state, "The immediate purpose of my speech is to have the audience stop buying deodorants in aerosol cans"; "The immediate purpose of my speech is to persuade the audience to oppose the idea of a lower drinking age in this state"; "The immediate purpose of my speech is to persuade the audience not to vote in the upcoming student body elections."

The relationship among the general purpose, the ultimate goal, and the immediate purpose of a speech is illustrated in figure 4.1.

Figure 4.1 Purposes
and goals of public
speaking.

Purposes and Goals of Public Speaking.

General purpose	Ultimate goal	Immediate purpose
To persuade	To persuade people to oppose nuclear power as an energy source	To have the audience recall three dangers of using nuclear power plants as a source of energy
To inform	To have the audience understand and appreciate the language used by some blacks	To have the audience state six expressions that are part of the ''street language'' used by urban blacks
To persuade	To discourage the audience from eating junk food	To have the audience describe the nutritional value of two popular junk foods

In order to gain experience in formulating general purposes, ultimate goals, and immediate purposes, complete the following exercise. For each of the topics specify the missing information. Remember to write the immediate purposes in behavioral terms.

Topic	General Purpose	Ultimate Goal	Immediate Purpose
Edible plants	To persuade	To convice the audience to eat plants they find in the wild.	_____ _____ _____ _____
Waterbeds	_____	_____ _____ _____ _____	To have the audience list three benefits of sleeping on a waterbed.
Marijuana	To persuade	_____ _____ _____ _____	_____ _____ _____ _____
Shoplifting	To inform	_____ _____ _____ _____	To have the audience state how much shoplifting costs the consumer.
Selection of the pope	To inform	To give the audience an understanding of how the pope is elected.	_____ _____ _____ _____ _____
Animal abuse	_____	_____ _____ _____ _____	To have the audience distinguish between animal abuse and animal discipline.

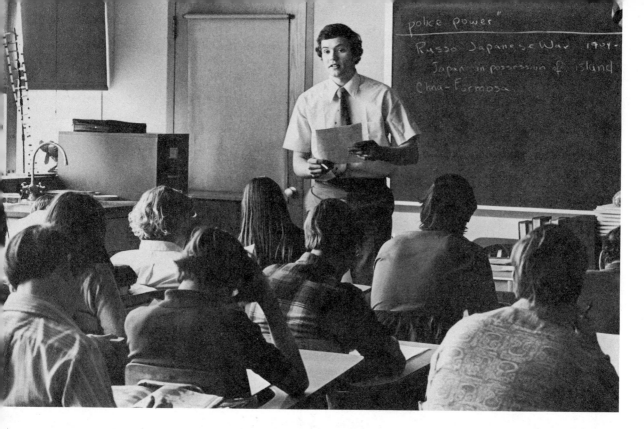

Conclusion

In this chapter you examined ways of selecting a topic and stating a purpose. You learned two methods of generating topic ideas: brainstorming and taking personal inventories. After you have tentatively selected a topic using one of these methods, you determined the appropriateness of your topic. The topic must be one with which you have *involvement* and in which you have some degree of *competence*. The topic should be of *interest* to the listeners and be *worthwhile*. The topic should be *significant, timely,* and appropriately *narrowed and limited* for the speaking situation.

You also learned that the statement of purpose includes the general purpose—most often to inform or to persuade; the ultimate goal—the long-range change you want from the audience; and the immediate purpose—the action you want from your audience right after your speech. The immediate purpose should be written in behavioral terms so you can determine your effectiveness in the speech.

Select a topic that you found through brainstorming or taking personal inventories. Make sure that the topic is appropriate for you, the audience, and the speech occasion. See that it is interesting and worthwhile to the audience as well as significant, timely, and appropriately narrowed and limited. At the top of your paper write your name and your topic. Then indicate your general purpose, your ultimate goal, and your immediate purpose for the speech. Your paper should look like this:

Topic: Carver Hall—the Man Behind the Building
General Purpose: *to inform* the audience about a campus building and the person after whom it was named.
Ultimate Goal: to encourage classmates *to read* a brief book that tells the stories behind the names of campus buildings.
Immediate Purpose: to provide information about Carver Hall and George Washington Carver that my classmates can *tell* roommates and acquaintances, by remembering at least three of the five facts I will relate about the black scientist after whom the building is named.

Make sure that your ultimate goal and immediate purpose include ways that your audience will behave differently as a result of your speech.

brainstorming A technique in which one lists or names as many possible ideas as one can in a limited amount of time.

general purpose The overall response a speaker seeks from an audience; usually to persuade or to inform.

immediate purpose What the speaker wants the audience to know, understand, or do immediately.

topic competence A characteristic of an appropriate topic for the speaker; a speaker's knowledge of or expertise in his or her chosen topic.

topic interest A characteristic of an appropriate speech; the topic's ability to hold the audience's attention.

topic involvement A characteristic of an appropriate speech topic for the speaker; the speaker's interest in the topic, often accompanied by a willingness to devote time and energy to the topic.

topic narrowness A characteristic of a speech topic that is appropriate to the occasion. The limiting of a topic to the time allowed, the setting, and the general assignment.

topic significance A characteristic of an appropriate speech topic for the occasion; the topic's concern with a major idea or issue rather than a minor one.

topic timeliness A characteristic of an appropriate speech topic for the occasion; the topic is current or relevant to the present.

topic worthwhileness A characteristic of an appropriate speech topic for the audience; the topic warrants the audience's time and attention.

ultimate goal The long-range purpose or end product a speaker wants from an audience.

1. Alex F. Osborn, *Applied Imagination: Principles and Procedures of Creative Thinking* (New York: Scribner's, 1953), pp. 300–301.

Chapter 5

Objectives

After completing chapter 5, you should be able to answer the following questions:

1. Which of your experiences should you speak about?
2. How can you get information and ideas from other people?
3. Where can you find written information on your topic?
4. How do you correctly record information from interviews and printed sources?
5. What kinds of supporting materials can you use in your speech?
6. How do you correctly outline the content of your speech?
7. What are some organizational patterns from which you can choose?

When you have completed chapter 5, you should have practiced skills in

1. Interviewing another person for ideas and information;
2. Using indexes to find printed information;
3. Recording information from interviews and printed sources;
4. Citing sources in correct footnote and bibliographic form;
5. Evaluating supporting materials;
6. Outlining your own speech by following the principles of subordination, division, and parallelism; and
7. Choosing organizational patterns that are appropriate to the topic and to the audience.

Application Exercises

1. Evaluating personal experience.
2. Interviewing for information.
3. Library scavenger hunt.
4. Getting your sources in shape.
5. Subordination, division, and parallelism.

Finding, Evaluating, and Organizing Support Material

Order and simplification are the first steps towards mastery of a subject.

Thomas Mann

You have selected and narrowed your speech topic to fit the occasion. You have analyzed your audience and know how they are likely to respond to your topic. Now, what will you include in your speech? What will be its main ingredients? Where will you find the arguments, statements, and supporting materials? How will you organize the information so that the audience will comprehend and remember it?

This chapter is devoted to increasing your confidence as a public speaker by helping you find, evaluate, and organize information. Even after you have selected a topic, you are unlikely to have enough current information to fulfill the assignment. Therefore, you need to know how to find more information on the topic. Once you find the information, you need to be able to evaluate it so that you use only the best and most effective support material in your speech. Finally, when you have the best support materials on hand, you need to know the most effective way to organize those materials in your speech.

In this chapter you will find the answers to three questions: Where can you find ideas and information for your speech? What kinds of support materials can you use in your speech? and How can you arrange your materials effectively?

Where Can You Find Ideas and Information for Your Speech?

Once you have your narrowed topic in mind and know what your general purpose, long-range goal, and immediate purpose are, the detective work begins—you have to find information and ideas. Where do you find them? The three main sources of information for public speeches are your personal experience, interviews, and printed materials.

Main Sources of Information for Public Speeches

1. Personal experience
2. Interviews
3. Printed materials

Personal Experience

One of the most powerful sources of information is you, yourself. You have gone to school for at least a dozen years; you may have worked at various jobs after school and during summers; and you may have gone places and met people who taught you some lessons in living. You may have married, returned to school after serving in the armed forces or after raising a family, or simply dropped out to "find yourself." Whatever your story, it is not *exactly* like anyone else's. In your own personal experience you can find the materials that will provide ideas, supporting materials, and arguments for your speeches.

Unfortunately, many students do not see themselves as unusual or unique. Often on the first day of class the authors have students identify themselves by name, major, hometown, year in school, age, and any other demographic information they wish to supply. That part is easy. It is more difficult to answer the question, "Why are you unique?" If anyone in the class has the same characteristic, then the person has to think of another "unique" feature. The class decides if the characteristic or experience is really unique.

A first step in seeking information for your topic is to consider your unusual or unique experience with the topic: Do you want to talk about alcoholism because someone in your family is an alcoholic? Do you want to talk about cloning because you are a biological science major? Do you want to discuss hydroponics because you are interested in plant production?

You may need to probe your own background to discover topic-relatedness. One of the authors spent two years as the pre-law advisor at a university. Part of the job was to write the "Dean's Recommendation" for students who wanted to enter law school. In order for the author to write the recommendation, students were interviewed for unusual information about themselves that might help them appear attractive to law schools. Often the students were unable to identify their own unusual or unique experiences until after the interview. One student called to ask if it made any difference that he had been a student for one summer in the Soviet Union. Another showed up a few days after the interview to ask if it made any difference that she was a concert pianist. Still another wondered if he should apply to anything other than the local law school. He did not see himself as unique. He was a national merit scholar finalist who finished college in three years with a straight "A" average. What have you done? What have you experienced? What is distinctive about you that could increase your credibility or supply you with information for your speech? Look first to yourself.

Application Exercise 1: Evaluating Personal Experience

A second important source of ideas and information is interviews. Whatever your college, you are likely to be surrounded by faculty members who are knowledgeable about hundreds of topics. Your community, too, is probably full of people who know a great deal about certain topics: government officials such as

Interviews

mayors, councilpersons, and city managers; members of the clergy; physicians; engineers; owners and managers of business and industry. These people can provide information for your speech.

A student once came to our office without a speech topic the day before he was to give his speech. He had actually selected a topic but could find nothing on it because another student had cut out all the information from magazines, newspapers, and books in the library. The first student was very angry. Together we decided that he should explore the topic he felt so passionately about at the moment: the destruction of library resources.

The student made an appointment that morning with the associate director of the library. He hit a gold mine. The associate director was part of a national study team investigating the destruction of library resources. He was enthusiastic about finding a student who was also interested. After two hours with the associate director, the student knew the average number of pages destroyed in the popular magazines, the cost of replacing or repairing the damaged sources, and the extent of damage at his own university. He had more information than he could have ever found in written sources. When he gave his speech, he was still passionate about the topic and was armed with the facts and figures from an authoritative source. For him, the interview had provided all the information he needed.

You may not find all the information you need in just one interview, but you may discover that interviewing is the most efficient way to gather information on your topic. The interviewee can share the results of his or her work with you, provide you with opinions you can quote in your speech, and lead you to other sources you would be unlikely to find on your own.

How do you go about conducting an interview? Before you interview someone, you may need to review some basic principles. The first is that *interviewing requires planning and preparation:* you need to know in advance what you are going to ask. Well-planned questions will provide information you can use, while a rambling conversation may yield nothing. If you have just a few questions that can be answered quickly, you may be able to interview over the phone simply by stating who you are, why you want information, and what information you want. If you have many questions that will take some time to answer, you should ask for an appointment, telling the person who you are and what information you seek.

Planning and Preparation

Here are some possible interview questions and a rationale for each:

1. How do you happen to know so much about this topic? Rationale: You want to determine the interviewee's background and level of expertise.
2. What facts and figures are most important to know on this topic? Rationale: You need facts, figures, and supporting materials for your speech. You should take careful notes and repeat back opinions and statements that you can quote in your speech, so that they will be accurate.
3. Do you have any suggestions for finding additional information on this subject? Rationale: Usually an expert on any topic will have or know of books, articles, and journals with specific information. These sources may be available in the library or borrowed from the interviewee. He or she may also refer you to another person for further information.
4. Have you found any particularly good ways to transmit information on this topic to others? Rationale: Sometimes your interviewee will have visual aids—posters, slides, films, videotapes—that he or she will let you use. If the interviewee does not offer them, you can at least find or make some of your own.

A second principle of interviewing is that you should *record information accurately.* The simplest method is to tape record the interview with the other person's permission. If either you or the interviewee feels uncomfortable about this, then notetaking is your alternative. In either case, strive for accuracy. Toward the end of the interview you may wish to read or "play back" those portions you expect to use in your speech to verify their accuracy.

Record Information Accurately

Since you are unlikely to use all the information you gather in an interview, you need to know how to select direct quotations. If you leave out some portion of what the interviewee said, you need to make sure the omission does not distort the meaning. To indicate an omission at the beginning of a written sentence, use three periods: ". . . watching football games has become a substitute for regular exercise." Similarly, at the end of a sentence, three periods indicate omission, and a fourth indicates the end of a sentence: "However, watching TV and drinking beer don't help your heart. . . ." Deleting information from the middle of a sentence is also indicated with three periods: "Far from overjoyed . . . he was despondent."

Indicating omissions in the spoken word is more difficult and ordinarily unnecessary. You can, however, state that you are omitting some material by saying, "Dr. Stronghart said, *in part:* '[. . .] exercise programs are a must for students who want to ensure good health in their future.' "

Just as you would in a written report, you must cite the source for information given in your speech. You do this by means of an oral footnote. In this case the oral footnote should include the name of the interviewee, the person's rank or title, and the basis of her or his expertise. In a speech the oral footnote might be worded this way: "According to Dr. Joseph Stronghart, Director of the College Exercise Clinic and author of two manuals on the subject. . . ." In an outline or document accompanying the speech, the citation would look like this:

[1]Dr. Joseph Stronghart, Director of the Exercise Clinic, Central College, August 1, 1983.

Application Exercise 2: Interviewing for Information

Ask your teacher or fellow students if they know anyone who is knowledgeable about your topic. Make an appointment with that person. Develop some specific questions that will provide information you can use in your speech. Take careful notes or record the interview. Select information and direct quotations you can cite in your speech along with oral footnotes.

Printed Materials

A third source of information for your speech is printed materials: newspapers, magazine and journal articles, government documents, pamphlets, books, and so on. How to find and record information from these materials is the subject of this section.

Every library has a card catalog that contains information on each book in the library, arranged by author, title, and subject. If you do not know the name of an author or the exact title of a book, you can look up the subject to see what available books deal with that subject. If your speech topic is water pollution, look not only under the subject "Water Pollution" but also under related subjects like "Conservation," "Environment," or "Natural Resources." Only under rare circumstances should you have to read an entire book for information. Instead, you can use a book's index or table of contents to lead you to the specific information you need.

Locating
Information

Every library also has the *Reader's Guide to Periodical Literature*. The *Reader's Guide* is usually located among the reference books and contains the titles of articles, listed by subject, from about 150 magazines and journals. By checking your topic and related subjects, you can usually find a significant number of appropriate articles.

Most college and city libraries have a large number of reference works that can be useful in discovering information for your speeches. You can often find background information in encyclopedias like *Encyclopaedia Britannica* or *Encyclopedia Americana*. However, information on current issues is unlikely to be found here. For information on people, you can use *Who's Who in America* or the *Dictionary of American Biography*. For statistics, facts, and details about

such subjects as demographics, the economy, or even the weather, consult *Statesman's Yearbook, Statistical Abstract of the United States,* or the *World Almanac and Book of Facts.* All these sources are located in the reference section of the library.

If your topic is very current, it may not be covered extensively in any book or general reference work. You may have to secure your information from a newspaper. The *New York Times* is widely regarded as an authoritative source among newspapers, and it is indexed. Current issues of local and state newspapers also often contain late-breaking stories. General and specialized indexes will lead you to books and periodicals on many topics.

If your topic is highly specialized, you will have to go to a specialized index. For example, if you are going to give a speech criticizing the school grading system, the most likely index to use is the *Education Index,* a guide to 150 magazines and journals dealing with education. If you are planning a speech about human behavior or literature, you may turn to the *Index to Behavioral Sciences and Humanities.* Keep in mind that most articles referred to in specialized indexes are written by experts and may need simplifying for your classroom audience.

The dictionary is useful for spelling, pronunciation, and meanings. Your library may have general dictionaries, like Webster's *Third New International Dictionary* and the exceedingly thorough *Oxford English Dictionary,* as well as more specialized dictionaries.

A partial list of reference works is shown in figure 5.1. This list gives an idea of the wealth of information the enterprising student can find in a library.

Figure 5.1 Printed resources for the public speaker.

Written Resources for the Public Speaker.

General indexes to periodicals
Reader's Guide to Periodical Literature. 1900-. (Author, title, subject)
Book Review Digest. 1905-. (Author, title, subject)
Social Sciences and Humanities Index. 1965-. (Author, subject)
New York Times Index. 1913-. (Author, subject)

Special indexes to periodicals
Art Index. 1929-. (Author, subject)
Bibliographic Index. 1937-. (Subject)
Biography Index. 1946-. (Subject)
Book Review Index. 1965-.
Catholic Periodical Index. 1930-. (Subject)
Education Index. 1929-. (Author, subject)
Biological and Agricultural Index. 1964-. (Subject)
Engineering Index. 1884-. (Subject)
Quarterly Cumulative Index Medicus. 1927-. (Author, subject)
Index to Book Reviews in the Humanities. 1960-.
Index to Legal Periodicals. 1908-. (Author, subject)
Business Periodicals Index. 1958-. (Subject)
Music Index. 1949-. (Author, subject)
Public Affairs Information Service. 1915-. (Subject)
Technical Book Review Index. 1935-.

Specialized Dictionaries
Fowler, H. W. *A Dictionary of Modern English Usage.* 2d ed., 1965.
Partridge, Eric. *Dictionary of Slang and Unconventional English.* 7th ed., 1970.
Roget's International Thesaurus. 4th ed., 1977.
Webster's New Dictionary of Synonyms. 1978.

Specialized Encyclopedias
Buttrick, George A., and Keith R. Crim, eds. *Interpreter's Dictionary of the Bible.* 5 vols. 1976.
Dictionary of American History. 8 vols. 1976.
Encyclopedia of World Art. 15 vols. 1959-68.
Illing, Robert. *Dictionary of Musicians and Music.* 2 vols. 1976.
Mitzel, Harold, ed. *Encyclopedia of Educational Research.* 4 vols. 1982.
Munn, Glenn G. *Encyclopedia of Banking and Finance.* 7th rev. ed., 1973.
Turner, John, ed. *Encyclopedia of Social Work.* 17th ed. 2 vols. 1977.

Yearbooks
Americana Annual. 1923-.
The Annual Register of World Events. 1958-.
Economic Almanac. 1940-.
Facts on File. 1940-.
Information Please Almanac. 1947-.
New International Year Book. 1907-.
Statesman's Year-Book. 1864-.
Statistical Abstract of the United States. 1878-.
World Almanac and Book of Facts. 1868-.

Application Exercise 3: Library Scavenger Hunt

You are much more likely to use reference works if you know where they are in the library and if you know what kind of information is in them. The following exercise is designed to better acquaint you with the library and its reference works.

1. From the card catalog find the author and title of one book that deals with your topic.

   Author _____ Title _____

   _____

2. From the *Reader's Guide to Periodical Literature* find the title and author of one article on your topic.

   Author _____ Title _____

   _____

3. Using the *Education Index* or other specialized index, give the author, title, and name of publication for an article on the topic you have selected.

   Author _____ Title _____

   _____ Publication _____

4. Using an encyclopedia or a yearbook, find specific information about your topic. In one sentence explain what kind of information you found.

   _____

   _____

   Source _____

Recording Information

The simplest and most efficient method of gathering information from printed sources is by taking notes on 3″ × 5″ or 4″ × 6″ index cards. At the top of the first card for a particular source, record complete bibliographical information. On any subsequent cards for the same source, abbreviate this information. Complete bibliographical information for a book includes author, title, place of publication, name of publisher, and date of publication. Here is an example.

Underhill, Robert. *The Truman Persuasions*. Ames, Iowa: Iowa State University Press, 1981.

If your source is a magazine or journal article, your bibliographical information will include article author, article title, magazine, volume number and/or date, and the pages on which the article appears.

Deming, Caren J. "Two Dream Machines: Television and the Human Brain," *Public Communication Review* 1(Fall 1981):5–9.

Figure 5.2 Correct
form for a research
note card.

```
"A Bitter Pill for Aspirin Makers."  Business Week, July 5, 1982, p. 78.


                         Aspirin and Children

Tylenol, an analgesic alternative to aspirin, has captured 37% of the
market.  Now aspirin is facing another problem:  it has been linked to
Reye's syndrome, a disease that affects 600-1200 children per year and
has a fatality rate of 20-30%.  Richard Schweiker, Secretary of Health and
Human Services is pressing for a warning label.  Business Week reports
that "The effect of such labeling would be to throw open the $100 million
children's analgesic market, of which Children's Tylenol has the largest
share."
```

Beneath the bibliography, record the topic and information relevant to it. Be sure to place quotation marks around material you take directly from the source. At the top of the card note the specific page or pages from which the information came.

The completed card should look something like the one shown in figure 5.2. A second note card from this same source would need only an abbreviated entry such as "Aspirin, *BW,* p. 78." This method of taking notes permits you to cite your source accurately, to record information accurately, and to indicate both paraphrasing and direct quotations.

When writing a paper, indicate in footnotes where you found your information. When delivering a speech, indicate where you got your information in oral footnotes, which are considerably simpler and briefer than those used for writing. Oral footnotes are indicated by italics in figure 5.3. Whatever form a footnote takes, the principle remains the same: give credit to others when you use their words and ideas.

Not all sources of material receive the same respect or believability. For instance, if you were to give a speech on the changing nature of sex roles in the United States, *Ladies Home Journal* would not be granted the same respect as the scholarly publication *The Journal of Consulting and Clinical Psychology* or the highly relevant journal *Sex Roles.* We will discuss the kinds of support materials you can use—and some questions you should ask about the evidence found in surveys and studies—in the next section. At this point, and before you complete the exercise that follows, you should understand that some sources of material are superior to others in believability or credibility.

Figure 5.3 Oral
footnotes for public
speaking.

Oral Footnotes for Public Speaking

Citing a source for paraphrased information:
According to *Consumer Reports*, the Federal Trade Commission has cracked down on the STP Corporation for violating its 1976 cease-and-desist order.

Citing a source for a direct quotation:
Theodore White in his book entitled *In Search of History* states, ''What I learned was that people accept government only if the government accepts its first duty—which is to protect them.''

Citing a magazine, a reference work, and a speech:
In his speech on campus one month ago, Andrew Young. . . .

Last week's *Time* magazine reported. . . .

According to *World Almanac*, the number of people in. . . .

''. . . yet how is it these vital facts are virtually unknown in this country today?''

© 1952 Punch/Rothco

To be sure your sources are accurate, you must state them in correct form. Can you, from the models shown earlier, correctly place the following two sources in correct bibliographical form?

Source A: Title of article is Black Student's Guide, author is Dennis A. Williams, page is 108, magazine is Newsweek, volume is C–19, date is November 8, 1982.

_____

_____

Source B: Publisher is Congdon & Weed, book is Growing Up, date is 1982, author is Russell Baker, place of publication is New York.

_____

_____

Record three sources for your topic in correct bibliographical form:

_____

_____

_____

_____

_____

_____

Your personal experiences, your interviews with knowledgeable people, and your use of written resources can provide the content for your speech. However, you should also know exactly what kinds of information and ideas to seek in preparing a speech. In this section you will find seven forms of supporting material: examples, explanations, quotations, narrations, statistics, comparisons, and analogies. Accompanying each of these forms of support will be some questions about each, to help you determine its strength or appropriateness for your speech.

Forms of Supporting Material

1. Examples
2. Explanations
3. Quotations
4. Narrations
5. Statistics
6. Comparisons
7. Analogies

Examples

Examples are particular instances that illustrate or clarify a concept; they can be actual or hypothetical. Actual instances are those that really occurred; hypothetical instances are those that (while they might *actually* have occurred) have been created by the speaker and identified as instances that might only *possibly* occur. Sometimes a single example will be sufficient because your audience either easily understands or accepts your point; at other times several examples may be necessary to gain audience understanding. Let us imagine that you are delivering a speech claiming that much advertising is sexist. You might need some actual sexist advertisements to help prove your point. You could provide further examples by mentioning that males are often portrayed as beer drinkers and women as tea drinkers. A third approach using examples might be to use a hypothetical example to illustrate how men or women could feel left out by an advertisement.

Some questions to ask about the example as a form of support in a speech are: Is the example actual or hypothetical? Is the example typical or is it highly unusual? Is the example relevant to the claim it is supporting? An actual example should be an accurate statement of what occurred; a hypothetical example should be identified as a statement of what could possibly occur. The less typical or common an example, the less believable it becomes as proof; the more relevant the example to the point being made, the stronger it stands as support.

Explanations

A second form of supporting material is the explanation. **Explanations** clarify a concept or idea for an audience by revealing how or why something occurs or what it is. The best explanation is brief, to the point, and insightful in advancing audience understanding. A student in electrical engineering was faced with the problem of explaining how electricity gets from the power plant to the light bulb in your home. She did so by following the enormous amount of electricity produced in a coal-fired power plant along the high-power lines, through the transformers, and into the home. She clarified, for an audience that knew very little about electricity, the many reductions and routes it must travel for effective use.

Some questions to ask of explanations in your speech include: Is your explanation long enough to clarify but short enough to retain audience interest? Is your explanation insightful, so that it invites the audience to think, "Aha, now I understand?" Finally, is your explanation really simpler and more understandable than the concept or idea that it is designed to explain? Length is important in explanations because many speakers are tempted to take the listener "on a long road to a small house;" insight is necessary in an explanation in order to produce clarity; and simplicity and understanding are the means by which you can render difficult or complex ideas palatable to your audience.

Reprinted by permission: Tribune Company Syndicate, Inc.

Quotations, or testimony, are a third form of supporting material frequently found in speeches. A quotation is the words of someone else, stated and attributed to support some idea or argument of your own. Two reasons for using someone else's words are most common: first, it lets you show that you are not the only one who thinks the way you do, by quoting important persons who agree with you. If you can show that a research physician from Mayo Clinic supports the idea you are trying to communicate to your audience, then you might have a better chance of gaining their acceptance as well. Second, quotations can often state an idea or argument so well that their eloquence can help you gain audience acceptance. The giants of literature, stars of stage and screen, and even some experts might have stated an idea in a way that will catch the ear of your audience—and add luster to your speech as well.

Some questions to ask of quotations or testimonial support materials include: is the person you quote an expert whose opinions are worthier than those of other people? Is the person being quoted about a subject in his or her area of expertise? Is the person more qualified than you or others, by virtue of education, experience, or both? And will your audience find your ideas clearer or more convincing because you used the quotation? Often a quotation is only as good as the person who uttered it; so the public speaker needs to carefully assess both what is said and who said it.

Narrations—stories or anecdotes—are a fourth form of supporting material that occur often in public speeches. Narrations are usually regarded as relatively weak when used as evidence or proof, but they are regarded as relatively strong as a method of clarification. Narrations, like examples, can be actual or hypothetical, real or created. They are good for conveying the feelings and emotions that accompany an issue. An army of numbers about poverty and quotations from famous sociologists might not convey the feelings and emotions of unemployment as well as a single story about a family of five trying to live through their third month without an income.

Not all narrations are worthy of use in a speech. The following questions should be asked: Is the story completely relevant to the point it is supposed to support? Is the story actual or hypothetical and identified as such? Is the narrative specific, concrete, detailed, and possibly even dramatic in its impact? And does it add enough to the audience's understanding to justify the time that it takes in the speech? Effective speakers are always watchful for a good narration that might be useful in a speech.

Statistics

Statistics are a fifth form of supporting material used in public speeches. Statistics is a method of numerical shorthand that summarizes large quantities of data for easy consumption by the audience.

Among the most useful applications of statistics are interpretations, averages, and percentages. An interpretation translates the numbers into the audience's perspective. A speaker giving statistics on the relationship between overweight and heart trouble, for instance, might make the statistics relevant to the audience by stating that if the audience conforms to national norms, eight of its twenty-five members can expect to have a heart attack before the age of fifty; and if everyone in class were ten or more pounds overweight, then seventeen might expect to suffer heart attacks before the age of fifty.

Averages and percentages are also used to summarize and simplify larger quantities of data that might otherwise be very difficult for an audience to comprehend. An average is the sum total of individual values, divided by the number of values. Hence, the average of 5, 7, 11, 2, and 22 is the sum total—47—divided by the number of values—5—giving a (rounded-off) average of 9. A percentage is a number expressed as a part of 100. Hence, the percentage .50 or 50% means that something occurs half the time. Both averages and percentages are best rounded off in a speech (the actual average above was 9 2/5) because fractions and slight variations from whole numbers tend to confuse the listener and are usually not very important, anyway.

Also, remember that both averages and percentages can be deceiving. The average grade in a class that received an equal number of A's and F's would be a C, even though no one even came close to that actual grade. Similarly, a 500% increase in sales can be a high-sounding percentage for a low amount of change: a company that sold one car last year and five this year had a 500% increase in sales. The problems with averages and percentages can be easily overcome if the speaker provides the information necessary to help the audience interpret the figures.

Some questions to ask yourself about your use of statistics in a speech include: have you provided sufficient information or context to help the audience interpret your numbers? Have you avoided distortion in the use of averages and percentages? Have you rounded off or simplified your figures for easier understanding? And have you done some translating of your statistics, some interpreting of the figures in ways that will aid audience comprehension? Because statistics are easy to misuse in a speech, the effective speaker assumes the burden of insuring that numbers and statistics are used to enlighten rather than baffle the audience.

A sixth form of supporting material used in public speaking is the comparison. **Comparisons**
By definition, **comparisons** draw literal similarities between two or more items
that are basically alike. The comparison is most useful in instructing the audience
about the unknown by showing its similarity to the known. A general comparison
of two universities that are very much alike in size, admissions policies, location,
and type (residential or commuter) can lead to particular comparisons that indicate desirable change. For instance, commuter campus X and commuter campus Y may both have serious parking problems. A speaker can compare the two
schools and argue that the parking plan adopted by campus X has been such a
success that campus Y should adopt the same plan.

A comparison is only as strong as the similarities between the two items being
compared; so the speaker needs to ask of every comparison: are the items being
compared literally similar in all important respects? To the extent that they are
not similar in all important respects, the comparison breaks down, and this weak-
ens the argument that they should be alike in one more respect. The speaker must
make a case for comparisons by showing first how very similar the items being
compared are. Only then is it possible to claim that two governments, two schools,
two persons, or two plans should be alike in still another way.

The seventh form of support is used more often for clarification than for proof. **Analogies**
Figurative **analogies** compare two things that are basically *unlike:* human social
structure is figuratively analogous to that of the bees, with their workers, queens,
and drones. The student cited earlier who gave a speech on how electricity moves
from the power plant into the homes used the analogy of the movement of electricity to the movement of water. Although water and electricity are basically
unlike in their physical properties, they do share important similarities: one is
contained in wires, the other in pipes; both are dangerous when they escape; and
both need to be constantly controlled by human beings if they are to serve rather
than destroy. But most people understand the movement of water better than the
movement of electricity; so the speaker made an analogy between these basically
unlike things precisely because their few important similarities improved the audience's understanding of the less-understood item—electricity.

The important question to ask is whether the similarities between two items
are *literal* or *figurative.* The *figurative* analogy just described proves very little
but may enlighten very much. The comparison, on the other hand, which deals
with *literal* similarities, is more important as proof, but its strength rests on the
extent to which the items being compared are similar.

As you read through the seven forms of supporting material used in public
speaking, you may have noted that different forms of support serve different purposes in the speech. Some—like statistics, examples, and comparisons—are regarded as relatively strong support when used as proof in an argument; others—
like narratives, explanations, and figurative analogies—are regarded as good
clarifiers or conveyors of feelings, but not appropriate as proof. Quotations fall

somewhere in between on the clarification-proof continuum because a quotation could be an excellent communicator of feelings and emotions, a clarifier, and even strong proof for an argument.

Now you know that the content of speeches comes from personal experience, from the experience and knowledge of others gained through interview, and from written and visual resources. Further, you know that the content of public speeches often appears in the form of examples, explanations, quotations, narrations, statistics, comparisons, and analogies which vary in their value as conveyors of clarification or providers of proof. Next you will find out how to arrange these supporting materials in your speech.

How Do You Arrange Your Materials Effectively?

In the previous section we concentrated on what materials you could use in your speech; in this section we will focus on the arrangement of those materials. Effective organization can be approached in several ways. You can examine the overall organization of a speech according to its form, as in an outline or a problem-solution design, or through its content, as in a chronological or topical design. This is often called the **macroorganizational approach** because it emphasizes the overall organization of the speech.

You can also examine the parts within the overall organization, such as inductive or deductive order in an argument, arrangement of evidence from strongest to weakest, or arrangement of pro-con arguments. This is called the **microorganizational approach.** In the chapter on persuasive speaking you will find information on the microorganization of a speech. In this section you will be examining the overall, or the macroorganization.

The Outline

Outlining is a useful compositional skill for preparing your speeches. Before finding out how to make an outline, you should know why they are useful, what role they play in organizing your speech, and how they function in presenting your speech. Outlines are useful because they provide you with a visual indication of how your speech is organized. By looking at your speech in outline form, you can easily see what and how many main points you have, what and how much evidence and explanation you have, and, perhaps, where you need to add or delete items from your speech. Many speakers use an outline as their main guide in delivering a speech because it includes the important verbal message they want to communicate.

In formulating an outline, you need to keep these three principles in mind: subordination, division, and parallelism.

Principles of Outlining

1. Subordination
2. Division
3. Parallelism

If you follow the **principle of subordination,** your outline will indicate which material is more important and which is less important. More important materials usually consist of generalizations, arguments, or conclusions. Less important materials consist of the supporting evidence for your generalizations, arguments, or conclusions. In the outline Roman numerals indicate the main points, capital letters indicate the subpoints under the Roman numeral statements, and Arabic numbers indicate sub-subpoints under the subpoints. Figure 5.4 shows a typical outline format. Notice, too, that the less important the material, the greater the indention from the left-hand margin.

Symbols and Margins Indicating Subordination

I. Generalization, conclusion, or argument is a main point.
   A. The first subpoint consists of illustration, evidence, or other supporting material.
   B. The second subpoint consists of similar supporting material for the main point.
      1. The first sub-subpoint provides additional support for the subpoint stated in "B."
      2. The second sub-subpoint also supports subpoint "B."
II. The second generalization, conclusion, or argument is another main point in the speech.

Figure 5.4 Symbols and indentions indicating subordination.

The principle of subordination is based not only on the symbols (numbers and letters) and indentions, but also on the content of the statements. The subpoints are subordinate to the main points, the sub-subpoints subordinate to the subpoints, and so on. Therefore, you need to evaluate the content of each statement to determine if it is broader or narrower, more important or less important than the statements above and below it. The student outline in figure 5.5 illustrates how the content of the statements indicates levels of importance.

Content Subordination

I. Jumping rope is a cardiovascular (CV) activity.
  A. A cardiovascular activity is defined by three main requirements.
    1. Large muscles must be employed in rhythmic, continuous motions.
    2. The heart beat per minute must be elevated to an intensity that is approximately 85% of a person's maximum rate.
    3. The elevated heart rate must be maintained for twenty to thirty minutes to achieve a CV "training effect."
  B. Other CV activities include running, swimming, and handball.
II. Jumping rope requires simple, inexpensive equipment.

Figure 5.5 Content should reflect subordination.

The second principle of outlining is the **principle of division,** which states that if a point is to be divided it must necessarily have at least two subpoints. For example, the outline illustrated in figure 5.5 contains two main points (I, II), two subpoints (A, B) under main point I, and three sub-subpoints (1, 2, 3) under subpoint A. All items are either undivided (II) or divided into two or more parts. The principle of division can, however, be applied too rigidly: sometimes a main point will be followed by a single example, a solo clarification, or an amplification. Such cases can be regarded as exceptions to the general rule: points, if divided, must be separated into two or more items of approximately equal importance.

The third principle of outlining is the **principle of parallelism,** which states that main points, subpoints, and sub-subpoints must use the same grammatical and syntactical forms. For instance, the student outline in figure 5.5 includes complete sentences for all divisions. An outline can also be composed of single words, phrases, or clauses as long as they are used consistently throughout. A sentence outline usually gives the most information, but for an extemporaneous speech a word or phrase outline might be sufficient to remind you of what you are going to say.

To illustrate how the principles of subordination, division, and parallelism work together, look at the complete outline, on the topic of macrame, as shown in figure 5.6. Figure 5.7 summarizes this discussion of outlining.

Form and Content Unite Through Subordination, Division, and Parallelism

AN INFORMATIVE SPEECH ON MACRAME

Statement of purpose: My purpose is to inform the audience about the art of macrame. At the conclusion of my speech the audience should be able to name the two basic knots used in a hanger and to list at least two uses for macrame.

I. Macrame is an ancient art that is gaining modern acceptance.
   A. Macrame was first used by medieval Arabian weavers to finish the edges of fabric.
   B. In the 1800s, sailors passed their time at sea by doing macrame.
   C. Macrame is a fast growing hobby in the twentieth century.
II. Macrame can be learned in two basic ways.
   A. Macrame can be learned from a book that can be obtained at a local craft shop.
   B. Macrame can be learned by attending classes offered by various organizations.
III. Macrame consists of two basic knots.
   A. The square knot is the fundamental macrame knot.
      1. The square knot consists of four cords, two holding cords and two working cords.
      2. The square knot is constructed in four simple steps.
   B. The half knot is a variation of the square knot involving only the first two steps.
IV. Macrame is a hobby with many uses.
   A. Macrame's most prominent use is as plant hangers and wall hangings.
   B. Macrame can also be used to make many accessories and unusual home furnishings.

Figure 5.6 Form and content unite through subordination, division, and parallelism.

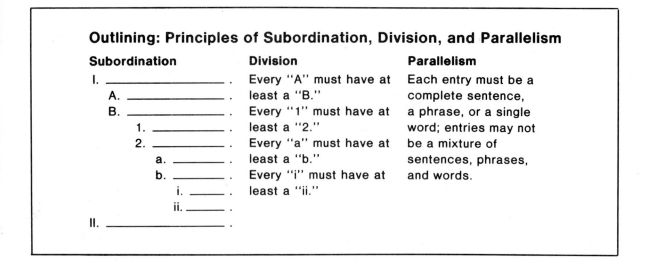

Figure 5.7 Outlining: Principles of subordination, division, and parallelism.

Outlining: Principles of Subordination, Division, and Parallelism

Subordination	Division	Parallelism
I. _____ .	Every "A" must have at	Each entry must be a
A. _____ .	least a "B."	complete sentence,
B. _____ .	Every "1" must have at	a phrase, or a single
1. _____ .	least a "2."	word; entries may not
2. _____ .	Every "a" must have at	be a mixture of
a. _____ .	least a "b."	sentences, phrases,
b. _____ .	Every "i" must have at	and words.
i. ___ .	least a "ii."	
ii. ___ .		
II. _____ .		

Application Exercise 5: Subordination, Division, and Parallelism

Using the following information, construct an outline. Show subordination and division by including main points, subpoints, and sub-subpoints. State your points in parallel form.

"Progressive" radio emerged in the late 1960s as younger people began to demand more variety in their music. Some stations began to play album cuts instead of Top 40 "hits." As listeners demanded more variety, some stations played newer, less well-known cuts which became known as "progressive" rock. Other stations expanded beyond "pure" rock to include contemporary jazz, jazz–rock fusion, "classical" rock, and "acid" rock. These "progressive" FM radio stations are attractive to advertisers because 95% of all households have at least one FM radio, the average home has the FM radio on for two hours and twenty minutes per day, and the FCC has licensed over three thousand FM stations. Their appeal is mainly to young adults. The "progressive" stations, together with the album-oriented rock stations, are the first choice of men between 18 and 24 years of age and the second choice of women in the same age group.

Transitions

In this section of the chapter, we are considering the arrangement of the information in your speech. So far, we have discussed dividing up the speech into its component parts through the principles of subordination, division, and parallelism. We turn now to a method of binding these parts into a whole. The method used to join the various elements of the speech is the use of transitions.

What are transitions? Where are they used in a speech? And how can they make a speech more effective? **Transitions** are the mortar used to bind the substantive ideas in a speech; they are the verbal lubricant that moves the speech

Finding, Evaluating, and Organizing Support Material

smoothly from point to point. They connect the introduction and conclusion to the body of the speech, link main points to subpoints, and even bring the speaker into and away from the visual aids.

Transitions come in at least three forms: the preview, the review, and the signpost transition. The **preview transition** forecasts the development of the speech: "Next, we will learn how the City Council got us into this financial mess." The **review transition** is an "instant replay" in abbreviated form of whatever just transpired in a speech: "So as you can see, the City Treasurer's mistake is one of the main reasons for the problem." The **signpost transition** enumerates the main points of the speech: "The second reason for this monetary mockery is the procedure that the Council used in securing the grant." These various kinds of transitions are not mutually exclusive; all three can be combined in a single transition: "The procedures for securing the grant, then, were unorthodox [review], but they were not as serious as the third [signpost] reason for the Council's money problems, which was the lack of responsible local taxation [preview]."

Transitions are designed to help your audience follow your ideas. You can help your audience recognize your most important points by numbering (signposting) them and by employing parallel sentence structure. The content can change from point to point, but the form becomes similar, familiar, and recognizable:

"Your first duty as a citizen of these United States is . . ."
"Your second duty as a citizen of these United States is . . ."
"Your third, and final, duty as a citizen of these United States is . . ."

"Now that we are familiar with the map of campus town, we can locate the best places to eat."

The form is parallel—each sentence starts with and continues with the same or similar wording; the main points include a signpost (first, second, third); and each main point can be announced with pauses before and after, and with a louder voice or different tone to indicate importance.

Subpoints should be signaled in a different manner to avoid audience confusion. You should not, for instance, use enumeration (signposting) for examples, subpoints, or other supporting material. Instead, you should lead into your supporting material with lines like these: "An example of this problem is . . . ;" "To clarify this main point I will share the story of . . . ;" "The best evidence to support this idea comes from *Consumer Reports* and Common Cause." Just as the parallel form and the signposting signaled main points in the speech, the subpoints are announced with words that indicate their relationship to the main point (an example, evidence, clarification) and with parallel structure ("The evidence from *Consumer Reports* says . . . ," "the evidence from Common Cause says . . . ," and so on.)

Transitions are a danger point for beginning speakers. They are the most common point for speakers to forget their place in the speech. For that reason, many speakers—including experienced ones—write out their transitions on their outline. You are unlikely to forget where you are in a speech when you are right in the middle of an exciting story, but you might falter when you get to the end of the example and are expected to move to the next point.

Finding, Evaluating, and Organizing Support Material

Figure 5.8 A sampling of transitions.

Speech Transitions

My first point is that . . .

Another reason why you should . . .

One of the best examples is . . .

As I have demonstrated . . .

To illustrate this principle, I will . . .

Today I will present three arguments . . .

Let us look at this picture . . .

A second, and even more convincing, argument is . . .

The evidence you have just seen would be . . .

One last illustration will show . . .

To synthesize what you have heard today . . .

I have shown that . . .

A public speech is full of transitions. They are needed at every turn to make your organization clear to the audience. Your skill at using transitions can help you face your audience with confidence. Figure 5.8 shows a number of transitions that may be used for various purposes.

Patterns of Organization

Among the possible organizational patterns for your speech are the time-sequence and the spatial-relations patterns—which are commonly employed in informative speaking—and the problem-solution, cause-effect, and climactic or anticlimactic patterns—which are frequently used in persuasive speaking. Another pattern of organization, the topical-sequence pattern, may be used in either informative or persuasive speeches. Let's look at each of these in detail.

Patterns of Organization

1. Time-sequence
2. Spatial-relations
3. Problem-solution
4. Cause-effect
5. Climactic and anticlimactic
6. Topical-sequence

Figure 5.9 An example of the time-sequence pattern of organization.

Time-Sequence Organization

Immediate purpose: To instruct class members about registration procedures for the next session so that they can complete the process without difficulty.

Introduction   I. Registration for classes is a process that can be completed without difficulty by following certain steps.

Body   II. The steps for completing registration include selecting forms, securing signatures, and turning in papers at the correct place.
         A. Go to Central Administration to pick up your registration forms.
         B. Complete your own registration forms including all of the classes you wish to take.
         C. Find your advisor for a signature.
         D. Turn in your registration packet at Window 3 in the Central Administration Building.

Conclusion   III. After you follow the appropriate steps cited above, you must wait for two weeks until the computer sorts out all of the class requests.

Time-Sequence Pattern

The **time-sequence pattern** is chronological; that is, it states in what order events occur over time. This pattern, obviously, is most appropriate for topics that are time-oriented. For instance, stating the steps in constructing a cedar chest, in making French bread, or in the development of a blue spruce from seed to maturity would all be appropriate topics for a time-sequence pattern.

An example of an outline for a speech employing the time-sequence pattern would look like the one shown in figure 5.9. The organization of most "how to do it" speeches of this type is crucial because the audience will be unable to "do it" unless all steps are noted in the correct order.

Spatial-Relations Pattern

The **spatial-relations pattern** indicates how things are related in space. Topics that lend themselves to a spatial pattern include how to arrange furniture on a stage set, how to design a lighting board, or where to place plants when landscaping. A spatial-relations pattern of organization is shown in figure 5.10.

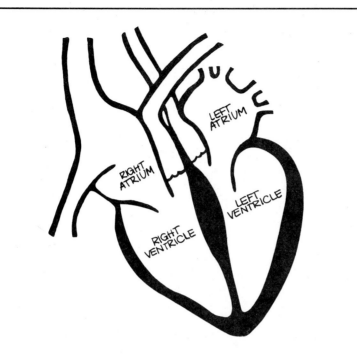

Figure 5.10 An example of the spatial-relations pattern of organization.

Spatial Relations Pattern of Organization

Immediate purpose: To teach my audience to recognize the form and function of the human heart.

Introduction

    I. The human heart is the part of the body that fails or falters in more than a million people per year.

   II. Learning about how your heart is structured and how it functions can help you keep it healthy.

Body

  III. As shown on the visual aid, the heart consists of four chambers, the right and left atrium and the left and right ventricle.

  IV. The atria and the ventricles have different functions.

     A. The right atrium and left atrium are thin-walled receiving chambers for blood.

     B. The right and left ventricles are thick-walled pumping chambers that pump eighteen million gallons of blood in seventy years.

Conclusion

   V. The heart's structure and functions are simple, but heart failure ends life.

  VI. Name the parts and the functions of the heart as a first step in guarding your own health.

Figure 5.11 An example of the problem-solution pattern of organization.

Problem-Solution Pattern of Organization

Immediate purpose: To convince students that they should not allow the Scholastic Aptitude Test (SAT) to limit them; instead, students can and should do well in college whatever their SAT scores.

Introduction

I. Over two million students take the SAT and the PSAT every year as part of their admission requirements for universities, colleges, and trade schools.

II. Heavy reliance on these tests may prove unwarranted according to recent studies of the test.

Body

III. The problem with the SAT is that it dominates the market, it is a poor predictor of college success, and it is used too often for admission and reward.

A. The Educational Testing Service of Princeton, New Jersey, dominates the field of diagnostic testing.

(Problem)

B. The SAT by itself is a poor predictor of college success and is, therefore, a questionable instrument to use for admission to college.

C. The SAT is used almost universally to determine college admission and financial awards like the National Merit Scholar awards.

(Solution)

IV. Some solutions to the problem include more competition, more emphasis on high school grades, and reduced emphasis on the SAT for college admission and awards.

A. The field of diagnostic testing invites more competition that could result in better, more predictive tests.

B. High school grades are a better predictor of college success than is the SAT.

C. The SAT should not be used as the most important criterion for college entrance or for financial awards.

Conclusion

V. You should not allow a score on a diagnostic test to limit your confidence concerning college achievement.

A. If you did well in high school, you are very likely to do well in college, regardless of your standardized test scores.

Finding, Evaluating, and Organizing Support Material

The **problem-solution pattern** is employed more often in persuasive than informative speeches because it is difficult to speak either on problems or solutions without intimating a position on the issue. The problem-solution pattern raises one serious question for the speaker: how much should you say about the problem or the solution? Usually you can work out a proper ratio based on what the audience knows about the issue. If the audience is unaware that a problem exists, you may have to spend time telling them about it. On the other hand, if the problem is well known to all, you can spend most of your time on the solution. This pattern lends itself nicely to outlining, with the problem being one main head and the solution the other. A problem-solution pattern of organization is shown in figure 5.11.

Problem-Solution Pattern

The **cause-effect pattern** of organization describes or explains a problem and its ramifications. Some examples include the cause of Parkinson's Disease and the effects that it has on the body, the causes of urban blight and one local government's solution, or the causes of low-and-high-pressure systems and their effect on ground temperature. As with the problem-solution pattern, this one lets you decide how much time you should spend on the cause(s) and how much on the effect(s). A cause-effect pattern of organization is shown in figure 5.12.[1] This outline suggests that the speaker will spend about two-thirds of the allotted time talking about the "causes" for high income occupations (education and family background) and about one-third talking about the effect of those factors.

Cause-Effect Pattern

The **climactic** and **anticlimactic patterns** hinge on the placement of your strongest arguments or best evidence. If you place your strongest or best material early in your speech and your weaker material at the end, you are using anticlimactic order. If you place the strongest and best material late in the speech, you are using climactic order, because the speech builds to a more dramatic conclusion. A recent study indicates that with a one-sided persuasive message, climactic order is superior to anticlimactic order in securing positive audience evaluation. In the climactic organizational pattern shown in figure 5.13,[2] the speaker moves from the least striking to the most impressive information on the role of women in the future.

Climactic and Anticlimactic Patterns

Figure 5.12 An example of the cause-effect pattern of organization.

Cause-Effect Pattern of Organization

Immediate purpose: To persuade the class that who you are can determine financial success as much as higher education can by having them tell me at the conclusion of the speech about the effects of family and education on finances.

Introduction

   I. Idealists believe that education is the primary force that moves people upward in society.

  II. Christopher Jencks argues persuasively that education alone is not the only important process that contributes to upward mobility.

Body

 III. More education often means higher pay.
- A. Past history shows that people who wanted to earn high incomes usually went to college.
- B. According to Jencks, male workers with four years of college take home almost 50% more in earnings than do workers with the same amount of experience but without college degrees.

 IV. Who you are can be as important as education in determining your occupation and income.
- A. Jencks's book on family and schooling in America states that "Those who do well economically typically owe as much as half their occupational advantage to family background."
- B. People from disadvantaged families are less likely than the privileged to join high paying occupations.

Conclusion

  V. The effect of education and family background is to help those people who are already favored with money and high paying jobs.

 VI. In order to find out what you learned from this speech, I am going to call on a couple of you to tell me what determines financial success in America.

Finding, Evaluating, and Organizing Support Material

Figure 5.13 An
example of the
climactic pattern of
organization.

A Climactic Pattern of Organization

Immediate purpose: To have classmates recognize the difference between media-perpetuated views of the attitudes of college students and the actual attitudes shown in a recent study.

Introduction

I. Our elders often think that college students are seeking high paying jobs and the life of single bliss.
   A. The press headlines stories about the materialistic goals of youth.
   B. Books and magazines emphasize the lives of the swinging singles.
II. A new study indicates that these views of today's youth may be incorrect.

Body

III. A national survey of first-year students indicates that their top goals focuses on relationships.
   A. The Institute for Social Research at the University of Michigan finds that 80% of the students sought a good marriage and family life.
   B. Seventy percent of the first-year students cite strong friendships as a top goal.
IV. The Michigan study shows that nearly 100% of the first year students want to marry and have children.
V. The study reveals at least one possible contradiction in student attitudes toward top goals.
   A. Two-thirds of the students say the mother of preschool children should be at home with them.
   B. Only 4% of the women expect to be full-time homemakers at age thirty.

Conclusion

VI. First-year students seek good marriages and strong friendships as their top goals in life.
VII. First-year students do not live up to the stereotype portrayed in the media.

Finding, Evaluating, and Organizing Support Material   107

Figure 5.14 An example of the topical sequence pattern of organization.

A Topical-Sequence Pattern of Organization

Immediate purpose: To invite prospective students to measure themselves against the criteria for being a communication major by stating whether or not they qualify on their evaluation of the speech.

Introduction	I. Crowded conditions and shortage of faculty have resulted in new admission standards.
	  A. The College of Communication has 2300 majors.
	  B. The College of Communication has fifty faculty.
	II. The new admission standards are more rigorous than those of the past.

Body	III. Direct admission to the College of Communication depends on class rank and SAT scores.
	  A. Direct admission students must be in the top half of their high school graduating class.
	  B. Direct admission students must have SAT scores of at least 1000, combined verbal and quantitative.
	IV. Transfer students must have a 2.5 cumulative grade point average after forty-five quarter credits for admission.

Conclusion	V. Use your evaluation form to indicate whether or not you qualify for direct or indirect admission to the College of Communication.

Topical-Sequence Pattern

The **topical-sequence pattern** is employed when you want to divide your topic into a number of parts, such as advantages and disadvantages, different qualities, or various types. Examples of such speeches might be the pros and cons of capital punishment, four qualities necessary in a leader, or three types of local transportation. This pattern is equally useful in informative and persuasive speeches. A topical-sequence pattern of organization is shown in figure 5.14. The speaker who uses this particular topical-sequence is asking each person in the audience to decide whether he or she meets the criteria or standards for becoming an honors student.

We have surveyed six organizational patterns you can use in your public speeches. The one you select for your own speech should be determined largely by the topic you select, by how much the audience knows about the topic, and by which arguments or evidence the *audience* will perceive as strongest or best.

Finding, Evaluating, and Organizing Support Material

Do not conclude from this discussion that these are the only ways to organize a speech. A recent article in a speech journal tells how storytelling is used in criminal trials by lawyers who need to convince jurors to make sophisticated judgments about complex information.[3] In another case, a student delivered a highly effective speech by telling a series of five stories about himself, interspersed with a refrain that was his main point. His organization was effective, but the speech defied the principles of outlining. The number of ways in which you can organize your speech is limited only by your imagination.

Conclusion

In this chapter you have discovered ways of finding ideas and information for your speeches through personal experience, interviews, and printed materials. You have learned how to evaluate your personal experience for its appropriateness in a speech, how to set up and conduct an interview, and how to locate and record written information in correct bibliographical and note-taking form. You have read about the principles of subordination, division, and parallelism to guide you in outlining, and surveyed six organizational patterns: time-sequence, spatial-relations, problem-solution, cause-effect, climax or anticlimax, and topical-sequence patterns.

In addition, you have practiced your skills in application exercises designed to help you to evaluate and use your personal experience, interview for information, find library sources in a scavenger hunt, cite sources in correct bibliographical form, and formulate an outline.

Application Assignment

Sentence Outline

On separate paper write your name, the title of your speech, and your immediate purpose. Then compose a sentence outline with at least three main points (generalizations, conclusions, or arguments) introduced with Roman numerals. Develop at least one of these main points by including subpoints and sub-subpoints. In addition to the outlines in this chapter, a student's outline also appears in Appendix B.

Vocabulary

analogies Support materials that establish similarities between basically unlike items.

anticlimactic pattern An organizational arrangement in which the strongest arguments and supporting materials are presented first and then descend in order of lesser importance.

cause-effect pattern An organizational arrangement in which part of the speech deals with the cause(s) of some problem or issue and part of it deals with the effect(s) of the problem or issue.

climactic pattern An organizational arrangement in which the arguments and supporting materials are presented in increasing order of importance, with the strongest arguments and evidence presented last.

comparisons Support materials that point out similarities between items that are basically alike.

examples Illustrations using specific instances, either actual or created (hypothetical).

explanations Supporting materials in which the speaker clarifies or simplifies a concept for easier audience comprehension.

macroorganizational approach The overall organization of an entire speech. Problem-solution, cause-effect, and time-sequence are all macroorganizational.

microorganizational approach The arrangement of materials *within* the parts of a speech, such as the order of inductive or deductive arguments or the arrangement of evidence from strongest to weakest.

narrations Stories or anecdotes used as support material, either for proof or clarification or as an attention-gaining technique in the introduction.

preview transitions Transitions that forecast the development of a speech: "Next, we will learn. . . ."

principle of division An outlining principle which states that every point divided into subordinate parts must be divided into two or more parts. A point cannot be divided into one part. Hence, in an outline, every I must have at least a II, every A at least a B, every 1 at least a 2, and so on.

principle of parallelism An outlining principle which states that all points must be in the same grammatical form. In a sentence outline all points must be stated in sentence form; in a phrase outline all points must be given in phrase form, with all phrases beginning with the same part of speech (for example, infinitives, prepositions, participles); and in a word outline all points must be given in single words.

principle of subordination An outlining principle which states that all points must be given in order of importance, as indicated by symbols (I . . . A . . . 1 . . . a . . . i) and indentions (the less important the material, the greater the indention).

problem-solution pattern An organizational arrangement in which part of the speech is concerned with the problem(s) and part with the solution(s) to the problem(s).

quotations The testimony of someone other than the speaker, used because of its eloquence or because it lends credibility to the speaker's point.

review transitions "Instant replays" of what has just been discussed in a speech: "You can see from what I've just said that. . . ."

signpost transitions Enumerations of the main points of a speech: "The *second* cause of our current problem is. . . ."

spatial-relations pattern An organizational arrangement in which things are related in terms of placement or location.

statistics Support material that summarizes numerical information or compares quantities.

time-sequence pattern An organizational arrangement in which events or steps are presented in chronological order.

topical-sequence pattern An organizational arrangement in which the topic is divided into reasonable parts, such as advantages and disadvantages or various qualities or types.

transitions The links in a speech that connect the introduction, body, and conclusion, as well as main points and subpoints; that provide previews, signposts, and reviews; that lead into and summarize visual aids; and that otherwise indicate where the speaker is in the organization of the speech.

Finding, Evaluating, and Organizing Support Material

1. Some of the information in this outline came from: Christopher Jencks, *Inequality: A Reassessment of the Effect of Family and Schooling in America* (New York: Basic Books, 1979).
2. The information about the national survey of freshmen came from Jerald G. Bachman and Lloyd D. Johnston, "The Freshmen, 1979," *Psychology Today* 13 (September 1979): 79–87.
3. W. Lance Bennet, "Storytelling in Criminal Trials: A Model of Social Judgment," *Quarterly Journal of Speech* 64 (February 1978): 1–22.

Chapter 6

Objectives

After completing chapter 6, you should grow in confidence because you understand the answers to these questions:
   1. What are you to accomplish in an introduction?
   2. How do you gain and maintain audience attention?
   3. What are some methods of relating the topic to the audience?
   4. What are some methods of relating the speaker to the topic?
   5. Which factors improve source credibility and which do not?
   6. What should you include when you introduce another speaker?
   7. What are you to accomplish in a conclusion?

When you have completed chapter 6, you should have grown in confidence because you will have practiced skills in
   1. Gaining and maintaining attention in an introduction;
   2. Describing your own qualifications as a source;
   3. Improving your own credibility;
   4. Checking your introductory strategies; and
   5. Delivering a speech that fulfills the functions of an introduction.

Application Exercises

1. Gaining and maintaining attention.
2. Describing your qualifications.
3. Signaling the conclusion.
4. Concluding a speech.

112

Introducing and Concluding Your Speech

It is with eloquence as with a flame; it requires fuel to feed it, motion to excite it, and it brightens as it burns.

Tacitus

Introduction

You have already moved through a number of steps in the preparation of your speech. You have analyzed your audience, selected a topic, and stated your purpose. In the last chapter, you learned how to find, evaluate, and organize your information. You probably observed that the section on arrangement of materials in the last chapter considered only the body of the speech. We discussed how to subdivide your materials through the principles of subordination, division, and parallelism, and we explained that transitions are used to join the parts after they have been divided. However, we did not discuss how to begin or end the speech. In this chapter you will learn how to introduce and conclude your speech.

Your introduction is crucial to an effective speech because the audience quickly decides if you are credible. One researcher determined that much of the sizing up occurs in the first fifteen seconds of the speech.[1] Therefore, it is important for you to understand what occurs in an introduction. Toward that end you will be examining four functions of an introduction, an example of a student introduction, and a summary of strategies you can use to introduce your speeches.

You will also have an opportunity to learn how to introduce another speaker. Research indicates that another person's introduction of a speaker can be a determining factor in the speaker's credibility. You will discover the rationale for introducing another person and examine an example of a student's speech introducing another speaker.

In the last section of this chapter, Concluding Your Speech, you will find answers to the following questions: What are you supposed to achieve in the conclusion of a speech? Are there any differences between the endings of informative and persuasive speeches? Are there any endings you should avoid?

Introducing Your Speech: Four Functions of an Introduction

Outside the classroom you may be introduced by someone else. In the classroom you will probably introduce yourself and your topic to the audience in that part of the speech called the introduction. An introduction serves four functions. You will examine these along with examples from student speeches. The four functions are to (1) gain and maintain attention, (2) relate your topic to your audience, (3) relate yourself as speaker to the topic, and (4) reveal the organization and development of your speech.

Introductory Functions

1. Gain and maintain attention
2. Relate topic to the audience
3. Relate speaker to topic
4. Forecast organization

Gaining and Maintaining Attention

Let us consider the first function of an introduction, gaining and maintaining attention. Have you ever watched someone try to teach a group of very small children? As the teacher talks, the children turn around and look at each other. Sometimes they just start talking about something else. Occasionally they touch someone. Getting children to pay attention is a very difficult job. Adults are no different. True, adults have learned to look as if they are listening. Their eyes are correctly directed, and their bodies may not move as much as children's bodies do. But the adults have replaced their overt physical activities with mental activities. When you speak to your classmates, their minds will be flitting from your speech to plans for the weekend, to the test the next hour, to the attractive person in the next seat. You will have to gain and maintain their attention.

Spend some time planning your introduction. Often students spend too much time thinking of a topic. Chapter 4 should have helped with this problem. After you have chosen your topic, you must take the time to develop your main points. As the class hour approaches, you may find you have little time left to prepare your introduction and conclusion. This is a mistake, however, because your introduction often determines whether the audience listens to your message. The introduction and conclusion are the bookends of your speech. If either or both fall, then the core of the speech may very well fall, too.

There are twelve ways you can gain and maintain attention. As you read through the variety of ways that you can use to accomplish this function of an introduction, you may feel overwhelmed. Which method should you select? How will you decide the way in which you will gain and maintain the attention of your audience? It is critical at this point that you understand the principles of audience analysis and adaptation discussed in chapter 3. If everyone in your class has used striking facts and statistics, for instance, you may want to choose a different method. If your class meets near lunch time, you may want to consider bringing some object of food that they can eat. You may wish to review chapter 3 before you determine the specific method you will use in gaining and maintaining the attention of your audience.

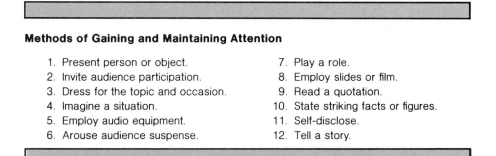

Methods of Gaining and Maintaining Attention

1. Present person or object.
2. Invite audience participation.
3. Dress for the topic and occasion.
4. Imagine a situation.
5. Employ audio equipment.
6. Arouse audience suspense.
7. Play a role.
8. Employ slides or film.
9. Read a quotation.
10. State striking facts or figures.
11. Self-disclose.
12. Tell a story.

Some effective ways to gain and maintain attention are:

1. Bring with you the person or object about which you are going to talk. This method is used more often for informative speeches than for persuasive ones, but it can be used for both. A student speaking on health food may give everyone a granola bar to eat while listening to the speech. A student who works at a bank may begin a speech about the dangers of a checking account by distributing one blank counter check to each member of the audience. Or, a student who informs the audience about classical ballet may bring a ballerina to class to demonstrate a few turns on point during the speech. All of these are effective ways to gain and maintain attention.

2. *Invite audience participation at the beginning of your speech.* Arousing an audience to react very early in your speech attracts their attention and interest in your topic. One student who was speaking about some of the problems of poverty asked his audience to sit crowded elbow-to-elbow during his presentation. Another asked the audience three questions about energy and requested they indicate by a show of hands whether they knew the answers. Because most members of the audience were unable to answer the questions, they listened carefully for the answers. One energetic student wrote a draft notice for every person in class, which summoned each one to meet with his or her draft board. As the student began his speech, each person in the audience opened up a plain white envelope with the unwanted message inside. Such audience participation gained and maintained their attention.

3. *Dress in a way that will arouse audience interest in you and the topic.* One enterprising student turned up in front of the class with a hardhat on his head, heavy boots on his feet, a sweat rag around his neck, and a flashlight in his hand. He was encouraging his classmates to take up the somewhat questionable "sport" of exploring the university's steam tunnels. A woman who was encouraging college students to lose weight delivered her speech in a warmup suit.

4. *Get your audience to imagine a situation.* You might have the audience imagine that they are standing on a ski slope, flying through the air, burrowing under the ground, and so on. As one student wrote in her plan for an introduction: "In order to gain audience attention, I will ask them to picture in their minds a hospital scene in which they are the patient on the operating table. They must watch their own death and subsequent resuscitation. This picture will prepare them for my topic on a second existence and raise the question in their minds of what actually happens in the interim." Inviting the audience to imagine a hypothetical situation is an effective method of gaining and maintaining attention.

5. *Use audio equipment and start with sound.* A student who was delivering a speech on classical music began with a one-minute excerpt from a famous work. Another, speaking against illegal abortions, played an actual tape of a woman being interviewed on her deathbed by a county sheriff. Both students immediately gained the audience's attention through the use of sound.

6. *Arouse audience suspense and whet their curiosity about the topic.* One student began his speech by saying, "A new sport has hit this state, yet it is a national tradition. It is held in the spring of the year in some of our most beautiful

timbered areas. It is open to men and women alike, with women having the same chance of success as men. It is for responsible adults only and requires common sense and patience. This sport of our ancestors is. . . ." Arousing curiosity captures the audience's attention.

7. *Role-play.* A student who was giving a speech on the dangers of using the crosswalks near campus thought of three role-playing introductions that he could use. First, he portrayed himself as a world war veteran of the crosswalks, a person with medals and old "war" stories to relate to the audience. Second, he described himself as a person who had just narrowly missed being hit while in the crosswalk—and the audience was the "person" responsible. Third, he acted as the relative of a person who was hit in the crosswalk. In each case the student was using role-playing to gain and maintain the audience's attention.

8. *Use slides or film.* A student who was speaking on big city slums began with a rapid series of twelve slides showing trash heaps, crowded rooms, rundown buildings, and rats. An international student from the Phillipines showed attractive photographs of her native land. A varsity football player, who was speaking on intentional violence in the sport, showed a film of two kickoff returns in which he and others were deliberately trying to maim their opponents with their face guards. The audience—seeing the slums, the tropical beaches, and football violence—was attentive.

9. Read a short excerpt to the audience. The reading can be hypothetical, literary, poetic, dramatic, or real. A woman who belonged to Tau Beta Pi, Chi Epsilon, Alpha Pi Mu, Phi Beta Phi, Mortar Board, and Alpha Lamba Delta honorary societies began her speech with this letter:

```
Dear Honor Student:

   Congratulations! You have been chosen to
become a member of Eta Delta Iota Kappa Mu Phi.
You have proven your academic abilities. You
have character. You have demonstrated
leadership qualities which will pave the way to
success. You have served the field affiliated
with this organization. And, you also have $45
that we want.

   Sincerely,


   Membership Chair
```

The purpose of the speech was to induce students to reject some of the invitations to join clubs and societies that simply want the students' money.

10. State striking facts and statistics.

We use almost nineteen million barrels of oil in this country every day.
In 1930, 25% of the population were farmers; today, farmers make up only 2% of the population.

Such statements are like headlines: they are designed to grab the eye or ear to pay attention. Most topics you explore will have such facts and statistics that you can use as "headlines."

*11. Use **self-disclosure;** that is, tell the audience something about yourself that they would not know if you did not tell them.* Usually a daring self-disclosure is confessional: "I had malaria," "I was an alcoholic," "I was a robbery victim." This method has considerable impact on an audience mainly because it violates the audience's expectations. A most daring disclosure in a public speaking class came when a mild-mannered young man revealed that he had been in prison in Louisiana for six years on a drug offense. He spoke with great feeling about the effects of our penal system on the individual.

Not all self-disclosures do have to be so dramatic. Indeed, some of the best pose a common problem, such as this one:

```
I am a Catholic girl and I have a Baptist
boyfriend. Our different religions have
challenged us both but have strengthened rather
than weakened our relationship because we have
to explain our faiths to each other. With that in
mind, I'd like to share with you the similarities
between two seemingly different religions.
```

Another student spoke on structural barriers to the handicapped and revealed that she knew about the subject because of a hip operation which forced her to learn how to walk all over again. Both of these students disclosed information that the audience had not known but that enhanced their credibility and captured the audience's attention.

Self-disclosure must be used carefully in the public speech. Most self-disclosure occurs in interpersonal communication when only two or three people are engaged in conversation. Be sure that you can handle the disclosure. One woman decided to tell a class about her sister's recent death from leukemia, but she found she could do nothing but cry. The speaking situation is one that is already filled with a certain amount of tension, and you do not want to overload yourself with more emotion than you can handle.

Self-disclosure must be considered carefully for a second reason. As we stated, self-disclosure generally occurs when one person provides personal information to one or two others. In general, we do not tell a large number of other people highly personal information. Perhaps the story of a suicide in your own family will gain the attention of the audience, but do you want twenty of your peers knowing such information? Do not self-disclose information that is potentially embarrassing to yourself or to people who care about you.

Self-disclosure must be honest information. Don't invent an event or exaggerate an experience beyond recognition. You will not be viewed as a trustworthy speaker if you practice deception and dishonesty in your speeches. One student began his speech by telling a story of how a friend of his had set his body on fire to protest U.S. involvement in conflicts in other parts of the world. He went on to say that the friend had suffered first-, second-, and third-degree burns and that he had to have plastic surgery later. When the students in the class expressed their regrets to him after the speech, he laughed and said he had made up the story and the friend. This particular student quickly learned the error of his ways, however. Nearly everyone in the class gave him a grade of "F" for the speech! In a classroom in which the students' grade did contribute to the grade received, the penalty was immediate and direct. In addition, the student was not perceived favorably on later assignments.

12. Tell a story (narration). Telling a story to gain the audience's attention is one of the oldest and most commonly used methods. Often the story can be humorous. This story is an analogy from the introduction to a student speech:

```
I'd like to share with you a story about a man
who, every morning, took his horse and wagon out
into the woods to gather firewood. He would later
take the wood to a nearby town and sell it for his
only income. He was by no means wealthy, yet he
lived a comfortable life. One day, in his greed,
the man found that if he doubled his load of wood
each day, he could earn twice as much money. He
also found that if he spent half as much on feed
for his horse, he could save even more money.
This worked fine until one day the extra loads
and the reduced food proved too much for the
horse, and it collapsed from exhaustion and
hunger.
```

The student revealed in his speech that the man represented farmers who find that they are expected to produce more and more goods despite government controls limiting their capacity to do so. The analogy got the audience involved in a speech that might have drawn less attention if it had been an openly announced speech on government control of farmers.

These twelve methods of gaining and maintaining attention in the introductory portion of a speech are not the only ones. There are dozens of other ways. Just think of imaginative ways to involve the audience. You can start by stating a problem for which your speech is the solution. You can create a dramatic conflict between seemingly irreconcilable forces: business and government, teachers and students, parents and children, grading systems and learning. You can inform the audience about everyday items they do not understand: stock market reports, weather symbols, sales taxes, savings accounts, and automobiles.

One word of warning: always make sure your attention getter is related to the topic. Jokes told for their own sake are a weak way to begin a speech because they do not relate to the topic. Another undesirable way to start is to write some provoking word on the board and then say, "I just wanted to get your attention." All of the examples in the twelve methods of gaining attention are from student speeches. They show that students can be creative in order to gain and maintain audience attention.

Think of a speech topic. Then take any three of the twelve methods of gaining and maintaining attention listed in the text to introduce your topic.

Relating the Topic to the Audience

A speaker can relate almost any topic to an audience in some way, preferably in the introduction of a speech. This assures the audience that there is a connection between them and the topic. A speaker should find helpful many of the examples given in the previous section on audience attention. A student gave a speech on women's rights, a topic the audience cared little about. However, in her introduction she depicted the plight of married women who have fewer job opportunities and receive less pay than their male co-workers. The speaker asked the audience how they would feel under such circumstances. How would the men like their wives and girl friends to earn less than men in the same jobs? Most of the men wanted their girl friends and wives to be able to earn as much money as possible. The audience listened to the speech with more interest because the speaker took pains to relate the topic to both men and women in class.

A common way for a speaker to put an issue into perspective for an audience is to state the issue in their terms. Here is an example from a student speech on the effect of drinking laws:

> How many of you have been to a house party recently? I'm sure everyone enjoyed the good music, the friends, and all the beer going around. If your house is like ours, almost everyone will be drinking, but what if the police were to come in checking I.D.s? I know of six people in our house who are minors, and I'm sure there are more around campus. Next year will be worse. The new drinking age has caught some college students this year and has made college parties more complicated and maybe a thing of the past.

The speaker was relating the topic to her particular audience. Her assumptions that many in the class went to parties, many knew illegal drinkers, and many were confused by the new laws ensured a relationship between audience and topic.

Introducing and Concluding Your Speech   121

Relating the Speaker to the Topic

In the last section, we discussed relating the topic to the audience. A public speaker also needs to relate the topic to himself or herself. You should help your audience to see you as a credible speaker on the topic. In chapter 2 you explored four dimensions of source credibility. In this chapter you will discover some principles of source credibility which have been derived from experimental studies. From the earlier discussion you should remember that speakers earn the right to speak; credibility is the audience's perception of the speaker and can change before, during, and after a speech; and credibility is related to topics, audiences, and situations.

A Speaker Earns High Credibility . . .

1. through perceived competence, trustworthiness, coorientation, dynamism;
2. through perceived status;
3. through good delivery.

A Speaker Can Lose Credibility . . .

1. through perceived incompetence, untrustworthiness, dissimilarity, lethargy;
2. through perceived low status;
3. through poor organization;
4. through nonfluencies.

Principles for Improving Source Credibility

Four principles will be useful for you to keep in mind as you attempt to improve your source credibility. First, *a highly credible speaker will achieve more opinion change from an audience than will a speaker with low credibility.*[2] This first principle means that your audience will have more of a change of opinion about you if they perceive you to be competent, trustworthy, cooriented, and dynamic. Since the audience makes many judgments on this matter early in the speech, it is in your best interest as speaker to relate yourself to your topic so that the audience will see the connection. For example, the speaker who can say, "I am the mother of five adolescent boys. Today I want to tell you which advice on disciplining children is nonsense and which makes sense," seems to be a more credible person than a single nineteen-year-old speaking on the same topic. The point behind this principle is that you need to make the connection between yourself and the topic in your introduction.

How do you help the audience to accept you as a highly credible source? Describe your qualifications early in the speech and tell the audience the connection between you and the subject. Research indicates that you should make your

statement descriptively, that is, without being judgmental or evaluative. For example, you can say, "I was an operator for the telephone company for seven years before I returned to college," which is objective and descriptive. It is different from a statement such as, "I was one of Northwestern Bell's best troubleshooters as an operator for seven years," which is judgmental and evaluative.

To improve your credibility as a speaker, be well prepared, practice, know your material, deliver it well, and show consistent confidence in your information. After a few successful speeches, your reputation and credibility in the class will expand.

The second principle is that *the perceived status of a speaker can make a difference in source credibility*. For example, those students who are identified as graduate students get higher ratings for competence than do undergraduates. Graduate students are also thought to be higher in fairmindedness, likeableness, and sincerity.[3] Your classification as a sophomore, junior, or senior might contribute to your credibility with a student audience. In another study, high-status speakers were consistently rated as more credible than low-status ones. Even more striking was the finding that listeners made their judgments on credibility and status during the first ten or fifteen seconds of a speech.[4] The probable explanation for this result is that the audience receives a barrage of cues about the speaker in the first few seconds of a public speech: they see the speaker's attire; make judgments about the speaker's appearance; hear the speaker's voice; and get an initial impression of the speaker's confidence, competence, trustworthiness, and dynamism.

Who has high status in the public speaking classroom? Status varies from classroom to classroom and from school to school. In one of the author's summer session classes the status lines were clear: the three veterans in class, who were older and more experienced than the other students, were accorded more respect than the others. Of the three veterans, the one who emerged with the highest status was the one who had been specially trained to work in nuclear submarines. He gave some of the very best speeches, based on his experiences. Your class may be different, but the status that your classmates accord you can positively affect your credibility as a speaker. You can affect your status with your classmates by letting them know if you are linked to whatever they admire, respect, or desire.

A third principle is that *poor organization of your speech can lower your credibility.* Students who listened to a disorganized speech thought less of the speaker afterwards than they did before.[5] Strangely enough, good organization of your speech does not increase your credibility,[6] but poor organization can lower it. When you relate yourself to the topic, you will want to demonstrate early a mastery of organization. Your introduction will give the audience its first indications of your ability to organize.

A fourth principle is that *good delivery can improve your credibility.*[7] When you relate yourself to the topic, the audience apparently judges you on how fluently you express yourself on the subject. **Delivery** consists of your use of voice, movement, and gesture. **Fluency** is the smoothness of your delivery—the lack of unintentional pauses. The presence of vocal fillers or pauses like "Ahhhh," "You know," or overuse of "Now," "Well," or "Then," to fill silence are signs of **nonfluency.** Research on the subject shows that such nonfluencies decreased speaker ratings in competence and dynamism, but did not affect the speaker's trustworthiness.[8] To achieve high credibility, you need to know your material well, start your introduction with confidence, and avoid any nonfluencies.

Factors That Do Not Affect Source Credibility

We have determined that a number of factors do affect source credibility. In addition, we also know that some factors do not appear to affect source credibility. Popular myth maintains that certain factors influence source credibility when, in fact, they do not. You, as a public speaker trying to link yourself to your topic in an introduction, need to know both the factors that do influence credibility (the principles cited in the previous section) and those that do not. For instance, does good organization increase source credibility? As we have seen, it does not. The evidence indicates only that poor organization decreases speaker credibility.[9] Other myths concerning source credibility are dispelled in the next section.

High Source Credibility Is. . .

1. unrelated to good organization;
2. unrelated to learning;
3. unrelated to conciliatory remarks;
4. unrelated to self-praise.

Source credibility does not appear to affect learning. The previous section showed that a high-credibility speaker receives more change of opinion from an audience than a low-credibility one. That principle is based on attitude change, not on learning. **Learning** is the cognitive dimension concerned with what you know, not with your attitude toward something. This principle means that an audience can learn from either a high- or low-credibility source and might learn equally well from either.[10] You can recollect, recall, and recount information from a speech regardless of the source's credibility. Learning, which is unaffected by source credibility, is influenced by some other factors. Is the listener motivated to understand? Is the speaker presenting information that the listener can relate to? Is the speaker organizing the content for understanding? Is the presentation of the message clear? These factors are related to learning even if source credibility is not.

A second principle that is especially important in the introduction of a speech is that *conciliatory remarks and obvious attempts to influence the audience, such as the use of self-praise, do not improve a speaker's credibility.* Common sense and popular belief might dictate that if a speaker uses compliments and self-praise, an audience's positive evaluations would increase. Studies, however, indicate that they do not.[11] You should *describe* your qualifications in the introduction and avoid evaluative and judgmental statements about them.

Use checklist 4 to ensure that you have considered the possible ways to improve your source credibility. Place a check in the blank on the left to indicate that you have considered the implications of the statement for your speech.

**Checklist 4:
Checklist for
Strategies for
Improving
Source
Credibility**

_____ 1. Can you ask your teacher or a fellow student who introduces you to mention any praiseworthy statements or comments about your qualifications? Such evaluative information appears to have more impact on an audience when it comes from someone besides the speaker.

_____ 2. Have you reminded your audience descriptively of your qualifications for speaking on the subject? Remember that self-praise does not help your credibility, but you may improve your credibility by reminding the audience of your experience, expertise, and qualifications.

_____ 3. Are you dressed appropriately for the occasion and the audience? What you wear when you speak and how you appear should be conscious strategic choices in a public speaking situation, just as they are when you go out with someone you wish to impress.

_____ 4. Given the classroom situation, your classmate audience, and the topic you have selected, is the audience likely to think of you as competent, trustworthy, dynamic, and interested in them?

_____ 5. Have you carefully pointed out how your topic is related to the audience, selected appropriate supporting materials, organized the content, and determined a means of delivery that will help your audience learn and retain the content of your speech?

**Application
Exercise 2:
Describing Your
Qualifications**

Think of a topic. Then describe your qualifications that could be mentioned in a speech on that topic. Carefully avoid judgments and evaluative language.

Topic _____

I am qualified to speak on this topic because _____

_____

_____

_____

_____

**Forecasting
Organization and
Development**

The fourth and final function of an introduction is **forecasting** the organization and development of your speech. This step should be done late in the introduction because it sets up the audience's expectations about the length and direction of the speech. The forecast reveals when and what you are going to cover in your speech.

Several forecasts from student speeches are cited here for your examination. Read each of them carefully so you can use them as models in your own speech.

"Pets are great! And this morning I'd like to give you some suggestions on how to pick a Pet . . . and when you've picked one; how to get along with it."

With these few hints you, too, can make ten dollars an hour painting houses, barns, and other buildings. First, you will have to find the right painting job for you. Next, you will have to know how to bid on the house or object to be painted. Finally, you will have to learn some tips on how to paint well.

In the remainder of my campaign to convince you of the seriousness of the poverty question, I will discuss the issues of (a) government poverty programs, (b) jobs for the poor, and (c) medical care for the poor.

In my speech on checking accounts, I will explain the numbers on your checks, the stamps on your checks, the procedure for stopping payment, and a way to prove your check was paid.

Forecasts can also take other forms. A problem-solution statement, "Last time you heard my explanation of why we have a problem with inflation; this time I will reveal some solutions to the problem." A spatial relations format, "Today I

An Example of an Introduction

DEATH RACE

Begins with a narrative, a story to gain attention.

Role-plays a veteran checking out his gear to maintain attention.

Story is a subtle means of relating himself to the topic: He has had the experience.

Arouses curiousity about the topic to maintain attention.

With sweat beading on my forehead and adrenalin gushing through my body, I solemnly survey my mission. Gusting winds cut through my jeans as a cloudy sky casts shadowy figures on the surroundings. I check through my gear one final time, for a failure on any items can spell certain death for me. Let's see. Good tread on tennis shoes. Check. Florescent vest turned on. Check. I take time to reflect on my previous missions. Yes, you could say that I am a veteran. I've been there and back many times. Two hundred or so successful assignments without a serious injury. A good record. A couple of close calls, but never anything more than a sprained ankle or a hurt ego. But today is a new day. I must not let my record lull me into carelessness. I'm ready. The time is now, for if I wait one minute longer, I'll be late for class!

Story employs drama, adventure, and conflict.

The thoroughfare is crowded and I can barely see my destination. Cautiously I look both ways up and down the street, once, twice, three times before I venture out. An opening breaks and I begin to hurry. Wait! A Mack truck just pulled out and is rushing toward me. Will he see the flashing warning lights? Will he read the big yellow sign proclaiming my right of way? As he rumbles recklessly toward me, I realize that the answer is no. I cover the remaining twenty feet in a couple of leaps and bounds. Exhausted, my mission is complete. I have successfully crossed a campus street.

Begins to announce the topic.

Relates topic to audience.

Does this story sound familiar to you? How many times a day do you have to risk life and limb to cross a campus street? How often have you been angered by the drivers who ignore the pedestrians, the crosswalks, and the warning lights? We have all had the experience.

Announces topic and forecasts development of speech.

Today I want to discuss with you what can be done to end this terror for the innocent pedestrian on campus. I want to talk about three suggestions that I have for alleviating the problem of crosswalk warfare.

Figure 6.1 An example of an introduction.

will show you how electricity gets from the power plant to your house." A chronological arrangement, "How does an insect develop from a worm to a flyer?" Each format indicates to the audience how the speaker plans to discuss the topic.

To see how the four functions operate together in a single introduction, examine the student introduction in figure 6.1. The side notes indicate which function is being fulfilled. Notice that the speaker gains and maintains attention, relates the topic to himself and to the audience, and forecasts the development of the speech. Remember that using a story is just one strategy that can be used in an introduction.

An Example of the Four Functions in a Student Introduction

Thus far in this chapter we have focused on the introduction of a public speech. In this section we will turn our attention to introducing another speaker.[12] Introductions are beneficial for building confidence because two people are in front of the room at the same time, and the focus is on the person being introduced, not on the person who is doing the introducing. Introductions also provide the speaker practice in selecting materials that are important to establish credibility. A side benefit is that the speaker has the opportunity to practice interviewing skills in order to decide what to say about the person he or she is introducing.

Introducing Another Speaker: The Functions

What are you to say when you introduce someone else? In most cases you (a) recognize the audience and any important dignitaries that may be present, (b) state your own name and affiliation, (c) state the name of the person being introduced, (d) announce the topic and enumerate the person's qualifications for speaking on that topic, and (e) present the person who is going to speak. Notice that in introducing another person, you fulfill some of the same functions you ordinarily fulfill in the introductory portion of your own speech. You relate the speaker to the topic, and you announce the topic of the speech.

One important difference between introducing someone else and introducing yourself in the first part of your own speech is that you do not have to be objective, descriptive, and nonjudgmental in introducing another. You do, however, have to be careful about what you say. When the person you are introducing is a friend, you should not disclose information that would damage your friend's credibility. When you are being introduced by another person, you should provide that person with some information in writing from which he or she can choose. This increases accuracy and decreases casual but potentially damaging remarks.

Carefully read this student's speech, which introduces another student speaker. The student doing the introducing gathered her information in a single interview with the speaker. Notice how she speaks warmly of the speaker, repeats his name frequently so that the audience will remember it, and emphasizes his interests that are related to the topic.

Professor Willis and fellow students. My name is Jennifer Speer, and I am here to introduce my new friend, easygoing Joe Myhre. Joe is a Norwegian from Hanlontown, a small town near Mason City with a population of 175. He attended high school in Manly, where his graduating class had 65 students. He is a sophomore majoring in industrial administration. He started out in forestry, but he changed majors when he discovered that even being a forestry major didn't guarantee one an outdoor job, which is what he wants. Industrial administration doesn't guarantee him an outside job either, but Joe thought that major would be as good as anything else.

Joe's biggest interest and his greatest love is the out-of-doors. In the summer he works for the Department of Transportation cleaning up the rest area at Clear Lake. When he is not doing that, he bales hay for farmers in the area.

One of Joe's favorite hobbies is hunting, as you might expect. He hunts everything from pheasant to fox. He owns two hunting dogs, black labradors. Joe raised and trained the dogs himself. He claims that his only reasons for going home are his dogs and his hunting.

Joe is also a fishing enthusiast. He tries to get to Minnesota for this purpose at least twice a year. He owns backpacking equipment which he likes to use year round. However, he usually has some trouble finding someone to accompany him in the winter. He also has his own canoe, which he uses on the Winnebago River near his home. And he owns a Yamaha 500 motorcycle that he says he rides in rain, sleet, and snow. It could be because Joe doesn't own a car.

Joe, who is nearly as open as the outdoors he loves, also enjoys some other outdoor sports. He does some water skiing when the opportunity arises. He does downhill snow skiing, too. In fact, over spring break he went to Steamboat, Colorado, to do some skiing.

Today Joe is going to speak to you about how to
survive in the out-of-doors when you have to fend
for yourself. He will tell us how to find food and
water and how to provide lodging that will keep
you alive in winter or summer. [13]

Jennifer introduced Joe as a person who knows about outdoor survival. The slightly negative material about Joe's choice of majors may have made him even more likeable to the audience. Joe turned out to be very much as he was described: open as the out-of-doors and wildly enthusiastic about outdoor living.

We have discussed the introduction of the speech very thoroughly. Let us now consider the ending or conclusion of the speech. Just like the introduction, the conclusion of a speech fulfills certain functions: (1) to forewarn the audience that you are about to stop; (2) to remind the audience of your central idea or the main points in your message; (3) to specify precisely what the audience should think or do in response to your speech; (4) to end the speech in an upbeat or memorable manner that will make the audience members want to think and do what you recommend.

Concluding Your Speech: The Functions

Conclusionary Functions

1. To forewarn the audience that you are about to stop
2. To remind the audience of your central idea or main points
3. To specify what the audience should do
4. To end the speech in an upbeat manner

Let's examine each of these functions of a conclusion in greater detail. The **brake-light function** warns the audience that you are about to stop. Can you tell when a song is about to end? Do you know when someone in a conversation is about to complete a story? Can you tell in a TV drama that the narrative is drawing to a close? The answer to these questions is usually "yes," because we get verbal and nonverbal signals that songs, stories, and dramas are about to end. But, how do you use the brake light function in a speech?

The most blatant, though trite, method of signaling the end of a speech is to say "In conclusion . . ." or "To summarize . . ." or "In review. . . ." Another way is to physically move back from the lectern. Also, you can change your tone of voice to have the sound of finality. There are hundreds of ways to say, "I'm

coming to the end." For instance, as soon as you say, "Now let us take my four main arguments and bring them together into one strong statement: you should not vote unless you know your candidates," you have indicated an impending ending.

Application Exercise 3: Signaling the Conclusion

Watch your professors for a few days. How do they indicate that classes are over? How many of them use ordinary ways to signal the end, such as saying, "For tomorrow read pp. 229–257"? What are some more imaginative ways that your teachers conclude their classes and lectures? Do any of them use methods that you could imitate in a public speech?

The second function of a conclusion—to remind the audience of the central idea in your message—is the **instant replay function.** You could synthesize a number of major arguments or ideas into a single memorable statement. A student giving a speech on rock music concluded it by distributing to each classmate a sheet of paper that had the names of local rock stations and their locations on the radio dial. You could also simply repeat the main steps or points in the speech. For instance, a student who spoke on the Heimlich Maneuver for saving a choking person concluded his speech by repeating and demonstrating the moves for saving a person's life.

The third function of a conclusion is to clearly state the response that you seek from the audience, the **anticipated response.** If your speech was informative, what do you want the audience to remember? *You* tell them. If your speech was persuasive, how can the audience show their acceptance? A student who delivered a speech on peridontal disease concluded by letting her classmates turn in their candy for a package of sugarless gum. Other students conclude by asking individuals in the audience to answer questions about the content of the speech: "Judy, what is the second greatest cause of lung cancer?" Whether your speech is informative or persuasive, you should be able to decide which audience behavior satisfies your goals. You do not want to find yourself in the position of the woman who has just finished talking with Blondie.

The fourth function of a conclusion—the **upbeat ending function**—is to end the speech in an upbeat or memorable manner so that the audience will remember it and want to do what you recommend. A student many years ago gave a speech with a clever ending that summarized his arguments and gave it a memorable ending. His speech was on car accidents, the wearing of seat belts, and the disproportionately large number of college-aged people who die on the highway. He talked about how concerned we are that an accident not be our fault. His conclusion: "It does not matter who is right in the case of an automobile accident. It is not who is right that counts in an accident; it is who is left." It was a grim conclusion that made the main point memorable. A student gave a more upbeat conclusion to her speech on cookies. She had the audience sample homemade, partially made, and ready-made cookies at the end of her speech to see if they could tell the difference. Many students had to eat dozens of cookies before they could draw a conclusion.

Avoid endings that are overly dramatic. A student at a large midwestern university was giving a speech on the fourth floor of a large classroom building. His topic was insanity. As he gave the speech, it became increasingly apparent to the class that he might have been speaking from personal experience. The longer he spoke, the more obvious it became: his words became increasingly slurred, his eyes went from restless to slightly wild, and his mouth and eyelids went slack. At the very end of the speech, he walked to an open window and jumped out. The class rushed to the window to see the speaker safely caught in a net held by his fraternity brothers. Had there been a mixup in communication and the fraternity brothers had appeared at the wrong time or window, overdramatization could have led to a permanent conclusion.

Between class sessions, develop a conclusion that can be tried on a small group of class-mates. See if you can fulfill the four functions given in the text. Try especially to develop skill in summarizing, synthesizing, and stating the main point of your message in language that will be striking and memorable.

Application Exercise 4: Concluding a Speech

This chapter has concentrated on beginnings and endings, the skills necessary for developing the introduction to a speech, introducing another speaker, and concluding a speech.

Conclusion

In the first section, you learned that there are four functions of an introduction: to gain and maintain attention, to relate the topic to the audience, to relate the speaker to the topic, and to forecast the organization and development of the speech. You were also given twelve methods of gaining and maintaining attention and encouraged to reveal explicitly to an audience how the speech topic is related to them. You learned four principles relating source credibility and opinion change, status, organization, and delivery, and found out that source credibility is unrelated to learning, self-praise, and conciliatory remarks.

In the second section you learned how to introduce another speaker, and why doing so is an important way to increase a speaker's credibility, especially when he or she is relatively unknown.

In the last section you learned four functions of the conclusion of a speech: the brake-light, the instant-replay, the anticipated response, and the upbeat-ending functions.

You should be cautious about overdramatization in both introductions and conclusions. The primary function of both is to focus audience attention and concern on your message.

Application Assignment

Performance

Deliver a two- to four-minute introduction to a speech. Be sure your introduction fulfills the functions explained in this chapter. The criteria for evaluation are the extent to which you

1. Gain and maintain the audience's attention through some means relevant to the topic;
2. State the topic of the speech and its relationship to the immediate audience;
3. Describe your qualifications for delivering a speech on this topic (i.e., the relationship between you and the topic);
4. Arouse interest, generate information curiosity, or highlight the need for the audience to hear the body of the speech;
5. Forecast the subject, development, and organization of the body.

Do not go beyond the introduction in this performance; instead, try to make the audience eager to hear more. See Appendix C for an example of a student speech that fulfills the assignment.

Written Script

Write a script of your introduction. Include side notes that indicate how it fulfills its functions. See Appendix C for an example of a student script with side notes.

brake-light function A function of the conclusion of a speech in which the speaker indicates an impending ending by verbal and nonverbal means.

conciliatory remarks Comments made by a speaker to show the audience that he or she has high regard for them; a factor that appears to be unrelated to source credibility.

delivery Characteristics of a speech, including gestures, movement, rate, pitch, voice variety, eye contact, and fluency.

fluency The smoothness of delivery; the lack of vocalized pauses such as "Ahhh" and verbal fillers such as "you know." Refers to a flow of words without unintentional pauses.

forecasting A function of the introduction, which reveals to the audience the organization and development of the speech.

instant-replay function A function of the conclusion of a speech, in which the speaker summarizes, synthesizes, or repeats the main points of the message.

learning Cognitive dimension characterized by the ability to remember ideas, facts, figures, and principles.

narration An introductory method of gaining and maintaining attention that depends on a story with a theme related to the speech topic.

nonfluency Needless repetition of words and phrases and the use of vocalized pauses ("Ahhh," "Well," "You know") to fill silence with sound; negatively affects credibility.

opinion change The altering of an audience's position on an idea or issue.

self-disclosure A speaker's revelation of a characteristic that the audience is unlikely to know already; a device used in public speaking to gain and maintain an audience's attention.

status The esteem in which an audience holds a speaker, based on age, experience, or special competence. One of the characteristics on which source credibility depends.

1. L. S. Harms, "Listener Judgments of Status Cues in Speech," *Quarterly Journal of Speech* 47 (1961): 168.
2. Ralph L. Rosnow and Edward J. Robinson, *Experiments in Persuasion* (New York: Academic Press, 1967), p. 18. See also, Kenneth Andersen and Theodore Clevenger, Jr., "A Summary of Experimental Research in Ethos," *Speech Monographs* 30 (1963): 59–78.
3. Andersen and Clevenger, pp. 59–78.
4. Harms, p. 168.
5. Harry Sharp, Jr., and Thomas McClung, "Effects of Organization on the Speaker's Ethos," *Speech Monographs* 33 (1966): 182–83.
6. Andersen and Clevenger, p. 77, and Sharp and McClung, pp. 182–83.
7. Wayne N. Thompson, *Quantitative Research in Public Speaking* (New York: Random House, 1967), p. 54.
8. Ibid.
9. Sharp and McClung, pp. 182–83.
10. Andersen and Clevenger, p. 77.
11. Ibid., p. 78.
12. For further research on introductions, see Thompson, p. 54.
13. A speech delivered by Jennifer Speer in Fundamentals of Public Speaking, Iowa State University.

Chapter 7

Objectives

After you have completed chapter 7, you should be able to answer the following questions:

1. What are some differences between spoken and written language?
2. What are eight different ways to share meanings by defining words, phrases, and concepts?
3. What kinds of language behavior should you avoid if you want to be a literate speaker?
4. What are five ways to improve your powers of description?
5. What is information overkill?

When you have completed chapter 7, you should have practiced skills in

1. Employing the language of spoken discourse;
2. Defining a word or concept in front of an audience by using some of the eight ways to share meaning;
3. Avoiding errors of language and thought that signal a lack of spoken literacy; and
4. Effectively describing a person, place, or object.

Application Exercises

1. Concrete and abstract language.
2. Defining your terms.
3. Translating euphemisms.
4. Comparisons.

Language in Your Speech

Proper words in proper places, make
the true definition of a style.

Jonathan Swift

W e like to think that other people share our own meanings for words. "When **Introduction**
I say *dog,* I mean dog!" We fully expect others to think the same thing we do
when we say the word *dog*. If we should get into a dispute over the meaning of
a word, we turn to "the final arbiter," the dictionary. Unfortunately, our commonly held beliefs—that others share the same understanding of words that we
do and that the dictionary settles all disputes—are both incorrect. Actually, language is an arbitrary symbol system that has developed over time and is full of
inconsistencies, because it was built not to please grammarians but to serve as a
functional means of communication.

Language is important for you to study in public speaking because much of the message you communicate to an audience depends on the words that you choose to express your intended meaning. You should remember that language is arbitrary, that words vary in their ability to be understood and in their availability for an audience, that words are often ambiguous, and that words are strategic choices that you have to make as a speaker.

The **arbitrariness** of language refers to the fact that meanings for words have developed over time, and that the relationship between a word and its various meanings is the product of people's inventiveness with the language. To one person a carbonated sweetened drink in a bottle or can is "pop," to another "soda," to still another "a soft drink."

Very likely you have learned a specialized vocabulary from your experience or field of study that is not shared by everyone in your audience. You cannot consult the dictionary as the final arbiter of meaning because what really matters to you as a speaker are the audience's interpretations of words and the meanings. Fortunately, as a public speaker, you will be in a position to share meanings with the audience.

A second set of characteristics of language is its ability to be understood and its **availability** to an audience. A word is highly understandable if the speaker and audience use it frequently in their everyday lives. One measure of a word's ability to be understood is its length: the words that we use most often tend to be abbreviated. "Motion pictures" become "films" or "flicks." "Television" becomes "TV" or "the tube."

Availability refers to the word we most likely will use to state a perception. We use words to describe various courses, such as *ag, home ec, double E,* and *stat,* which are not only highly understandable, but the most available, the most likely ones we select to talk about those courses. The public speaker who uses language effectively is sensitive to both the ability to be understood and the availability of the words he or she selects for a speech.

A third characteristic of language is **ambiguity.** Ambiguity is the difficulty of determining exactly what a word is likely to mean to an audience. In certain circumstances, a person uses words as signals to reduce ambiguity. For example, a sign that says "Stop" is not supposed to be ambiguous, because it means that everyone should come to a complete halt, check for safety, and proceed. On the other hand, a sign that says "Yield" is somewhat more ambiguous because in some cases you should stop completely and wait, while in others you need only slow down to check the flow of traffic.

Much of our everyday language is highly ambiguous. For instance, suppose someone calls you a conservative. What does that term mean? The word is ambiguous because there is no universally agreed-upon meaning for it. Similarly, if you say that someone is beautiful, the term is ambiguous because reasonable persons may disagree on what beauty is. As a public speaker you will have to learn ways to lessen ambiguity and to increase the chances that the audience shares your intended meanings.

Finally, language in public speaking involves **strategic choice.** That is, you as speaker must choose words deliberately, intentionally, and purposefully. You must choose words strategically so they accurately describe what you have in mind and so the audience shares enough of the meaning to understand your message. For example, suppose you were to describe the building in which you grew up as a child. Would you call it an apartment, a shack, a mansion, a hovel, a high-rise, a condominium, a townhouse, or a tenement? These words all have a certain similarity, but they do not communicate the same message. The word you choose depends on both the meaning you intend to communicate and the codability and availability of the word for your audience. You gain nothing by calling the building a condominium or a hovel if your audience is unfamiliar with those words. They may be accurate descriptors, but they may fail to communicate because of low codability and availability.

In this chapter you will find ways to overcome some of the most common problems of using language in a public speech. Language may be arbitrary, high or low in ability to be understood and availability, ambiguous, and strategic, but it is also functional. You can learn ways to use language more effectively in your public speeches.

One approach to the study of language is to discuss it at a theoretical level, as we did in the preceding section. Another approach is to consider what language problems arise when student speakers actually deliver their speeches in class. This is the approach we will take in the rest of this chapter. The examination is not exhaustive; you or your instructor may know of language problems that are peculiar to your classmates, your college, or your region. Language problems that are discussed here are among the most common in the public speaking classroom.

Solutions to Language Problems in Public Speaking

Using Spoken Rather Than Written Language

What are some of the language problems that confront student, instructor, and audience in the public speaking class? One problem arises when *the speaker uses written rather than spoken language* in the speech. Many students are more comfortable if they write out their speeches. When they deliver them in front of the class, they have either partially memorized the speeches, or they are reading them. The result is stilted language.

Compare, for example, these three excerpts from student speeches. Which seem more like written language? Which, on the other hand, seem more like spoken language?

A. The designer's art is probably the least appreciated and truly understood craft of the modern day. Truly fine design is inherently unobtrusive but crucial to the utility of a given object; only when bad design is present do most people notice design at all. . . .[1]

B. The story of the Salem witch trials is an allegory for modern times. The urge to hunt witches has not vanished. Replace the idea of the wicked witch dressed in black with concepts such as race or nationality. . . .[2]

C. "Hey man, let's get high!" Is this a familiar scene with you? I bet as a student in this college you have at one time or another come into contact with "cannabis." You say, "What's cannabis?" Well, what about "pot" or "grass?" Ah yes, I see they sound familiar. . . .[3]

There is nothing incorrect in any of these student speeches. However, if you guessed that sample C was the most like spoken language, you would be correct. The passage is conversational. It invites audience response by asking questions and is the only passage to directly address the audience. Samples A and B seem to be more literary—more like written than spoken language. Sample A is full of long words. Sample B assumes that the audience knows what an allegory is. Neither sample is conversational nor directly addresses the audience, though sample B does ask us to consider our attitudes toward nationality and race as being similar to earlier attitudes toward witches.

You can make your speeches sound more like spoken than written language if you recognize the distinction between concrete and abstract words. **Concrete language** evokes a more specific image in another person's mind. It is "closer" to its referent (the concept or object for which it stands). All words "stand for" or

"As I have often said in moments of tranquility 'pride cometh before a fall' and 'he who is at the top has farthest to fall'."

symbolize something else, but a concrete word "stands for" or symbolizes something in particular. **Abstract language** consists of less specific references to ideas for which you may be unable to point to anything in particular. In this sense, the abstract term is "farther from" its referent: it does not tend to evoke a specific image in the listener's mind.

The word *justice* is an abstract term. If you asked your classmates their meaning for the term, you would receive many answers. However, if you told the class how your car broke down in the parking lot and received twenty dollars in fines for which there was no appeal, then you would be rendering the concept of justice—or injustice—in concrete terms.

You should consider how to translate some of our earlier examples into more concrete language. Sample A is probably the most abstract of the three selections. Here it is again:

```
The designer's art is probably the least
appreciated and truly understood craft of the
modern day. Truly fine design is inherently
unobtrusive but crucial to the utility of a given
object; only when bad design is present do most
people notice design at all.
```

A Comparison of Abstract and Concrete Language	
Abstract	**Concrete**
Dog	Spot
Some people say	*Time* reports
Recent reports	Today's *New York Times* says
Music	Joe Jackson's "I'm the Man"
Fast	Ninety miles per hour
Department store	Sears
Killed	Murdered in cold blood
Runner	Sprinter in 100 yard dash
Far away	Four hundred and ninety miles away

Notice the abstractions: *the designer's art, craft, modern day, truly fine design, utility, object, bad design,* and *people.* These terms are all so broad that the images evoked in the audiences' minds are practically uncontrolled.

See what happens in your mind when this passage is "translated" into more specific, concrete language:

```
Are you comfortable in the chair you are sitting
in? Someone designed that chair for you; yet, you
are unlikely to think about the chair you sit in,
the table you eat at, or the clothes that you wear
unless the chair is too small, the table too
narrow, or the collar too tight.
```

Is it easier for you to see and feel your chair, your table, and your clothes than to envision the "designer's art"? Now look at some of the examples of abstract and concrete language in figure 7.1. The concrete examples have much more impact than their abstract counterparts. Similarly, in your own speeches, you will find that the audience responds better when you "translate" abstract ideas and concepts into more concrete terms. No speech will be without some abstractions, but you should learn to recognize the difference between concrete and abstract language so that you can speak more effectively.

The use of stilted language is only one indication that a speaker is using written rather than oral style in a speech. Additional differences between oral and written style spring from the fact that the language of public speaking is closer to the language of conversation than to that of literature. Just as a speech is likely to consist of specific, concrete language rather than abstract language, it is also likely to consist of simple rather than complex words, of short rather than compound or complex sentences, and of short paragraphs rather than long and convoluted ones. A speech is also likely to employ questions or interrogative sentences rather than an army of declarative ones; it is likely to use relational or personal pronouns (we, our) rather than impersonal ones (one, they); it is likely to use the everyday language of colloquial expression rather than the formal language of the high court; it is likely to use blatant transitions ("Now that we have covered that point, let's move to the second point"); it is likely to be repetitive; and it is likely to contain language adapted to the particular audience.[4]

"Translate" the abstract terms in the column at the left into more specific, concrete terms in the blanks at the right.

1. A recent article . . .   _____
2. An allegory for modern times . . . _____
3. Race or nationality   _____
4. A $4 billion profit   _____
5. She is intelligent   _____
                                     _____
                                     _____
                                     _____
                                     _____

Application Exercise 1: Concrete and Abstract Language

Using Shared Meanings

A second trouble spot for speakers comes from using words the audience does not understand. The student who is interested in canoes speaks of "straight strokes," "j-strokes," and "sweep strokes." The student who makes his own butter talks about the "dasher" and the "clabber," "bilky" milk and butter that "gathers." The student who speaks on aerobics uses terms like "arteriosclerosis," "cardiovascular-pulmonary system," and "cardiorespiratory endurance." Do you know what these students are talking about? The words they are using are all specialized terms, sometimes called *jargon,* that are used by people who know more than the ordinary person does about canoeing, buttermaking, and exercise.

At the outset you should recognize that there is nothing particularly wrong with using terms that the audience does not understand—as long as you explain the terms in language they *can* understand. Another way of stating the principle involved is that you should explain your terms in the audience's language. The student giving a speech on buttermaking explains that "The dasher consists of a stick similar to a broom handle. A cross made of two slats, four inches long and two inches wide, is nailed to the end of the handle. The dasher is inserted into the churn, and the churn's opening is covered by a tightly fitting wooden lid with a hole in the middle for the dasher."[5] The student speaker defines a word his audience is unlikely to know by comparing it to a broomstick and revealing how it is constructed.

You can make your speeches more effective by learning various methods of communicating meaning to an audience. The following eight methods are a sampling of ways to evoke the meanings you intend. Each method is labeled, defined, and illustrated.

Types of Definitions

1. Comparison	5. Etymology
2. Contrast	6. Differentiation
3. Synonyms	7. Operational definition
4. Antonyms	8. Experiential definition

Comparison

Something unfamiliar can be defined by showing how it is similar to something else with which the audience is more familiar. A student who was defining "was-sailing" explained that the term meant "going on a spree or a binge, or 'painting the town red.' As the Bible puts it, 'eat, drink, and be merry.' "[6]

Contrast

Something unfamiliar can be defined by showing how it is different from something else with which the audience is more familiar. A speaker who was attempting to communicate the meaning of "assertiveness" explained the concept like this:

```
Assertiveness can be contrasted with the more
familiar idea of aggressiveness. Aggressiveness
is characterized by pushiness and threats, while
assertiveness is characterized by clarity. The
aggressive person might say "Get over here and
help me"; the assertive person might say "I need
your help."[7]
```

Synonyms

To define a term with synonyms is to use words that are close to or similar in meaning and more familiar to the audience. "Being spaced out," said a speaker who was defining the term, "is similar to having the mind go blank, being dumbfounded, or being disoriented."[8]

Antonyms

To define a term with antonyms is to use words that are opposite in meaning and that are more familiar to the audience. Hence, being "spaced out" is "not being alert, keen, or responsive."[9]

144   Language in Your Speech

To define a term by means of its etymology is to give its origins or history. A desk *Etymology*
dictionary will reveal the language or languages from which a word is derived.
More specialized sources like the *Dictionary of Mythology,* the *Oxford English
Dictionary,* and the *Etymological Dictionary of Modern English* will provide
more detailed accounts. In a speech of definition, a speaker used the etymology
of a word to explain its significance:

> What does *rhinoplasty* mean? Well, without a
> dictionary, you might feel that you're lost. But
> if you break up the word into its two parts, *rhino-*
> and *-plasty,* the meaning becomes clearer. You
> might not know the meaning of *rhino-* itself, but if
> you think of an animal whose name bears this
> prefix, namely the rhinoceros, and of the most
> distinctive feature of this beast, its rather
> large snout, you would probably guess correctly
> that *rhino-* refers to the nose. The meaning of the
> suffix *-plasty* also seems elusive, but a more
> common form of it, *plastic,* reveals its meaning of
> "molding or formation." Put together, these
> meanings have been modified to create the current
> medical definition of *rhinoplasty:* "a plastic
> surgical operation on the nose, either
> reconstructive, restorative, or cosmetic." Put
> quite simply, a *rhinoplasty* is a nose job. [10]

To define a term by means of differentiation is to distinguish it from other mem- *Differentiation*
bers of the same class. Notice how a student used differentiation to show the
difference between two things that many people would see as very much alike:

> Some people think a jury trial is a jury trial; they
> don't realize that a jury trial can be quite
> different, depending on whether the case being
> tried is a civil or a criminal case. If it is a
> criminal case, then the jury will have to decide
> guilt or innocence beyond a reasonable doubt; if
> the trial is a civil case, then the preponderence
> of evidence should decide whether the plaintiff or
> the defendant wins the case. The end result of a
> jury trial in a criminal case is guilt or
> innocence, with the former resulting in
> punishment. The end result of a jury trial in a
> civil case is damages, either granted or not. [11]

Operational
Definition

An operational definition reveals the meaning of a term by describing how it is made or what it does. A cake can be operationally defined by the recipe, the operations that must be performed to make it. A job classification, such as secretary, can be operationally defined by the tasks that the person in that job is expected to perform: a secretary is a person who takes dictation, types, and files papers. Here is an operational definition from a student speech:

> Modern rhinoplasty is done for both cosmetic and health reasons. It consists of several mini-operations. First, if the septum separating the nostrils has become deviated as a result of an injury or some other means, it is straightened with surgical pliers. Then, if the nose is to be remodeled, small incisions are made within each nostril, and working entirely within the nose, the surgeon is able to remove, reshape, or redistribute the bone and cartilage lying underneath the skin. Finally, if the nose is crooked, a chisel is taken to the bones of the upper nose and they are broken so that they may be straightened and centered. [12]

Experiential
Definitions

A term can be explained by revealing someone's experience with it. During the 1980 Winter Olympics the U.S. Hockey team won a gold medal after defeating the Soviet Union and Finland. The headline for the day stated: "Americans 'big doolies' after victory." The reporter explained the headline:

> "Is there one word," the players were asked now, "to describe what you've done?"
> "Well," replied Mike Eruzione, the captain, "we're all a bunch of big doolies now."
> To his listeners, doolies was a new word. Eruzione turned to Phil Verchota, from Duluth, Minn., who had coined the word.
> "I got a gold today so I'm a big doolie," Verchota explained. "It just means big wheel, big gun, big shot." [13]

The 1980 U.S. Olympic hockey team was a bunch of big doolies. Their surprise victories over the Soviet Union and Finland made them heroes in the United States. Their new term, "big doolies," may or may not become part of our vocabulary, but it was coined and defined through the experience of the team. "Big doolies" is an example of how a term can be made up by one person and spread to millions who read about it the next day in the newspapers.

Other methods of defining terms exist, but the eight we've discussed—comparison, contrast, synonyms, antonyms, etymology, differentiation, operational definition, and experiential definition—will help you share meanings with your audience. You communicate more clearly as a speaker when you define your terms.

You also can avoid the embarassment of communicating something that you do not intend. A student gave a speech in which she frequently used the word *cruising*. Every time she used it, the members of the audience looked at each other in amusement. At the time, the word *cruising* was used by students to mean "seeking a sexual partner." However, the speaker was using it as professional foresters do to refer to the marking and measuring of trees. Remember that defining your terms can improve your communication.

Examine the words in the column at the left. Consider which method of definition you would use to help your classmates understand your meaning by placing the name of the method in the middle column. Then in the column at the right show how you would use that method.

Application Exercise 2: Defining Your Terms

Word	Method	Application
1. Ugly	_____	_____
2. Hair stylist	_____	_____
3. Intelligent	_____	_____
4. Gentleman	_____	_____
5. Unfair	_____	_____
6. Slob	_____	_____

Literacy as applied to the written word means a person's ability to read and write at some minimally acceptable level. Literacy may also be applied to the spoken word. Some indications of oral illiteracy and how to overcome it are explored in the following sections.

Achieving Literacy

Signs of Oral Illiteracy

1. Mistakes in grammar and pronunciation
2. Vocalized pauses and verbal fillers
3. Use of the language and ideas of other people
4. Overattachment to your own words

ERNIE?...THE COPS HAVE ME FOR KNOCKING OVER A BANK.

© 1979 by NEA Inc. T M Reg U S Pat Off

THAVES 11-30

Reprinted by permission. © 1979 NEA, Inc.

Signs of Oral Illiteracy

One sign of oral illiteracy is that the speaker makes mistakes in grammar and pronunciation. The speaker who says "Him and I, we went," "If we was staying there," or "Everyone reaches a point in their life" is signaling those who know the rules of grammar that he or she does not know them. Similarly, a speaker who cannot pronounce the words in his speech is revealing to the audience that he probably does not know very much about the subject, because anyone knowledgeable about the topic would know how to pronounce the necessary words.

Less serious, but equally problematic, is the overuse of certain words, which may cause the audience to start listening for the next repetition. Some speakers repeat the word *now* every time they begin a new sentence; others repeat the word *so*. Certain words and phrases are often used as "fillers" or vocalized pauses. They change considerably from year to year, but one phrase that has been around for several years is *you know*. Undoubtedly, many of the people in your class have other words and phrases that they use as verbal fillers.

A third indication of oral illiteracy is the use of other people's language to explain your own position. One example is the use of **clichés** such as "You only get out of it what you put into it," "All's fair in love and war," and "Beauty is only skin deep." Another example is the use of **euphemisms** or socially acceptable expressions such as the words *bathroom, powder room,* or *ladies' lounge* for the word *toilet*. A third example is more difficult to illustrate, but it consists of mouthing the words of others every time you have to state your position on an issue. You might, for instance, explain your position on busing by using your father's argument and his words. You might cling to some other authority like William F. Buckley or John Kenneth Galbraith on the welfare issue. Perhaps you simply take your husband's, wife's, friend's, or roommate's position on issues when you are asked to articulate your own. In any case, oral illiteracy includes your being unable to explain your own position without merely adopting someone else's language, arguments, and words.

Speechmakers who speak frequently have a tendency to use the same words repeatedly until their entire speech becomes memorized and impervious to further thought. The politician has his stock speech, the athletic banquet speaker has hers, and the evangelist has his. Such frequent expression of one's own thinking can become little different from thoughtlessly mouthing the words of others. This is especially true when the words have been spoken so often that the speaker is unwilling to revise them even in the face of changing circumstances. Are the words you use in your speeches simply repetitions of expressions you have given time after time? Is there any new knowledge that should be taken into account since you began taking a particular position?

Oral literacy includes avoiding mistakes in grammar and pronunciation, the overuse of verbal fillers or vocalized pauses, clichés and euphemisms, the simple adoption of other's language and ideas without using your own mind, and avoiding repetition of your own words and ideas to the point that you are no longer open to new terms, new knowledge, or changes in circumstance. Why should you strive to become orally literate? Why should you avoid grammatical mistakes, clichés, and all of the other errors you have been warned against?

Why Should You Strive for Oral Literacy?

You should avoid grammatical and pronunciation errors because audiences may discount much of what you have to say simply on the basis of such errors. This does not mean that your language must sound stilted or affected. You can be relaxed and informal without making errors in grammar and pronunciation.

What can you do if you have a problem with grammar or pronunciation? You can observe how other people pronounce words and use language. You can turn to your instructor for help. You can turn to the dictionary or a grammar handbook. The student who habitually makes numerous grammatical errors is unlikely to find a quick cure, but poor language can be corrected by students who recognize the social and economic benefits of being able to express themselves correctly and effectively.

Why should you avoid clichés and euphemisms? Clichés are a substitute for thought. There are so many clichés that entire conversations and speeches can be strung together with them. Unfortunately, most clichés are only partial truths. "You only get out of it what you put into it." Is that always true? Have you ever met people, including fellow students, who put a great deal into their college education and get practically nothing out of it? Have you seen others who put nothing into their education and yet reap many more benefits than they seem to deserve? If beauty is only skin deep, is ugliness, then, clear through? The partial truths that we mumble in answer to difficult problems mask the complexity and invite simple answers that discourage the creative thought that might solve a problem or settle an issue.

What is wrong with using the language and words of others? Again, the problem centers on using other people's thinking as a substitute for your own. Your position on an issue may be like someone else's, but did you arrive at that position you call your own by inheriting it from your parents or borrowing it from your friends? You can be considerably more convincing as a speaker if you try to articulate your own ideas instead of simply imitating those you have heard or read. Likewise, you should occasionally take a close look at the positions you have held for a long time. Has a situation changed so much that your position on it is still viable? George Wallace, Alabama politician and two-time presidential contender, repeated segregationist ideas for years without recognizing the changes in circumstances (including the civil rights movement) that altered the country so much. He became politically, philosophically, and morally out of step with the times. The same circumstance could be true for us if we did not make the effort to re-examine our own ideas. Literacy in public speaking is more than avoiding grammatical errors—it means you must synchronize your own ideas and language and effectively communicate them.

Euphemisms often mask realities that we would prefer not to think about or express. Many a slum is called an urban-renewal area. Convert the euphemisms at the left into more direct words at the right.

Application Exercise 3: Translating Euphemisms

Euphemisms	Synonymous Expressions
1. "Passed on"	_____
2. "Perspiration"	_____
3. "Senior citizen"	_____
4. "With child"	_____
5. "Underachiever"	_____
6. "Sanitation engineer"	_____

How can you improve your use of language in the public speech? Public speakers need to have a large vocabulary and good **descriptive powers** in order to accurately and vividly convey their thoughts. The person who only knows the primary colors—blue, red, and yellow—is unable to describe a landscape as accurately as the person who knows how to differentiate mauve, chartreuse, indigo, violet, and purple. A person's descriptions typically relate size, shape, color, texture, or even feelings evoked by objects and people.

Improving Your Descriptive Powers

Let us look first at some examples of descriptions from student speeches. Is a basketball just a round thing usually orange in color? This student looked at a basketball from various perspectives:

```
Defining the surface texture is much more
crucial to understanding the object than is
naming the exterior material. Texture is not
only a quality of coarseness, but of typography.
At a viewpoint range of, say, one centimeter, a
basketball is an undulating surface infiltrated
by scores of bulging protuberances, like the
pebbly bottom of a backwoods stream. At a range
of one hundred meters, it becomes
indistinguishable from an orange ball bearing. [14]
```

A second student described an early snowfall:

> The harshness of the frozen earth had been transformed into a soft, rolling white carpet. The bare trees which had previously been stripped of their majestic, colored leaves now stood proudly flocked.
>
> The sun was beginning to push the night back— revealing a chilling blue sky. The early morning light glistened off the newfallen snow, dancing from one ice particle to another, creating thousands of diamonds everywhere. [15]

Finally, a third student described an accelerated maneuver stall in an airplane:

> The stall is initiated by tipping the plane into a 45° angle turn, pushing the throttle to full power, and pulling back on the stick. The once serene earth has tipped onto its side and is spinning dizzily around me. The spinning fields slowly sink out of sight as I continue to pull back on the stick until all I see is blue sky in the windshield. The force of gravity on my body is steadily increasing. When the maneuver began there were two G's on my body, the same as on the big hill of the tornado rollercoaster. Just before the stall there will be four G's pulling me in my seat. My blood rushes to my feet instead of staying in my brain where I need it. My stomach constricts so I won't throw up. The noise of the engine makes a lugging sound as the plane labors into a steeper and steeper climb. When the airspeed comes within five knots of stalling, an irritating horn blares out its warning.
>
> Suddenly the plane begins to buffet. The stall is imminent. The nose drops violently, and the earth pops up in front of the plane. The four positive G's turn to four negative G's. The force pushes my stomach into my throat. The blood

Reprinted by permission. © 1980 NEA, Inc.

```
rushes to my brain. I have to act fast, or the
stall will turn into a spin. Against instinct, I
push the stick forward, level the wings, and
apply right rudder. . . .¹⁶
```

These speakers could have said, "A basketball is a round plastic thing," "The ground was covered with snow," and "The plane went up fast, stalled, and fell." But such brief, abstract descriptions would give the audience very little opportunity to develop the pictures in their own minds. The specific details in the students' accounts help the audience to visualize and feel what the speakers experienced. The speeches also suggest some methods of description you can use in your own speeches.

Use Precise, Accurate Language

One method of describing something is to use precise, accurate language. In the description of the basketball, the speaker views the ball from distances of one centimeter and one hundred meters—not from close and far away. The language is very precise. The plane tips to a 45° angle; it does not simply turn on its side. The language is very specific.

Build Your Vocabulary

A second method of describing something is to use a variety of words and expressions. The basketball's surface texture is described as "coarseness," "typography," and "an undulating surface infiltrated by scores of bulging protuberances." The snow is "soft," "rolling," and "white." The "serene earth" in the stalling maneuver becomes "spinning fields" as the engine makes a "lugging sound" and "labors into a steeper and steeper climb." The vocabulary in each case is impressive in its variety and appropriateness.

*Employ
Denotative and
Connotative
Meanings*

A third method of describing something is to use the connotative dimension of words. **Denotative meaning** is the dictionary meaning, the objective meaning without an emotional component. **Connotative meaning** is what the word suggests, its emotional content. For instance, if you refer to a woman as a "broad," the denotative definition may mean a female, but the connotative definition probably means a sex object. The same thing holds for a man referred to as a "hunk."

A look at our student speeches shows how one uses connotative meaning to enliven a description. To refer to the "typography" of a basketball suggests a map with a raised surface to indicate mountains, hills, and valleys. To say that a tree was "stripped" suggests forceful removal, and "proudly flocked" might suggest the spray "snow" used to decorate Christmas trees.

Use Comparison

A fourth method of describing something is to use comparisons, to examine two or more objects for likenesses or similarities. The idea is to compare the unknown (that which the speaker saw) with the known (that with which the audience is familiar), as the student did when he said that two G's are the same as you would feel "on the big hill of the tornado rollercoaster."

The public speaker must be careful to avoid comparisons that have been overused—such as "smooth as silk," "as pretty as a picture," or "as hard as a rock." These overused similes or comparisons are called clichés. Instead, you should try to create comparisons that help the audience envision what the speaker describes—such as the student speakers who said that a basketball at one centimeter looks "like the pebbly bottom of a backwoods stream" or that snow became a "soft, rolling white carpet."

*State the Familiar
in an Unfamiliar
Way*

A fifth method of describing something is to state the familiar in an unfamiliar way to make it more striking and memorable. "The bird carried the sky on its wings" is more exciting imagery than "the bird flew across the sky." Similarly, in the student descriptions the imagery is more striking when a basketball at one hundred meters is "an orange ball bearing" and in the snow scene when "the sun was beginning to push the night back."

To make your speeches more effective, use precise, accurate language; employ a wide vocabulary; use both the denotative and connotative meaning of words; make comparisons; and state the familiar in an unfamiliar way. Learn new words by reading self-help books, stories, and poems; by listening carefully to how literate people use the language. Use resources like the dictionary, the thesaurus, and handbooks on grammar and usage. Learning how to express yourself through language is not an easy task, though people who do it well make it look easy. A public speaking class gives you the opportunity to start working on your vocabulary, the accuracy and precision of your language, and your descriptive powers.

Comparisons are an effective method by which to describe phenomena. Unfortunately, some speakers use comparisons that have lost meaning through overuse. Instead of using clichés, speakers need to employ effective comparisons that are fresh and insightful. In order to gain experience in this skill, complete the following exercise. Describe the phenomenon at the left with a new comparison rather than with a cliché. An example is provided for you. Keep in mind that a variety of different expressions may be appropriate in each case.

Words

Comparison

1. Strong temptation

   It was as attractive and forbidding as a desert cactus in bloom.

2. Starry night

3. Ugly building

4. Crowded beach

5. Stormy sky

6. Good friend

Language and Information Overkill

We have discussed difficulties that speakers have with language and some methods of overcoming those problems. We turn now, to one final area of concern which is **information overkill.** The primary point of this section is that it is relatively easy for a knowledgeable speaker to provide more information and ideas than a diverse audience, that does not have expertise in a particular area, can easily absorb. Usually this is exactly the type of audience you face in a public speaking class. The warning to avoid information overkill is not aimed at speakers addressing a homogeneous audience whose members, like the speaker, are well acquainted with the ideas and specialized language necessary to express them.

"And my twenty-seventh point about pollution is . . ."

An example of the problem of information overkill comes from a student who was delivering a speech in class on the topic of photovoltaics. His first three sentences were appropriate enough as an attention-getter, but observe what happened next:

```
With America's energy independence growing
weaker everyday because of dwindling oil
reserves, it is paradoxical that energy is
available in the United States at over 500 times
the United States' present rate of consumption.
Where does this energy come from? The sun, of
course. When the sun is high in the sky, energy
radiates on the earth's surface at a little more
than one kilowatt per meter squared. The
equivalent of one gallon of gas, 36 kilowatt-
hours, falls on the area of a tennis court every
ten minutes. In the least sunny part of the
United States, the northeast according to chart
1, one football field could provide all the
energy used by 66 average American families of
4.7 people during a year's time. . . .[17]
```

Language in Your Speech

Probably, for most members of the audience, the references to tennis courts and football fields did relate the unfamiliar to the familiar, but how many people in a classroom audience know the meaning of "one kilowatt per meter squared," "36 kilowatt-hours," or the significance of "66 average American families of 4.7 people during a year's time"? The information flow was too rapid for the introduction of a speech to a diverse, unspecialized audience. The language was too unfamiliar, undefined, and unpalatable. The problem of information overkill was caused by a density of ideas and language complexity.

The speaker did not improve his communication. By the middle of the speech, he was saying this:

```
I will use this silicon cell as my example.
Electricity is generated in the silicon cell
when electrons are freed from the valence on the
outermost shell of the silicon atom by light.
When the electron is freed, it creates a hole,
which is a positively charged carrier, whereas
the electron is a negatively charged carrier.
If the photovoltaic cell was of uniform
consistency, no current would be generated,
since holes and freed electrons would be in the
same proportion; hence, they would all
recombine. . . .
```

The speaker was clearly talking above the audience's capacity to understand. He used the language of electrical engineering and physics without considering that most audience members were unfamiliar with atoms, valences, positive and negative charges, currents, electrons, and photovoltaic cells. Even if the speaker had defined all of these terms, the speech would have been inappropriate for a generalized audience. The speech does, however, illustrate the meaning of information overkill through language.

Conclusion

In this chapter you learned that language is an arbitrary system of communication in which words evoke meanings in other people's minds. You found that public speakers face certain problems with language. One problem is that beginning speakers, and even some experienced ones, tend to use written rather than spoken language in their speeches. A solution to this problem is to understand the difference between abstract and concrete language and to follow the suggestions in chapter 8 on delivery. Another problem is how to establish shared meanings. This can be solved by means of comparisons, contrasts, synonyms, antonyms, etymologies, differentiation, and operational and experiential definitions. A third problem area is achieving oral literacy. This can be accomplished by avoiding (1) grammatical and pronunciation errors, (2) the overuse of certain words as verbal fillers or vocalized pauses, (3) the use of others' language and ideas to articulate your own position, and (4) over-attachment to your own stock ideas. A fourth problem is how to improve your descriptive powers. This can be done by (1) using precise, accurate language, (2) building vocabulary, (3) using both denotative and connotative meanings, (4) using comparisons, and (5) stating the familiar in an unfamiliar fresh way. Finally, you learned that you should avoid language and information overkill in public speeches.

Application Assignment

The Speech of Definition

Deliver a two- to three-minute speech in which you define a term unknown to a majority of your audience by using at least three of the methods of defining discussed in chapter 7. You can also explain the denotative and connotative meanings of the word or concept. Your speech will be evaluated according to how well you can use the three ways of defining and can achieve literacy in oral communication by avoiding grammatical and pronunciation errors, avoiding vocalized pauses and verbal fillers, and avoiding a dependence on others' language to express your definition. You are encouraged to use sources of information like the dictionary or a thesaurus to help you determine various ways of defining your terms. Chapter 5 cites other sources that you might use in this assignment.

Optional: Provide a manuscript of your speech with side notes indicating where you used the three different methods of defining and denotative and connotative meanings. *Note:* An example of a speech of definition can be found in Appendix D. This speech can serve as a model for this assignment.

The Speech of Description

Deliver a three- or four-minute speech in which you describe a person, place, object, or experience by indicating size, weight, color, smell, texture, and/or feelings. The speech will be evaluated according to your ability to use precise, accurate, specific, and concrete language; a diverse vocabulary; words with appropriate connotative and denotative meanings; at least two comparisons; and one familiar item described in an unfamiliar way. The speech does not require outside sources, but you may wish to use a thesaurus or dictionary to help you produce a description without using clichés.

Optional: Provide a script of your speech with side notes indicating where you used comparisons, connotative and denotative meanings, and a familiar item described in an unfamiliar way. *Note:* An example of a speech of description can be found in Appendix E. This speech can serve as a model for this assignment.

Vocabulary

abstract language The use of words that tend to be broad and unspecific and refer to ideas likely to evoke a variety of meanings; the opposite of concrete language.

arbitrariness A characteristic of language referring to the relationship between a word and the various meanings people assign to it over a period of time.

availability A characteristic of language referring to the likelihood of a word's being selected to describe a particular perception; words most likely to be selected as descriptors are high in availability.

cliché A statement that has lost its impact because it has been overused.

concrete language The use of words that are relatively close to their referent; words that tend to be precise and specific and evoke particular meanings; the opposite of abstract language.

connotative meaning What a word suggests to the listener or reader; subjective meaning resulting from emotional involvement.

denotative meaning The objective meaning of a word, standardized by such sources as a dictionary.

descriptive powers The ability to vividly convey one's thoughts; usually related to sensory matters (size, shape, weight, texture, smell, and feelings experienced) and relayed to others by means of precise, accurate language, a wide vocabulary, connotative and denotative meanings, comparisons, and fresh imagery.

euphemism An agreeable expression substituted for one that may offend or sound unpleasant.

information overkill The use of excessive jargon or specialized language and an oversupply of factual data for a particular audience.

oral literacy The ability to speak fluently without errors in grammar or pronunciation, repetitive vocalized pauses or verbal fillers, overdependence on the language and ideas of others, or a restricting reliance on only your own language and ideas.

Endnotes

1. From a speech delivered by Matthew Eash in Fundamentals of Public Speaking, Iowa State University.
2. From a speech delivered by Jana Milford in Fundamentals of Public Speaking, Iowa State University.
3. From a speech delivered by David Kastner in Fundamentals of Public Speaking, Iowa State University.
4. Based on Harold P. Zelco and Frank E. X. Dance, "Oral Style Characteristics," *Business and Professional Speech Communication,* 2nd ed. (New York: Holt, Rinehart, and Winston, 1978), pp. 152–154.
5. From a speech delivered by Warren Varley in Fundamentals of Public Speaking, Iowa State University.
6. From a speech delivered by Roberta Mau in Fundamentals of Public Speaking, Iowa State University.
7. From a speech delivered by Jergen Nelson in Fundamentals of Public Speaking, Iowa State University.
8. From a speech delivered by John Rector in Fundamentals of Public Speaking, Iowa State University.
9. Eckerman.
10. From a speech delivered by Mark DuPont in Fundamentals of Public Speaking, Iowa State University.
11. From a speech delivered by Barbara Tarter in the Communication and Persuasion course, Ohio University.
12. Dupont.
13. Dave Anderson, "Americans 'big doolies' after victory,". *The Des Moines Register Peach,* February 25, 1980, p. 15. Used with the permission of the *New York Times* News Service.
14. From a speech delivered by Matthew Eash in Fundamentals of Public Speaking, Iowa State University.
15. From a speech delivered by Susan Schiltz in Fundamentals of Public Speaking, Iowa State University.
16. From a speech delivered by Warren Varley in Fundamentals of Public Speaking, Iowa State University.
17. The speaker of this negative example will remain anonymous for obvious reasons.

Chapter 8

Outline

Introduction: The importance of delivery and visual aids in public speaking.
  I. Four modes of delivery.
     A. Manuscript mode.
     B. Extemporaneous mode.
     C. Impromptu mode.
     D. Memorized mode.
  II. Vocal and bodily aspects of delivery.
     A. Vocal aspects of delivery.
        1. Pitch.
        2. Rate.
        3. Pauses.
        4. Volume.
        5. Enunciation.
        6. Fluency.
        7. Vocal variety.
     B. Bodily aspects of delivery.
        1. Gestures.
        2. Facial expression.
        3. Eye contact.
        4. Movement.
  III. Visual aids.
     A. Rationale for using visual aids.
     B. Types of visual aids.
        1. Chalkboards.
        2. Posters.
        3. Movies and slides.
        4. Opaque and overhead projections.
        5. Living models and physical objects.
        6. Handouts.
        7. Yourself.
Conclusion: A review of delivery and visual aids.

Objectives

After you have completed chapter 8, you should be able to answer the following questions:
  1. What are four modes of delivering speeches?
  2. What should you be doing with your voice when you speak?
  3. What is a "vocalized pause"?
  4. How should you use your arms during your speech?
  5. Should you move while you speak?
  6. What kinds of visual aids are most effective?
  7. What are the kinds of visual aids from which you can choose?
  8. What will your audience be watching for when you deliver your speech?

After you have completed chapter 8, you should have practiced skills in
  1. Choosing an appropriate mode of delivery;
  2. Using your voice for a more effective delivery;
  3. Monitoring your own gestures and movement;
  4. Selecting appropriate visual aids for your speech; and
  5. Evaluating your delivery skills and use of visual aids.

Application Exercises

  1. Selecting a mode of delivery.
  2. Testing the vocal aspects of your delivery.
  3. Bodily aspects of delivery.
  4. Evaluating your delivery.

Delivery and
Visual Aids

Besides, as is usually the case, we are
much more affected by the words which
we hear, for though what you read in
books may be more pointed, yet there is
something in the look, the carriage,
and even the gesture of the speaker,
that makes a deeper impression
upon the mind.

Pliny the Younger

Demosthenes, the famous classical orator, was asked his opinion on the three **Introduction** most important aspects of public speaking. His answer was "Delivery, Delivery, Delivery." Although some experts question whether delivery is the most important aspect of public speaking, few doubt that good delivery can render a speaker and a speech more effective. Also, evidence indicates that audiences tend to downgrade speeches which have obvious delivery flaws.

Through the ages, literature has contained advice on delivery. Here is Shakespeare on the subject:

> Speak the speech, I pray you, as I pronounced it to you, trippingly on the tongue. But if you mouth it, as many of our players do, I had as lief the town crier spoke my lines. Nor do not saw the air too much with your hand, thus, but use all gently, for the very torrent, tempest, and (as I may say) whirlwind of your passion, you must acquire and beget a temperance that may give it smoothness. O, it offends me to the soul to hear a robustious periwig-pated fellow tear a passion to tatters, to very rags, to split the ears of the groundlings, who for the most part are capable of nothing but inexplicable dumb shows and noise. I would have such a fellow whipped for o'erdoing Termagant. It out-herods Herod. Pray you avoid it.
> *Hamlet* III, ii, 1

This chapter focuses on the nonverbal aspects of a public speech that influence the effectiveness of communicating your message. These include both the vocal and bodily aspects of your delivery and your use of visual aids to communicate your message more clearly. First we will examine four modes of delivering a speech; this will help you answer the question, "What mode of delivery is most appropriate for this topic, audience, and speaker?" Second, we will see what vocal and bodily behavior is effective and ineffective. Finally, we will identify a number of visual aids that you can use in your speeches. By the time you complete this chapter, you should have expanded your understanding of delivery and, through practice and the application exercises, your confidence as a public speaker.

Four Modes of Delivery

The four modes of delivering a speech are (1) manuscript, (2) extemporaneous, (3) impromptu, and (4) memorized. These modes are appropriate for different topics, audiences, situations, and speakers. When you complete this section, you should be able to decide which mode to use in each speaking situation.

Four Modes of Delivery in Public Speaking

1. Manuscript mode
2. Extemporaneous mode
3. Impromptu mode
4. Memorized mode

Let us now consider the first mode of delivery, the manuscript mode. The speaker writes out and reads *verbatim* a manuscript speech. The **manuscript mode** of delivery is most appropriate when a speaker has to be precise. A president who delivers a foreign policy speech in which a slip of a word could start a war, a minister who carefully documents his sermon with biblical quotations, and a politician who releases information to the press are examples of speakers who might adopt this mode.

An example of the use of this mode occurred one week on campus when the school invited several speakers to present their points of view on religion. Every lecture drew a huge audience. The speakers, all professors, were a humanist, a Protestant, and an atheist. The humanist presented his point of view in a speech virtually without notes. His speech was almost paternal, full of human virtue and devoid of conflicting opinions. The Protestant, a Lutheran, delivered his speech a few days later. Many students in the audience were also Protestants, mainly Lutherans, and the speaker had considerable support from his audience. He, too, delivered his speech with few notes. A few days later, the atheist presented his speech. Instead of standing on the well-lighted stage as the others had done, he delivered his speech seated in the middle of the auditorium with a single spotlight shining on him in the darkness. He read every word from a carefully argued manuscript. Though he argued well, he had few followers in the audience. The response was polite but restrained.

The following weekend all three speakers faced each other and the audience in a discussion of their positions. Because the atheist's position was unpopular with both his fellow speakers and the audience, he was asked most of the questions. He received the audience's reluctant admiration because, in verbal combat, his previous mode of delivery enabled him to have a solid position on almost every question. The humanist and the Protestant had difficulty remembering exactly what they had said, while the atheist answered nearly every inquiry *verbatim* from memory. It was difficult for anyone in the audience or on the stage to distort the atheist's position. It was clearly a case in which a manuscript delivery was the most appropriate mode for the speaker, audience, and situation.

The advantages of a manuscript speech are obvious: the manuscript prevents slips of the tongue, miswording, and distortion. Of course, there are also disadvantages. It is difficult to be spontaneous or to respond to audience feedback with a manuscript, and it is quite impossible to make any significant changes during delivery. Many of the bodily aspects of delivery are limited by the script. If you have to read every word accurately, you cannot be watching your audience at the same time or move about and gesture uninhibitedly, as you can when giving an extemporaneous speech.

While the manuscript mode requires dependency on the script, reduces eye contact, and makes adaptation to the audience difficult, the **extemporaneous mode** of delivery invites freedom from notes, encourages eye contact, and permits immediate adaptation to the audience. The Latin root of the word *extemporaneous*

"I accept this award on behalf of all the little people who did so much to make it possible."

means "on the spur of the moment." In actuality, the extemporaneous mode of delivery, in order to be spontaneous, requires considerable preparation. The speaker must carefully research and plan her speech. She must strategically select the most effective arguments, evidence, and visual aids. She must practice the speech, mastering the content without memorizing it. She selects alternative strategies in case the audience response is different than expected. The speaker delivers the speech from a sentence, clause, or key-word outline or plan so that she can use exact wording as she speaks. Only after all of this does the effective extemporaneous speech appear to be "on the spur of the moment."

The extemporaneous mode of delivery is the one that is most commonly taught in the public speaking classroom. It is most speech teachers' favorite because it is the most versatile mode, demands attention to all aspects of public speaking preparation, and is the mode a speaker is likely to use most often.

Impromptu Mode

The word *impromptu* means "in readiness." The **impromptu mode** of delivery actually *is* "on the spur of the moment." Unlike the extemporaneous mode, the impromptu mode really involves no planning, preparation, or practice. You may be ready for an impromptu speech because of your reading, experience, and background, but you do not have any other aids to help you know what to say.

You undoubtedly have already delivered impromptu speeches. When your teacher calls on you to answer a question, your answer—if you have one—is impromptu. You were ready because you read the assignment or prepared for class,

164   Delivery and Visual Aids

but you probably did not write out an answer or certain key words. When someone asks you to introduce yourself, explain something at a meeting, reveal what you know about some subject, or give directions, you are delivering your answer in an impromptu fashion.

One of the advantages of an impromptu speech is that it reveals what you are like in unplanned circumstances. In a job interview you might be asked to explain why you are interested in the company, want a particular job, or expect such a high salary. Your impromptu answers may tell a potential employer more about you than if you were given the questions ahead of time and had prepared your answers. Similarly, the student who can give an accurate, complete answer to a difficult question in class shows a mastery of the subject matter that is, in some ways, more impressive than it might be in an exam or other situation in which he or she may give partially planned answers. One advantage of the impromptu mode is that you learn how to think on your feet. A major disadvantage of impromptu delivery is that it is so spontaneous that it discourages audience analysis, planned research, detailed preparation, and prior adaptation to the audience.

The **memorized mode** of delivery is one in which the speaker has committed his or her speech to memory. It entails more than just knowing all of the words; it usually involves the speaker's rehearsal of gestures, eye contact, and movement. The speaker achieves this mastery of words and movement by practicing or delivering a speech over and over in much the same way that an actor or actress masters a dramatic script.

The memorized mode is common in oratory contests, on the lecture circuit, and at banquets. It is appropriate for ceremonial occasions where a minimum of spontaneous empathy with the audience occurs. Campus lecturers often earn

Memorized Mode

$1000 or more a night for merely filling in the name of a different college in their standard speech. Politicians usually have a stock speech that they have delivered so many times they have memorized it. Some speakers have delivered the same speech so many times that they even know when and how long the audience is going to applaud. The main advantage of the memorized mode is that it permits maximum use of delivery skills: every variation in the voice can be mastered, every oral paragraph stated in correct cadence, every word correctly pronounced at the right volume. With a memorized speech, you have continuous eye contact and you eliminate a search for words. On the other hand, a memorized speech permits little or no adaptation during delivery. If the audience appears to have missed a point, it is difficult for a speaker to explain the point in greater detail. Another disadvantage, especially for beginning speakers, is that a speech sometimes *sounds* memorized: the wording is too glib, the cadences are too contrived, and the speech is too much of a performance instead of a communicative experience. Nevertheless, there is still a place for the memorized speech in your public speaking repertoire. In some formal situations there may be little need for adaptation.

Your mode of delivery must be appropriate for you, your topic, audience, and situation. Memorizing five pages of print may not be your style. A manuscript speech is out of place in a dormitory meeting, a rap session, or any informal gathering. Ultimately, the mode of delivery is not the crucial feature of your speech. In a study to determine whether the extemporaneous or manuscript mode was more effective, two researchers concluded that the mode of delivery simply did not determine effectiveness. The speaker's ability was more important. Some speakers were more effective with extemporaneous speeches than with manuscript speeches, but others used both modes with equal effectiveness.[1]

Application Exercise 1: Selecting a Mode of Delivery

Examine each of the topics, audiences, and situations here and indicate which mode of delivery would be best by placing the appropriate letter in the blank on the left.

A = Manuscript mode, B = Extemporaneous mode,
C = Impromptu mode, D = Memorized mode.

_____ 1. You have to answer questions from the class at the conclusion of your speech.

_____ 2. You have to describe the student government's new statement of policy on student rights to a group of high-level administrators.

_____ 3. You have to deliver the same speech about student life at your college three times per week to incoming students.

_____ 4. You have to give parents a "walking tour" of the campus, including information about the buildings, the history of the college, and the background of significant places on campus.

_____ 5. You have to go door to door demonstrating and explaining a vacuum cleaner and its attachments that you are selling.

Delivery and Visual Aids

In the last section, we considered the various modes of delivery in the public speech. We turn now to a discussion of specific vocal and bodily aspects of delivery. Keep in mind the central goal of public speaking, which is to communicate a message to an audience as effectively as possible. Your knowledge of the content of your speech looms larger in importance than what you do with your hands or your eyes. Indeed, some authors have suggested that the best way to improve your delivery is not to emphasize it directly.[2] Instead, you should let your effective delivery flow naturally. As you grow in confidence in front of an audience, your delivery is likely to improve because you do not have to think about it. In an extemporaneous speech, for instance, the "best" delivery may be one in which you appear to be conversing with the audience. All of your delivery skills can be aimed at using your voice and body in ways that reflect a conversational quality in your speech.

In this section you will examine a relatively large number of variables that occur in delivering a speech. You should first learn to understand these aspects of delivery so that you can practice them in your continuing effort to grow in confidence as a public speaker.

We will now consider the vocal and bodily aspects of delivery. We shall begin with the vocal aspects. Studying the vocal aspects of speech delivery is like studying the music that comes from the musical notes. Musical notes are like the words of a speech; the music that results is like the paralanguage that we hear when someone says the words: pitch, loudness, and vocal variety. Different musicians can make the same musical notes sound quite different; different speakers can evoke different interpretations of words and produce different effects on the audience. We will now examine the music we hear when someone delivers a speech, by defining various vocal characteristics, referring to relevant studies, and offering some helpful suggestions about your delivery. The seven vocal aspects of delivery include pitch, rate, pauses, volume, enunciation, fluency, and vocal variety.

Vocal and Bodily Aspects of Delivery

Vocal Aspects of Delivery

Vocal Aspects of Delivery in Public Speaking

1. Pitch
2. Rate
3. Pauses
4. Volume
5. Enunciation
6. Fluency
7. Vocal variety

Pitch

Pitch is the highness or lowness of the speaker's voice, its upward and downward inflection, the melody produced by the voice. Pitch is what makes the difference between the "Ohhh" that you utter when you earn a poor grade on an exam and the "Ohhh" that you say when you see someone really attractive. The "Ohhh" looks the same in print, but when the notes become music, the difference in the two expressions is vast. The pitch of your voice can make you sound animated, lively, and vivacious, or it can make you sound dull, listless, and monotonous. As a speaker you can learn to avoid the two extremes: you can avoid the lack of pitch changes that result in a monotone and the repetitious pitch changes that result in a singsong delivery. The best public speakers use the full range of their normal pitch. They know when to purr and when to roar and when to vary their pitch between.

Pitch control does more than make a speech aesthetically pleasing. Certainly one of the more important features of pitch control is that it can be employed to alter the way an audience responds to words. Many subtle changes in meaning are accomplished by pitch changes. Your pitch tells an audience whether the words are a statement or question, sarcastic or ironic, and whether you are expressing doubt, determination, or surprise.

You learn pitch control in baseball or speech by constant practice. An actor who is learning to say a line has to practice it many times, in many ways, before he can be assured that most people in the audience will understand the words as he intends them. The public speaker rehearses a speech in front of a sympathetic audience to receive feedback on whether the words are being understood as she intends them. Perhaps you sound angry or brusque when you do not intend to. Maybe you sound cynical when you intend to sound doubtful. Possibly you sound frightened when you are only surprised. You may not be the best judge of how you sound to others. Therefore, place some trust in other people's evaluations of how you sound. Practicing pitch is a way of achieving control over this important aspect of delivery.

Rate, the second characteristic of vocal delivery, is the speed of delivery. Normally, American speakers say between 125 and 190 words per minute, but audiences can comprehend language spoken much faster. Four psychologists in an article entitled "Speed of Speech and Persuasion" noted that speech rate functions to improve the speaker's credibility, that rapid speech improved persuasion.[3] Another study, however, showed that when students shortened their pauses and increased their speaking rates from 126 to 172 words per minute, neither the audience's comprehension nor their evaluations of the speaker's delivery was affected.[4] Thus, you should not necessarily conclude that faster speaking is better speaking.

Rate

Instructors often caution beginning speakers to "slow down." The reason is that beginning speakers frequently vent their anxiety by speaking very rapidly. A nervous speaker makes the audience nervous as well. On the other hand, fluency comes from confidence. A speaker who is accustomed to audiences and knows the subject matter well may speak at a brisk rate without appearing to be nervous. An effective speaker sounds natural, conversational, and flexible. He or she can speak rapidly or slowly, depending on the circumstances.

The essential point, not revealed by the studies, is that speaking rate needs to be adapted to the speaker, audience, situation, and content of the speech. First, you should be comfortable with your rate of speaking. If you normally speak rather slowly, you might feel awkward talking like a competitive debater. If you normally speak at a rapid pace, you might feel uncomfortable speaking more slowly. As you learn to speak publicly, you will probably find a rate that is appropriate for you.

Second, you should adapt your rate to the audience and situation. A grade-school teacher does not rip through a fairy tale; the audience is just learning how to comprehend words. The public speaker addressing a large audience without a microphone might speak like a contest orator to make sure the audience comprehends his words. Audience, situation, and content help to determine your speaking rate.

The content of your speech may determine your rate of delivery. A story to illustrate a point can be understood at a faster rate than can a string of statistics or a complicated argument. The rate should depend on the effect you seek. Telling a story of suspense and intrigue would be difficult at a high rate of speed. Effective public speakers adjust their rate according to their own comfort, the audience, situation, and content of their speeches.

A third vocal characteristic is the **pause.** Speeches are often stereotyped as a steady stream of verbiage. Yet the public speaker can use pauses and silences for dramatic effect and to interest the audience in content. You might begin a speech with rhetorical questions: "Have you had a cigarette today? Have you had two or three? Ten or eleven? Do you know what your habit is costing you a year? A decade? A lifetime?" After each rhetorical question a pause allows each member of the audience to answer the question in his or her own mind.

Pauses

Another kind of pause—the **vocalized pause**—is really not silent at all. Instead, it is a way of delaying with sound. The vocalized pause is a nonfluency that can adversely affect an audience's perception of the speaker's competence and dynamism. The "ahhhs," "nows," and "you knows" of the novice speaker are annoying and distracting to most audiences. Unfortunately, even some highly experienced speakers have the habit of filling silences with vocalized pauses. One organization teaches public speaking by having members of the audience drop a marble into a can every time the speaker uses a vocalized pause. The resulting punishment, the clanging of the cans during the speech, is supposed to break the habit. A more humane method might be to rehearse your speech for a friend who can signal you more gently every time you vocalize a pause. One speech teacher helps her students eliminate vocalized pauses by rigging a small red light on the lectern. Every time the student speaker uses a vocalized pause, the instructor hits the light for a moment. Do not be afraid of silence; most audiences would prefer a little silence to a vocalized pause.

One way to learn how to use pauses effectively in public speaking is to listen to how professional speakers use them. Paul Harvey, the Chicago radio commentator, practically orchestrates his pauses. A long pause before the "Page Two" section of his news broadcast is one technique that has made him an attractive radio personality. Oral Roberts, Billy Graham, and television anchor persons similarly use pauses effectively.

A fourth vocal characteristic of delivery is **volume,** the relative loudness of your voice. You are accustomed in conversation to speaking at an arm's length. When you stand in front of an audience, some of them may be quite close to you, but others may be at some distance from you. Beginning speakers are often told to "project," to increase their volume so that all may hear the speech.

Volume is more than just projection, however. Variations in volume can convey emotion, importance, suspense, and subtle nuances of meaning. You whisper a secret in conversation, and you stage whisper in front of an audience to signal conspiratorial intent. You speak loudly and strongly on important points and let your voice carry your conviction. An orchestra never plays so quietly that the patrons cannot hear it, but the musicians vary their volume. Similarly, a public speaker who considers the voice an instrument learns how to speak softly, loudly, and at every volume in between to convey his or her intended meaning.

Enunciation, the fifth vocal aspect of delivery, is the pronunciation and articulation of words. Because your reading vocabulary is likely to be larger than your speaking vocabulary, you may use words in your speeches that you have never heard before. It is risky to deliver unfamiliar words. One student in a speech class gave a speech on the human reproductive system. During the speech he made reference to a woman's "vir–gín–yah" and her "you–teár–us." The suppressed laughter did not help the speaker's credibility as a competent commentator. Rather than erring in public, practice your speech in front of friends, roommates, or family who can tell you when you make a mistake in pronunciation or articulation, or check pronunciation in a dictionary. Every dictionary has a pronunciation key. For instance, the entry for the word *deification* in *Webster's New World Dictionary of the American Language* is:

de–i–fi–ca–tion (dē′ə–fi–kā′shən), n.[ME.; OFr.],1. a deifying. 2. deified person or embodiment.[5]

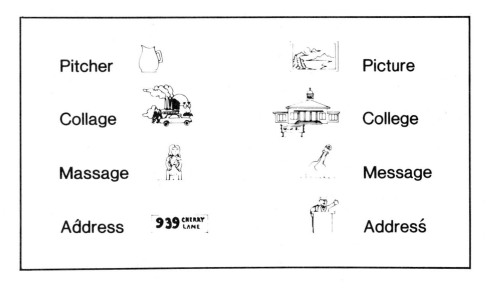

Pitcher

Picture

Collage

College

Massage

Message

Address

939 CHERRY LANE

Addresś

Wee Pals by Morrie Turner. © 1980 United Feature Syndicate, Inc. Courtesy of Field Newspaper Syndicate.

The entry indicates that the word has five syllables into which it can be divided in writing and which carry distinct sounds. The pronunciation key says that the e should be pronounced like the $\bar{e}$ in $\bar{e}$ven, the ə like the *a* in ago, and the $\bar{a}$ like the $\bar{a}$ in ape. The accent mark (′) indicates which syllable should receive heavier emphasis. You should learn how to use the pronunciation key in a dictionary, but if you still have some misgivings about how to pronounce a word, ask your speech teacher for assistance.

Another way to improve your enunciation is to learn how to prolong syllables. Such prolonging makes your pronunciation easier to understand, especially if you are addressing a large audience assembled outside or in an auditorium with no microphone. The drawing out of syllables can be overdone, however. Some radio and TV newspersons hang onto the final syllable in a sentence so long that the device is disconcertingly noticeable.

Pronunciation and articulation are the important components of enunciation. Poor **articulation,** poor production of sounds, is so prevalent that there are popular jokes about it. Some children have heard the Lord's Prayer mumbled so many times that they think that one of the lines is "hollow be thy name."

The problem of articulation is less humorous when it happens in your own speech. It occurs in part because so many English words that sound nearly alike are spelled differently and mean entirely different things. In consequence, words are conveyed inaccurately. A class experiment will illustrate this problem. One student whispered a phrase from a presidential address, and a line of students whispered the message from person to person. The phrase was "We must seek fresh answers, unhindered by the stale prescriptions of the past." By the time the message left the third person, it was "When we seek stale answers to the perscription." The eighth person heard the message "When the snakes now answer the question." Similar problems can occur in a public speech if a speaker does not take care to articulate words properly.

The sixth vocal characteristic of delivery is **fluency**—the smoothness of delivery, *Fluency* the flow of the words, and the absence of vocalized pauses. Fluency is difficult because it cannot be achieved by looking up words in a dictionary or by any other simple solution. Fluency is not even very noticeable. Listeners are more likely to notice errors than the seemingly effortless flow of words and intentional pauses in a well-delivered speech. You can, however, be too fluent. A speaker who seems too fluent is perceived as "a fast talker," "slicker than oil." The importance of fluency is emphasized in a study that showed that audiences tend to perceive a speaker's fluency, the smoothness of presentation, as a main ingredient of effectiveness.[6]

To achieve fluency, you must be confident of the content of your speeches. If you know what you are going to say, and if you have practiced it, then disruptive repetition and vocalized pauses are less likely to occur. If you master what you are going to say and concentrate on the overall rhythm of the speech, your fluency will improve. Pace, build, and time various parts of your speech so that in delivery and in content they unite into a coherent whole.

The seventh vocal aspect of delivery is one that includes many of the others— *Vocal Variety* **vocal variety.** Vocal variety refers to your ability to use voice quality, intonation patterns, pitch inflections, and syllabic duration to communicate your message. When you talk with your parents, friends, spouse, or roommate, you probably express surprise, anger, and affection. You probably do not talk in one unvarying tone of voice, nor do you warble like a lark. Instead, you use vocal variety to help express your meaning. In public speaking, as in lively conversation, the speaker learns to communicate naturally by using vocal variety.

Read to a classmate, roommate, relative, or friend the following excerpt from Carl Sandburg's *Smoke and Steel,* with special attention to the pitch, rate, pauses, volume, enunciation, fluency, and voice variety. Let your listener tell you how you can make your reading more effective.

Application Exercise 2: Testing the Vocal Aspects of Your Delivery

Four Preludes on Playthings of the Wind

"The past is a bucket of ashes."

I

The woman named Tomorrow
sits with a hairpin in her teeth
and takes her time
and does her hair the way she wants it
and fastens at last the last braid and coil
and puts the hairpin where it belongs
and turns and drawls: Well, what of it?
My grandmother, Yesterday, is gone.
What of it? Let the dead be dead.

II

The doors *were* cedar
and the panels strips of gold
and the girls were golden girls
and the panels read and the girls chanted:
    We are the greatest city,
    the greatest nation:
    nothing like us ever was.
The doors are twisted on broken hinges.
Sheets of rain swish through on the wind
    where golden girls ran and the panels
      read:
    We are the greatest city,
    the greatest nation,
    nothing like us ever was.

III

It has happened before.
Strong men put up a city and got
    a nation together,
And paid singers to sing and women
    to warble: We are the greatest city,
      the greatest nation,
      nothing like us ever was.
And while the singers *sang*
and the strong men listened
and paid the singers well
and felt good about it all,
    there were rats and lizards who listened
    . . . and the only listeners left now
    . . . are . . . the rats . . . and the lizards.
And there are black crows
crying, "Caw, caw,"
bringing mud and sticks
building a nest
over the words carved
on the doors where the panels were cedar
and the strips on the panels were gold
and the golden girls came singing:
    We are the greatest city
    the greatest nation:
    nothing like us ever was.
The only singers now are the crows crying, "Caw,
    caw,"
And the sheets of rain whine in the wind and
    doorways.
And the only listeners now are . . . the rats . . .
    and the lizards.

IV

The feet of the rats
scribble on the doorsills;
the hieroglyphs of the rat footprints
chatter the pedigrees of the rats
and babble of the blood
and gabble of the breed
of the grandfathers and the great-grandfathers
of the rats.

And the wind shifts
and the dust on a doorsill shifts
and even the writing of the rat footprints
tells us nothing, nothing at all
about the greatest city, the greatest nation
where the strong men listened
and the women warbled: Nothing like us ever
was.

Bodily Aspects of Delivery

We have considered the vocal aspects of delivery. Let us now examine the bodily aspects. Gestures, facial expression, eye contact, and movement are four bodily aspects of speech delivery—nonverbal indicators of meaning—that are important to the public speaker. In any communication, you indicate how you relate to the material and to other people by your gestures, facial expression, and bodily movements. When you observe two people busily engaged in conversation, you can judge their interest in the conversation without hearing their words. Similarly, in public speaking, the nonverbal aspects of delivery reinforce what the speaker is saying. Researchers have found that audiences who can see the speaker, and his or her visible behavior, comprehend more of the speech than audiences who cannot.[7]

Bodily Aspects of Delivery in Public Speaking

1. Gestures
2. Facial expression
3. Eye contact
4. Movement

Some persons are more sensitive to nonverbal cues than are others. Five researchers who developed a "Profile of Nonverbal Sensitivity" found that women were more sensitive to nonverbal communication than men were, as early as the third grade. However, men in artistic or expressive jobs scored as well as the women. The researchers' finding suggests that such sensitivity is learned. A second finding on nonverbal communication was that, until college age, young people are not as sensitive to nonverbal communication as older persons are.[8] This, too, supports the notion that we can and do learn sensitivity to nonverbal cues like gestures, facial expressions, eye contact, and movement.

Gestures

Gestures are movements of various parts of the body that we use to describe what we are talking about, to emphasize certain points, and to signal an advance to another part of the speech. Although you probably are quite unaware of your arms and hands when you converse with someone, you may find that they become bothersome appendages when you stand in front of an audience. You may feel awkward because standing in front of an audience is not, for most of us, a very natural situation. You have to work to make public speaking look easy, just as a

skillful golfer, a graceful dancer, and a talented painter all make their performances look effortless. Novices are the people who make golfing, dancing, painting, and public speaking look difficult. Paradoxically, people have to work diligently to make physical or artistic feats look easy.

What can you do to help yourself gesture naturally when you are delivering your speech? The answer lies in your involvement with the issues and with practice. Angry farmers and irate miners appear on television to protest low prices and poor working conditions. Untutored in public speaking, these passionate people deliver their speeches with gusto and determined gestures. The gestures look very natural. These speakers have a natural delivery because they are much more concerned about their message than about when they should raise their clenched fists. They are upset, and they show it in their words and actions. You can deliver a speech more naturally if your attention is focused on getting your message across. Self-conscious attention to your own gestures may be self-defeating: the gestures look studied, rehearsed, or slightly out of synchronization with your message. Selecting a topic that you really care about can result in the side effect of improving your delivery, especially if you concentrate on your audience and message.

Another way to learn appropriate gestures is to practice a speech in front of friends who are willing to make constructive comments. Constructive criticism is one of the benefits your speech teacher and fellow students can give you. Actresses spend hours rehearsing lines and gestures so that they will look spontaneous and unrehearsed on stage. You may have to appear before many audiences before you learn to speak and move naturally. After much practice, you will learn which arm, head, and hand movements seem to help, and which hinder, your message. You can learn, through practice, to gesture naturally in a way that reinforces your message instead of detracting from it.

Another physical aspect of delivery is **facial expression.** One of humanity's greatest thinkers, Socrates, said: "Nobility and dignity, self-abasement and servility, prudence and understanding, insolence and vulgarity, are reflected in the face and in the attitudes of the body whether still or in motion."[9] Some experts believe that neural programming connects the emotions and facial muscles and that what activates an emotion and the rules for displaying it is culturally determined.[10] Ekman and Friesen believe that our facial expression shows how we feel and our body orientation (e.g., leaning, withdrawing, turning) expresses the intensity of our emotion.[11] As a public speaker you may or may not know how your face looks when you speak. Others who watch you practice your speech can best check out this aspect of delivery. The goal is to have facial expressions that are consistent with your intent and message.

Facial Expression

A third physical aspect of delivery that is important to the public speaker is **eye contact.** This term refers to the way a speaker observes the audience while speaking. Studies and experience indicate that audiences prefer maintenance of good

Eye Contact

eye contact,[12] which improves source credibility.[13] Eye contact is one way you indicate to others how you feel about them. You may be wary of a person who in conversation will not look at you. Similarly, in public speaking, eye contact conveys our relationship with the audience. If you rarely or never look at your audience, they may be resentful of your seeming disinterest. If you look over the heads of your audience or scan them so quickly that you do not really look at anyone, you may appear to be afraid. The proper relationship between you and your audience should be one of purposeful communication. You signal that sense of purpose by treating the audience as individuals with whom you wish to communicate a message and by looking at them for responses to your message.

How can you learn to maintain eye contact with your audience? One way is to know your speech so well and to feel so strongly about it that you have to make few references to your notes. The speaker who does not know her speech well tends to be manuscript-bound. You can encourage yourself to keep an eye on the audience by delivering an extemporaneous speech from an outline or key words. One of the purposes of extemporaneous delivery is to help you adapt to your audience. Adaptation is not possible unless you are continually monitoring the audience's reactions to see if they understand your message. Other ways of learning eye contact include scanning or continually looking over your entire audience, addressing various sections of the audience as you progress through your speech, and concentrating on the head nodders. In almost every audience there are some individuals who overtly indicate whether your message is coming across. These individuals usually nod "yes" or "no" with their heads, thus the name *nodders*. You may find that you can enhance your delivery by finding the friendly faces and positive nodders who signal when the message is getting through to them.

Movement

A fourth physical aspect of delivery is **movement,** or what you do with your entire body during a speech presentation. Do you lean forward as you speak to demonstrate to the audience how serious you are about communicating your message? Do you move out from behind the lectern to show that you want to get closer to the audience? Do you move during transitions in your speech to signal physically to the audience that you are moving to a new location in your speech? These are examples of purposeful movement in a public speech. Movement without purpose is discouraged. You should not move just to work off your own anxiety like a caged lion.

Always try to face the audience even when you are moving. For instance, even when you have need to write information on the board, you can avoid turning your back by putting your notes on the board before class or putting your visual material on posters. You can learn a lot about movement by watching your classmates and professors when they speak. You can learn through observation and practice what works for others and for you.

Effective delivery has many advantages. Research indicates that effective delivery, the appropriate use of voice and body in public speaking, contributes to the credibility of the speaker.[14] Indeed, student audiences characterize the poorest speakers by their voices and the physical aspects of delivery.[15] Poor speakers are judged to be fidgety, nervous, and monotonous. They also maintain little eye contact and show little animation or facial expression.[16] Good delivery tends to increase the audience's capacity to handle complex information.[17] Thus, your credibility, the audience's evaluations of your being a good or a poor speaker, and your ability to convey complex information may all be affected by the vocal and physical aspects of delivery.

To put this section on the physical aspects of speech delivery in perspective, remember that eye contact, facial expression, gestures, and movement are important, but content may be even more important. The very same researcher who found that poor speakers are identified by their voices and the physical aspects of their delivery also found that the best speakers were identified by the content of their speeches.[18] Two other researchers found that more of an audience's evaluation of a speaker is based on the content of the speech than on vocal characteristics such as intonation, pitch, and rate.[19] Still another pair of researchers found that a well-composed speech can mask poor delivery.[20] Finally, one researcher reviewed studies on informative speaking and reported that, while some research indicates that audiences who have listened to good speakers have significantly greater immediate recall, other findings show that the differences are slight. His conclusion was that the influence of delivery on comprehension is overrated.[21]

What are you to do in the face of these reports that good delivery influences audience comprehension positively but also that the influence of delivery on comprehension is overrated? What are you to do when one study reports that poor vocal characteristics reveal a poor speaker and another states that good content can mask poor delivery? Until more evidence is available, the safest position for you as a public speaking student is to regard both delivery and content as important. What you say and how you say it are both important—and probably in that order.

Observe a talented public speaker—a visiting lecturer, a political speaker, a sales manager—and study his or her gestures, facial expressions, eye contact, and movement. Then answer the following questions.

1. Do the speaker's gestures reinforce the important points in the speech?
2. Does the speaker's facial expression reflect the message and show concern for the audience and the topic?
3. Does the speaker maintain eye contact with the audience, respond to the audience's reactions, and keep himself or herself from becoming immersed in the manuscript, outline, or notes?
4. Does the speaker's movement reflect the organization of the speech and the important points in it?
5. Are the speaker's gestures, facial expressions, and movements consistent with the occasion, the personality of the speaker, and the message being communicated?

Application Exercise 3: Bodily Aspects of Delivery

Visual Aids

Another aspect of speech delivery is the use of visual aids. Why should you use visual aids? What kinds should you use? How should you use them?

Rationale for Using Visual Aids

The main reason for using visual aids is that they can help an audience understand your message, and they can help you to inform and persuade an audience. We learn much of what we know through sight. For instance, we learn

1% through taste
1.5% through touch
3.5% through smell
11% through hearing
83% through sight

Furthermore, you are likely to remember

10% of what you read
20% of what you hear
30% of what you see
50% of what you see and hear
80% of what you say
90% of what you say and do

Finally, you are likely to retain

	3 hours later	3 days later
telling alone	70%	10%
showing alone	72%	20%
showing and telling	85%	65%

These data suggest that seeing is an important component of learning and retaining information.[22] That is exactly what you are trying to do in using visual aids—to help the audience see what you are talking about.

Fortunately, some fairly solid experimental studies also support the use of visual aids. University students in one study were exposed to a series of words and/or pictures and were tested later on their recall. When the subjects were exposed to two stimuli at a time (i.e., sound plus pictures or printed word plus line drawings), they remembered better[23] than they did with just one stimulus. Another study demonstrated that two-dimensional objects, simple figures against a background, were better remembered when they moved than when they were static.[24]

A third study used male and female subjects from junior high to college age and tested them for audio and visual cues. The experimenters determined that these audiences were more influenced by what they saw than by what they heard.[25]

In this section we'll explore different kinds of visual aids.

Types of Visual Aids

1. Chalkboards
2. Posters
3. Movies and slides
4. Opaque and overhead projections
5. Living models and physical objects
6. Handouts
7. Yourself

Chalkboards   One of the simplest visual aids you can use is the chalkboard. However, it can also be one of the most distracting. You can use the chalkboard most effectively if you follow these suggestions:

1. Ask your teacher whether he or she prefers that you place information on the board before class begins, rather than after the preceding speaker has finished. Some teachers and audiences dislike the delay when a speaker spends three or four minutes between class speeches writing information on the board. Others feel just as strongly that having information on the board before a speech is distracting. Few instructors or audiences, however, object to the speaker who writes his or her name and the title of the speech on the board immediately before delivering the speech.
2. Write information on the board in large print so that everyone in the audience can see it. Just as you have to speak loudly in a speech so that all can hear, so you have to write boldly and clearly so that all can see.
3. Use the board to supply information that is difficult to digest in oral form. If you are using technical vocabulary that many in the audience are unfamiliar with, write those words on the board so that the audience can both see and hear them. If you have statistics, facts, or details that are difficult to follow or remember, help your audience by putting them on the board.
4. Face your audience even when you are using the board. The simplest way to do this is to point with your hand, a yardstick, or a pointer.
5. Use the chalkboard as a "point clincher"[26] to make sure the audience understands your main ideas.

The chalkboard is one of your greatest opportunities for using visual aids effectively. It is inexpensive and easy to use.

Posters   A second kind of visual aid is the poster. You do not have to be a graphic artist to make good posters. All you really need is a large piece of poster paper and a marking pen that writes in dark ink. Simply follow the same directions we gave for using the chalkboard: write in large letters ahead of time, supply information that is difficult to convey orally, face the audience while using the poster, and use the visual message as a point clincher to highlight important points.

A student gave a speech on child abuse and used posters to highlight his speech. He had five main points and five posters, each with one true or false question on the front. He placed all five posters on the chalk tray and introduced the speech by asking his audience if they could answer the true or false questions: Most children who are abused come from poor families, True or False; Most children who are abused are abused by their own mothers, True or False; Most people now in prison were once abused children, True or False—and so on. The audience was uncertain of the answers, but the questions aroused their curiosity, and the speaker used each question as a main point in his speech. The posters also eliminated the speaker's need for notes—they were on the posters.

A student speaker who was delivering a speech on the relationship between students and religion placed the sayings, slogans, and statements shown in figure 8.1 around the room and incorporated them into his speech. When there was a furor over the use of nitrites to preserve meats, a student used the colored bar graph in figure 8.2 to show the percentage of nitrites that we actually get from meat. A speaker who knew that audiences are unlikely to remember numbers wrote out on her poster (figure 8.3) the number of calories that an ordinary person uses per hour in various activities. Notice that the numbers are rounded off for easier understanding. A student who was speaking on the sport of rappeling used the visual aid shown in figure 8.4 to state the main points of the speech for preview, explanation, and review. A poster can also give you or a friend a chance to use special talents. Figure 8.5 shows how one student drew a cartoon character beside the message to gain and maintain attention.

As figures 8.1–8.5 show, you can use posters to announce slogans and display pictures consistent with your message, to show ratios and proportions through pie charts and bar graphs, and simply to state the main points of your message. Here are some suggestions for the "content" of your posters:

Figure 8.1 Posters for speech on the relationship between students and religion.

1. Keep your poster's message simple, whether it is a montage of photographs and advertisements or a list of your main points. The audience should be able to grasp quickly what you are illustrating.
2. Use bar graphs rather than circle or pie charts whenever possible because audiences tend to underestimate the relative areas of circles.[27]
3. Use color and artistic or graphic talents to make the poster attractive—to gain and maintain attention.
4. Be sure that the poster is large enough for all to see.
5. Get hints on using photographs or ready-made posters, such as travel posters, from TV commercials—the world's most expensive persuasion. (TV advertisers tend to use outdoor daytime shots with one person, but no crowds.)[28]
6. Learn to use flip charts (a series of posters) and reveal information (uncover each item on the poster as you get to it) for special effects.

Whatever kind of poster you use, keep it (or them) in front of the audience as long as you are on the subject portrayed. In many cases it is appropriate to place the used poster on the chalk tray, so that you can refer to it again in the conclusion when you review the content of your speech.

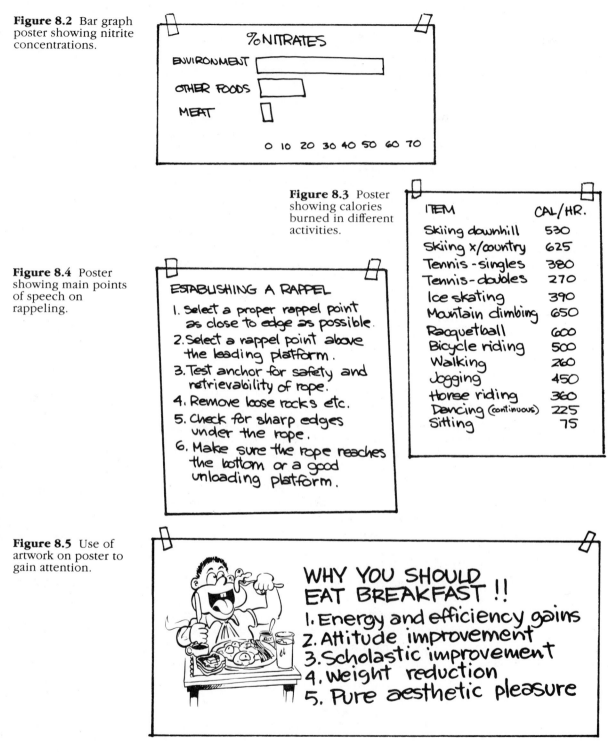

Figure 8.2 Bar graph poster showing nitrite concentrations.

Figure 8.3 Poster showing calories burned in different activities.

Figure 8.4 Poster showing main points of speech on rappeling.

Figure 8.5 Use of artwork on poster to gain attention.

A third set of visual aids are movies and slides. Movies and slides are good visual supplements to your speech as long as they do not *become* the speech. Both have the disadvantage of placing audience and speaker in the dark, with the resulting loss of visual cues. Even so, a one- or two-minute film showing violence on the basketball court or five or six slides showing alternate energy sources can add force to your speech. When you use slides and films you must check out equipment and rehearse. An upside-down slide or a jittery film can make you look like a mechanical idiot.

Movies and Slides

Another set of visual aids which you may wish to consider are opaque and overhead projections. These aids also demand special equipment and practice, but they, too, have special advantages in a speech. An opaque projector is a machine that can project a picture or print from a magazine or a book without your having to cut out the page. It can also be used for relatively small, flat objects. An overhead projector is a machine that can project transparencies or sheets of clear plastic on which the speaker can write with a special pencil. Transparencies are best prepared ahead of time, but short messages can be printed on them as the speaker talks. Both machines require dim lights and an empty wall or a screen.

Opaque and Overhead Projections

Living models and physical objects are still other kinds of visual aids. For your speech on body building, you might bring to class a 250-pound weight lifter to flex his muscles. In your speech on stringed instruments you might ask a musician to come to class and play several such instruments.

Living Models and Physical Objects

Physical objects, too, will interest the audience in your subject. You might bring in chemistry equipment to show the audience a simple experiment. You might bring in your collection of polished rocks or show the class your model cars.

Handouts

Handouts are another effective way to get your audience to focus on your speech. You might follow a speech on artificial resuscitation by handing out a single sheet that reviews the steps with illustrations. You might distribute copies of a contract used to will body parts to others. Or you could ditto a self-examination that the audience can use to demonstrate what they learned from your speech.

Handouts are an excellent way to remind your audience of your speech because they usually are carried out of the classroom for the audience members and others to see. They also let you "say" more than you can convey orally. For example, a student who gave a speech on rock music stations could not get class-mates to write the names and call numbers of all of the local stations, but he did list them all on a page for the audience to use.

Yourself

Finally, *you* can be your own visual aid. You can demonstrate karate, show some disco steps, or wear rappeling equipment. One student gave a speech on how tolerant students were about clothing. For two days he wore a large, wide-brimmed hat, short pants, one long and one short sock, and a crazy vest. Not one person asked him why he was dressed as he was. He made his point and was his own visual aid during his speech.

You can enhance your speeches by using visual aids: the chalkboard, posters, film or slides, opaque or overhead projections, living models and physical objects, handouts, or yourself. Consider the questions in Checklist 5 when you prepare your next speech.

Delivery and Visual Aids

_____ 1. How can you use the chalkboard? Can you place your name and the title of your speech on the board? Have you written out your main points prior to class? Are there any difficult words that you should write on the board? Is there any statement that you can place on the board that summarizes your speech for the conclusion?

_____ 2. What posters would help your audience understand your speech? Are there any picture posters that could be taped up during your speech? Can you state your main points on a flip chart? Are there any slogans that summarize your speech or any questions that you could state on a poster?

_____ 3. Are there any film clips or slides that would work well to gain and maintain your audience's attention? Have you reserved and checked out the equipment? Have you practiced with the machinery so that you know how it works? Can you set up the equipment between classes to save time?

_____ 4. Can you use an opaque projector to enlarge and show magazine or book illustrations or prints? Can you use transparencies on an overhead projector? Have you practiced with the equipment so that you can run it smoothly? Do you have someone who can help you with the lights?

_____ 5. Can you use a living model or physical object to help the audience understand your message? Can you make sure that the model or object will not be a distraction during your speech?

_____ 6. Can you use yourself as a visual aid? Can you dress in some way that will help communicate your message? Can you demonstrate by yourself what you are trying to explain?

Conclusion

You began this chapter on the nonverbal aspects of public speaking by learning the four modes of delivery: manuscript, extemporaneous, impromptu, and memorized. You next surveyed the vocal and bodily aspects of delivery. The vocal aspects include pitch, rate, pause, volume, enunciation, fluency, and voice variety. The bodily aspects include gestures, facial expression, eye contact, and movement. You learned that, in the final analysis, the content and delivery of your speech are both important in public speaking. Finally, you found out why you should use visual aids in your speeches, and you examined ten different kinds of visual aids that you can use to strengthen your public speeches.

Application Exercise 4: Evaluating Your Delivery

For your next speech, have a classmate, friend, or relative observe and evaluate your speech for delivery skills. Have your critic use this scale to fill in the blanks on the left.

1=Excellent, 2=Good, 3=Average, 4=Fair, 5=Weak

Vocal Aspects of Delivery

_____ Pitch: highness and lowness of voice; upward and downward inflections

_____ Rate: words per minute; appropriate variation of rate for the difficulty of content

_____ Pause: intentional silence designed to aid understanding at appropriate places

_____ Volume: loud enough to hear; variation with the content

_____ Enunciation: correct pronunciation and articulation

_____ Fluency: smoothness of delivery; lack of vocalized pauses; good pacing, rhythm, and cadence without being so smooth as to sound artificial, contrived, or overly glib

_____ Vocal variety: voice quality, intonation patterns, pitch inflections, and syllabic duration

Bodily Aspects of Delivery

_____ Gestures: natural movement of the head, hands, arms, and torso consistent with the speaker, topic, and situation

_____ Facial expression: consistent with message; used to relate to the audience; appropriate for audience and situation

_____ Eye contact: natural, steady without staring, includes entire audience, and is responsive to audience feedback

_____ Movement: purposeful, used to indicate organization, natural, without anxiety

Use of Visual Aids

_____ Speaker uses smooth transitions into and away from visuals.

_____ Visuals are easy to see, with large print and/or pictures.

_____ Visuals highlight message.

_____ Any equipment is used without difficulty.

_____ Visual aids are appropriate for the speaker, the audience, the topic, and the situation.

Application Assignment

Speech Using Visual Aids

Deliver a five-minute speech on a topic of your choice in which you (1) provide an introduction that fulfills its proper functions, (2) develop an idea through the use of visual aids, and (3) provide a conclusion that fulfills its proper functions. You may wish to review chapter 6, on introducing and concluding your speech. You should use Application Exercise 4 in this chapter to evaluate your delivery and use of visual aids.

Pay special attention to your delivery and your visual aids because this assignment will be evaluated not only on its introduction, conclusion, and topic appropriateness, but also on the extent to which you can maintain eye contact by freeing yourself from your notes; your use of facial expression, gesture, and movement to indicate important ideas and speech organization; and the clarity and usefulness of your visual aids. Often a visual aid can serve as your notes for the speech, so that you do not have to handle both note cards and visual aids, an activity that inhibits movement and gestures. Finally, consider all the possibilities for visual aids (chalkboard, posters, handouts, and so on) that are appropriate for your speech.

Optional: Provide an outline of your speech, in which you indicate where and what kind of visual aids you intend to use in the speech.

articulation A vocal aspect of delivery, indicating the effective production of sound. See *Enunciation*.   **Vocabulary**

enunciation A vocal aspect of delivery that involves the pronunciation and articulation of words; pronouncing correctly and producing the sounds clearly so that the language is understandable.

extemporaneous mode Delivery in which the speaker proceeds through careful preparation and practice to deliver a speech that appears spontaneous and conversational. This mode is characterized by considerable eye contact and minimal use of notes.

eye contact A bodily aspect of delivery that involves the speaker's looking directly at the audience in order to monitor their responses to the message. In public speaking, eye contact is an asset because it permits the speaker to adapt to audience responses and to assess the effects of the message.

facial expression A bodily aspect of delivery that involves the use of eyes, eyebrows, and mouth to express feelings about the message, the audience, and the occasion. Smiles, frowns, grimaces, and winces can help a speaker communicate feelings.

fluency A vocal aspect of delivery that involves the smooth flow of words and the absence of vocalized pauses.

gestures A bodily aspect of delivery that involves movement of head, hands, and arms, to indicate emphasis, commitment, and other feelings about the topic, the audience, and the occasion.

impromptu mode Delivery in which the speaker talks spontaneously without special preparation. Question and answer sessions after a speech follow this mode of delivery because the speaker has to address answers to questions that may not have been anticipated.

manuscript mode Delivery in which the speaker writes out every word of the speech and reads the speech to the audience with as much eye contact as possible; appropriate in situations where exact wording is very important.

memorized mode Delivery in which the speaker commits the entire manuscript of the speech to memory, either by rote or repetition; appropriate in situations where the same speech is given over and over to different audiences.

movement A bodily aspect of delivery that refers to a speaker's locomotion in front of an audience; can be used to signal the development and organization of the message.

pause An intentional silence used to draw attention to the words before or after the interlude; a break in the flow of words for effect.

pitch A vocal aspect of delivery that refers to the highness or lowness, upward and downward inflections of the voice.

rate A vocal aspect of delivery that refers to the speed of delivery, the number of words spoken per minute; normal rates range from 125 to 190 words per minute.

vocalized pause A nonfluency in delivery characterized by sounds like "Uhhh," "Ahhh," or "Mmmm" or the repetitive use of expressions like "O.K.," "Now," or "For sure" to fill silence with sound; often used by speakers who are nervous or inarticulate.

vocal variety An aspect of delivery that encompasses pitch, rate, pauses, volume, enunciation, and fluency; necessary in sustained discourse to promote interest and attentiveness in an audience.

volume A vocal characteristic of delivery that refers to the loudness or softness of the voice. Public speakers often project or speak louder than normal so that distant listeners can hear the message. Beginning speakers frequently forget to project enough volume.

Endnotes

1. Herbert W. Hildebrandt and Walter Stevens, "Manuscript and Extemporaneous Delivery in Communicating Information," *Speech Monographs* 30 (1963): 369–72.
2. Otis M. Walter and Robert L. Scott, *Thinking and Speaking* (New York: Macmillan, 1969), pp. 124–33.
3. Norman Miller et al., "Speed of Speech and Persuasion," *Journal of Personality and Social Psychology* 34 (1976): 615–24.
4. Charles F. Diehl, Richard C. White, and Kenneth W. Burk, "Rate and Communication," *Speech Monographs* 26 (1959): 229–32.
5. *Webster's New World Dictionary of the American Language—College Edition* (New York: The World Publishing Company, 1957), pp. 386–87.
6. Donald Hayworth, "A Search for Facts on the Teaching of Public Speaking," *Quarterly Journal of Speech* 28 (1942): 247–54.
7. Edward J.J. Kramer and Thomas R. Lewis, "Comparison of Visual and Nonvisual Listening," *Journal of Communication* 1 (1951): 16–20.
8. Robert Rosenthal et al., "Body Talk and Tone of Voice: The Language Without Words," *Psychology Today* 8 (1974): 64–68.
9. Socrates, Xenophon, *Memorabilia III* in *Nonverbal Communication: Readings with Commentary,* Shirley Weitz, ed. (New York: Oxford University Press, 1974), p. vii.
10. Paul Ekman, "Pan-cultural Elements in Facial Displays of Emotion," *Science* 164 (1969): 86–88.
11. Paul Ekman and Wallace V. Friesen, "Head and Body Cues in the Judgment of Emotion: A Reformulation," *Perceptual and Motor Skills,* 24 (1967): 711–24.
12. Martin Cobin, "Response to Eye-Contact," *Quarterly Journal of Speech* 48 (1962): 415–18.
13. Steven A. Beebe, "Eye Contact: A Nonverbal Determinant of Speaker Credibility," *Speech Teacher* 23 (1974): 21–25.
14. Erwin Bettinghaus, "The Operation of Congruity in an Oral Communication Situation," *Speech Monographs* 28 (1961): 131–42.
15. Ernest H. Henrikson, "An Analysis of the Characteristics of Some 'Good' and 'Poor' Speakers," *Speech Monographs* 11 (1944): 120–24.
16. Howard Gilkinson and Franklin H. Knower, "Individual Differences Among Students of Speech as Revealed by Psychological Tests—I," *Journal of Educational Psychology* 32 (1941): 161–75.
17. John L. Vohs, "An Empirical Approach to the Concept of Attention," *Speech Monographs* 31 (1964): 355–60.
18. Henrikson, pp. 120–24.
19. Ronald J. Hard and Bruce L. Brown, "Interpersonal Information Conveyed by the Content and Vocal Aspects of Speech," *Speech Monographs* 41 (1974): 371–80.

20. D.F. Gundersen and Robert Hopper, "Relationships between Speech Delivery and Speech Effectiveness," *Speech Monographs* 43 (1976): 158–65.
21. Charles R. Petrie, Jr., "Informative Speaking: A Summary and Bibliography of Related Research," *Speech Monographs* 30 (1963): 81.
22. Elena P. Zayas-Baya, "Instructional Media in the Total Language Picture," *International Journal of Instructional Media* 5 (1977–78): 145–50.
23. Bernadette M. Gadzella and Deborah A. Whitehead, "Effects of Auditory and Visual Modalities in Recall of Words," *Perceptual and Motor Skills* 40 (February, 1975): 255–60.
24. Delores A. Bogard, "Visual Perception of Static and Dynamic Two-Dimensional Objects," *Perceptual and Motor Skills* 38 (April, 1974): 395–98.
25. Bella M. De Paulo et al., "Decoding Discrepant Nonverbal Cues," *Journal of Personality and Social Psychology* 36 (March 1978): 313–23.
26. Kenneth B. Haas and Harry Q. Packer, *Preparation and Use of Audiovisual Aids* (New York: Prentice-Hall, 1955), pp. 163–68.
27. Michael MacDonald-Ross, "How Numbers Are Shown. A Review of Research on the Presentation of Quantitative Data in Texts," *AV Communication Review* 25 (Winter, 1977): 359–409.
28. Isbrabim M. Hebyallah and W. Paul Maloney, "Content Analysis of T.V. Commercials," *International Journal of Instructional Media* 5 (1977–78): 9–16.

Chapter 9

Objectives

When you have completed chapter 9, you should be able to answer the following questions:
  1. What are some general purposes of informative speeches?
  2. What two rhetorical principles can you apply to the informative speech?
  3. What principles of learning can you use for your audience?
  4. What are the major types of informative speeches?
When you have completed chapter 9, you should have practiced skills in
  1. Stating your informative purpose behaviorally;
  2. Applying the principles of rhetoric in an informative speech;
  3. Applying the principles of learning in an informative speech;
  4. Delivering a speech of definition, description, explanation, demonstration and/or investigation.

Application Exercises

  1. Applying a rhetorical principle: the speaker.
  2. Applying a rhetorical principle: the audience.
  3. Applying principles of learning.

Informative Speaking

The improvement of the understanding is for two ends: first, for our own increase of knowledge; secondly, to enable us to deliver and make out that knowledge to others.

John Locke

How do you know what you know? How do you know how to play football, make a dress, drive a car, read a book, or write an essay? For many years, parents, teachers, coaches, employers, and friends have helped you to increase your knowledge. In many cases, the vehicle for learning probably has been the informative speech. A physical education instructor may have taught you how to bowl, dance, and participate in team sports. Other teachers undoubtedly taught you how to read, write, and take examinations. Employers may have taught you how to serve a customer, type a letter, or give a sales pitch.

Introduction

After you complete your formal education, you may find yourself conveying what you know to your children, employees, or fellow workers. The purpose of this chapter is to examine the primary means of communicating information to other people: the informative speech. You will discover the purposes of informative speaking, the rhetorical principles for communicating information, and principles of learning that are especially important for communicating information to an audience. Elsewhere in this chapter you will find a checklist for the informative speech, examples of introductions to informative speeches (figures 9.1 and 9.2), an outline of an informative speech (figure 9.3), and a number of assignments in which you can apply what you have learned here.

Purposes of Informative Speaking

The four primary purposes of informative speaking are to generate a desire for information in your audience, increase audience comprehension, encourage audience retention of information, and invite audience application of new knowledge. Let us consider each of these in more detail.

Four Purposes of Informative Speaking

1. Generating information hunger
2. Increasing audience comprehension
3. Encouraging audience retention
4. Inviting audience application

Generating a Desire for Information

The first primary purpose of informative speaking is to generate a desire for information. Audiences, like students, are not always receptive to new information. You have observed teachers who were skilled and those who were unskilled at inspiring your interest in poetry, advanced algebra, chemistry, or physical education. You will have an opportunity in class to demonstrate whether you are skilled or unskilled at communicating information to an audience of classmates. If you read this chapter carefully, you should become an effective informative speaker. The first step is to arouse the audience's interest in your topic.

To generate a **desire for information** in your audience you must arouse their need for, or interest in, the information. Can you show how your information will improve their everyday lives? Can you demonstrate to the audience that they can gain the respect and admiration of their peers by knowing what you have to tell? Can you raise questions for which the audience will seek answers in the speech? One way you can learn to generate this hunger for information is to become a systematic observer of your own instructors. How do they arouse your interest?

How do they get you to learn information even in courses that you are required to take? You can adopt others' methods to improve your own ability to generate a desire for information.

How does a person generate a desire for information in a speech? One student began like this:

```
My speech today is on the subject of
hydroponics. [The class looked slightly
mystified.] How many of you know what hydroponics
is? [Two students out of twenty-two raised their
hand.] I see that only a few of you know what
hydroponics is. Our technology is ahead of our
ability to absorb it. Educated people should
know what it is. Today you will find out.
```

After this introduction, the audience was convinced that most of them did not know the topic of the speech, and, as educated people, they began to feel they *ought* to know. The speaker had successfully aroused their interest for information.

Another student generated a desire for information by posing questions to which the members of the audience would seek answers in the speech. She began: "Do you know what your chances are of getting skin cancer? Do you know when you are likely to get it? Do you know if anything can be done to cure it?" The

questions aroused the audience's curiosity about the answers, which were given later in the speech. Other student speakers have asked: "Do you know how to save money on food?" "Can you repair your own stereo?" "Can you tell a poor used car from a good one?"

The student who has carefully analyzed an audience's demographics, interests, and attitudes can find ways to instill a hunger for information that will make the audience want to hear the informative speech.

Understanding Information

The second general purpose of informative speaking is to increase the ways in which the audience can respond to the world. The more we know, the greater is our repertoire of responses. The poet can look at a boulevard full of trees and write about it in a way that conveys its beauty to others. The botanist can determine the species of the trees, whether their leaves are pinnate or palmate, and whether they are healthy, rare, or unusual. The chemist can note that the sulphur dioxide in the air is affecting the trees and know how long they can withstand the ravages of pollution. A knowledgeable person may be able to respond to the trees in all of these ways. Acquiring more information provides us with a wider variety of ways in which to respond to the world around us.

The informative speaker's goal is to increase an audience's understanding or **comprehension** of the topic. Research indicates that an audience's prior interest in a topic is unrelated to comprehension, but interest that is aroused during a speech is related to how much the audience will comprehend.[1] The effective informative speaker analyzes an audience to find out how much it already knows about a subject, so that he or she does not bore the informed or overwhelm the uninformed. The effective speaker narrows the topic so that he or she can discuss an appropriate amount of material in the allotted time. Finally, the effective speaker applies his or her own knowledge to the task to simplify and clarify the topic.

How can you encourage the audience to comprehend your topic? You can apply the following ideas to your own informative speeches:

1. Remember that audiences comprehend main ideas and generalizations better than specific facts and details.[2] Make certain that you state explicitly, or even repeat, the main ideas and generalizations in your own informative speech. Limit your speech to three to five main points.

Informative Speaking

2. Remember that audiences are more likely to comprehend simple words and concrete ideas than polysyllabic words and abstract ideas.[3] Review the content of your informative speech to determine if there are simpler, more concrete ways of stating the same ideas.
3. Remember that early remarks about how the speech will meet the audience's needs can create anticipation and increase the chances that the audience will listen and understand.[4] In your introduction be very explicit about how the topic is related to the audience. Unless your speech is related to their needs, they may choose not to listen.
4. Remember that the audience's overt participation increases their comprehension. You can learn by listening, and you can learn by doing, but you learn the most—and so will your audience—by both listening *and* doing.[5] Determine how to encourage your audience's involvement in your speech by having them raise their hands, stand up, answer a question, comment in a critique, state an opinion, or do whatever you are instructing them to do.

If you will remember and apply these four suggestions in your informative speech, you will probably increase the audience's understanding of your topic.

Retaining Information

The third general purpose of informative speaking is to help the audience remember important points in your speech. How can you get them to retain important information? One method is to reveal to the audience specifically what you want them to learn from your speech. A speaker can tell you about World War I and let you guess what is important until you flounder and eventually forget everything you heard. However, the audience will retain information better if the speaker announces at the outset, "I want you to remember the main causes of World War I, the terms of the armistice, and the immediate results of those terms." Similarly, a student speaker may say, "After this speech I will ask several of you to tell me two of the many causes for blindness that I will discuss in my speech." Audiences tend to remember more about an informative speech if the speaker tells them specifically at the outset what they should remember from the speech.

Methods of Encouraging Information Retention

1. Tell audience what you want them to remember
2. Indicate to audience which ideas are most important
3. Employ distributed repetitions
4. Repeat main idea early in the speech
5. Pause to indicate important points
6. Gesture to indicate important points

the small society   by Brickman

A second method of encouraging an audience to retain information (and one also closely tied to arousing audience interest) is to indicate clearly in the content of the informative speech which ideas are main ones and which are **subordinate,** which statements are generalizations to be remembered and which are details to support the generalizations. Careful examination of students' textbooks and notebooks shows that in preparing for examinations students highlight important points with marking pens. You can use the same method in preparing your informative speech. Highlight the important parts and convey their importance by telling the audience, "You will want to remember this point . . .", "My second main point is . . .", or "The critical thing to remember in doing this is. . . ."

Other methods that encourage an audience to retain important information are interspersing repetitions, repeating an idea two or three times throughout the speech, and pausing or using some physical gesture to indicate the importance of the information.[6] At least one experiment showed that speaking in a loud voice, repeating important matters infrequently, and repeating important matters too often (four repetitions) did *not* enhance the audience's ability to answer questions based on the information in the speech.[7] When you listen to your instructors' and classmates' informative speeches, try to determine what the speakers do to inspire you to remember the information. Then see if you can apply those same techniques in your own informative speech.

Applying Information

The fourth general purpose of informative speaking is to encourage the audience to use or apply the information during the speech or as soon afterward as possible. An effective speaker determines methods of encouraging the audience to use information quickly. Sometimes the speaker can even think of ways that the audience can use the information during the speech. One student, who was delivering an informative speech on the Japanese art of origami, for example, had everyone in class fold paper in the form of a bird with moveable wings. Another student speaker had each classmate taste synthetic foods made with chemicals. Still another student invited everyone to try one disco step to music. These speakers were encouraging the audience to apply the information during their speeches to ensure that they knew how.

198   Informative Speaking

Why should the informative speaker encourage the audience to use the information as quickly as possible? One reason is that information applied immediately is remembered longer. Another reason is that something that is tried once under supervision is more likely to be tried again. An important purpose of informative speaking is to evoke behavioral change in the audience. It is easy to think of informative speeches as simply putting an idea into people's heads, of increasing the amount they know about some topic. However, there is no concrete indication that increased information has been imparted except by observing the audience's behavior. Therefore, the informative speaker seeks **behavioral change** in the audience.

What behavioral change should the informative speaker seek? Many kinds are possible. You can provoke behavioral change by inviting the audience to talk to others about the topic, or to actually apply the information (e.g., trying a disco step) or to answer questions orally or in writing. If the audience cannot answer a question on the topic before your speech but can do so afterward, you have effected a behavioral change in your audience.

The four general purposes of informative speaking, then, are to generate a desire for information in the audience, to increase audience understanding of the topic, to encourage the audience to retain the information, and to apply the information as quickly as possible.

Next we will examine two rhetorical principles and five learning principles that relate to informative speaking.

Two **rhetorical principles** are related to any public speech, but they need special emphasis in informative speaking because they are so often overlooked. These two principles focus on the relationship between the speaker and the topic and the audience and the topic. The learning principles focus on the way people learn information.

Rhetorical Principles of Informative Speaking

The Relationship between the Speaker and the Topic

The first rhetorical principle states that you, the informative speaker, must show the audience the relationship between yourself and the topic. What are your qualifications for speaking on it? How did you happen to choose this topic? Why should the audience pay particular attention to you on this subject? As we pointed out in the chapter on source credibility, audiences tend to respond favorably to high-credibility sources because of their dynamism, expertise, trustworthiness, and coorientation. This credibility is unrelated to comprehension: an audience apparently learns as much from a low-credibility source as from a high-credibility source. However, the audience is more likely to apply what they do comprehend if they respect the speaker as a source.

Consider this hypothetical example. Suppose a husky male athlete gives an informative speech to your class on macrame, an activity that helps him relax. Would the men in the class comprehend the information as well if a female art major delivered the same information? Research says that the comprehension would be the same: they would learn about macrame equally well from a high- or low-credibility source.[8] But, would the men in the class be more likely to actually try macrame themselves if the male athlete suggested it? We believe that the athlete and art major would be equally successful at teaching macrame, but the athlete would be more likely to secure behavioral change from the men in the audience.

The point is that you must relate the topic to yourself, so that the audience will respect and apply the information you communicate. Giving a speech on street gangs? Let the audience know if you belonged to one. Giving a speech on sky diving? Tell the audience how many times you have dropped. Giving a speech on hospital costs? Tell the audience how much your last hospital stay cost.

The Relationship between the Topic and the Audience

A second rhetorical principle of informative speaking is to relate the topic to the audience early in the speech. We have already indicated that this tactic is a wise one for ensuring audience interest and comprehension. Again, you must be explicit. It may not be enough to assume that the audience understands the connection between themselves and the topic. Instead, it is best to be direct: specifically tell the audience how the topic relates to them. Remember, too, that many topics may be very difficult to justify to an audience. An informative speech on taxes is lost on an audience that pays none. An informative speech on raising thoroughbred horses is lost on an audience that has very little money. Therefore, the informative speaker is encouraged to scrutinize audience analysis information to discover indications of audience interest in a topic.

Here are excerpts from two speeches in which students applied the principles stated above. First, the rhetorical principle of relating the topic to the speaker:

> You heard the teacher call my name: Gary Klineschmidt. That is a German name. My grandparents came from Germany and the small community in which I live is still predominantly German with a full allotment of Klopsteins,

Kindermanns, Koenigs, and Klineschmidts. Many German customs are still practiced today in my home and in my hometown. Today I want to tell you about one German custom that has been adopted by many Americans and two German customs that are practiced primarily by people of German descent.

The speaker established a relationship between himself and his topic by stating explicitly the origins of his authority to speak on German customs.

The second example demonstrates the rhetorical principle of relating the topic to the audience:

Over half of you indicated on the audience analysis form that you participate in team sports. We have two football players, two varsity tennis players, one gymnast, three hockey players, and four persons in men's and women's basketball. Because you already possess the necessary dexterity and coordination for this sport, you are going to find out today about curling.

This speaker carefully detailed the many ways in which the topic was appropriate for the particular audience. When you deliver your informative speech, remember to relate the topic to yourself and your audience.

Think of three topics about which you could give a three-minute speech to inform. List the topics in the blanks at the left. In the blanks at the right explain how you relate to the topic in ways that might increase your credibility with the audience.

Application Exercise 1: Applying a Rhetorical Principle: The Speaker

Topics	Your Relationship to Topic
1. _____	_____
	_____
2. _____	_____
	_____
3. _____	_____
	_____

Application Exercise 2: Applying a Rhetorical Principle: The Audience

In the blank at the left, name one topic that you did not use in the previous exercise and explain in the blanks below how you would relate that topic to your own class in an informative speech.

Topic: _____

The audience's relationship to topic

_____

_____

_____

_____

Principles of Learning

Informative speaking is a type of teaching. Listening to informative speeches is a type of learning. If you expect an audience to comprehend your informative speech and apply the knowledge learned, you must treat the speech as a phenomenon in which teaching and learning occur. Because you, as an informative speaker, are inviting the audience to learn from you, you can apply these five **principles of learning** to your speech.

Principles of Learning

1. Relate new to old, strange to familiar, and unknown to known ideas
2. Relate wit to wisdom
3. Relate what you say to what the audience sees
4. Relate your information to your organization
5. Relate information to reinforcement

Relate New to Old, Strange to Familiar, and Unknown to Known Ideas

One principle of learning is that people tend to build on what they already know, and they accept ideas that are consistent with what they already know. An informative speech, by definition, is an attempt to "add to" what the audience already knows. If the audience is to accept the new information, it must be related to information and ideas that they already hold.

Suppose you are going to inform your audience about how to kill cockroaches. If many people in your audience live in old apartments, homes, or dormitories, they may have a need for this information. You have to consider what the audience already knows. The audience probably already knows that they can turn

202   Informative Speaking

on the lights quickly and step on the roaches as they flee for the cracks, but they probably do not know the very best chemical ingredients to wipe out roaches. So, you tell them about chlorpyrifos. You do not have to tell them that chlorpyrifos is actually the simple name for "O, O-diethyl O-3,5,6-trichloro-2-pyridyl phosphorothioate," but you can tell them what they do not know: that chlorpyrifos is an excellent cockroach killer that remains effective for weeks and is available in only three insecticides—Real-Kill Extra Strength in aerosol spray, and Rid-A-Bug and Real-Kill Liquid Extra in liquid spray.[9] In short, you can build on the audience's probable previous knowledge—manual means of killing insects and the general use of aerosols, sprays, liquids, powders, baits, and fumigant cakes— by adding to their knowledge the specific ingredient that they should look for and by giving them the names of the only three insecticides that contain the ingredient. You could elaborate by pointing out that Propoxur is also a good roach killer, but it both smells offensive and stains. Build on what the audience knows. Relate the new idea to the old, the strange to the familiar, the unknown to the known.

Relating New to Old Helps an Audience Learn

Gasohol is unleaded gasoline with 10% alcohol added.

Modern daycare institutionalizes the old practice of having aunts, uncles, and grandparents care for a child while the mother is at work.

Working with electrical wiring is like working with water pipes: you can shut off the supply of juice; you should always have something to contain it; and it is very destructive if it gets loose.

A second principle of learning to observe in informative speaking is to relate wit to wisdom. Any of us can find some topics about which we know more than our classmates. They may be our religion, hobbies, travels, political position, eating habits, or major in college. However, the aim in informative speaking is to make the information palatable to the audience and to present it in such a way that the audience finds the information attractive. Notice that the principle does not dictate that you must be funny. The principle says "relate wit to wisdom." Wisdom is the information that you know about the topic. Wit is the clever way that you make the information attractive to the audience. One pre-med student, for example, decided to give a speech on chiropractors, even though he was clearly prejudiced against them. He decided to handle his prejudice with wit rather than anger or bitterness. He entitled his speech "Chiropractors: About Quacks and Backs." Another student used wit in her speech about parenting. She was unmarried and well-known by her classmates. The audience could hardly hide its

Relate Wit to Wisdom

shock when she stated in the introduction to her last speech, "I did not think anything of parenting until I had my son." Her "son" turned out to be an uncooked hen's egg. She was taking a course on the family, in which she was required to care for her "son," the egg, for one week. When she went out on a date, she had to find a "babysitter" to care for the egg. She had to protect it from breaking as she went from class to class, take it to meals, and tuck it in at night. The introduction of her "son," the egg, added wit to the wisdom of her informative speech on parenting.

Often language choices help add vigor to your presentation. A student who was delivering a potentially boring speech on "TV and Your Child" enlivened his speech with witty language. He began this way:

> Within six years almost everybody in this room will be married with a young one in the crib and another on the way. Do you want your youngster to start babbling with the words SEX, VIOLENCE, and CRIME or do you want him to say MOMMY, DADDY, and PEPPERONI like most normal kids?

The speaker hit the audience with the unexpected. It was witty, and it made his speech more interesting to the audience.

A third principle of learning is to communicate your message in more than one way. Some people learn best by listening. Other people learn best by reading. Some people learn best when they do what the speaker is explaining. Still others learn best by seeing. Effective informative speakers recognize that different people learn best through different channels. Therefore, such speakers try to communicate their messages in a number of different ways.

Relate What You Say to What the Audience Sees

A student giving an informative speech about motorcycle safety included a three-minute film consisting of battered helmets, with a narrator explaining what happened to each motorcycle rider. The speaker also explained that he was a motorcycle safety instructor who had survived two serious accidents because he always wore his helmet. Finally, he distributed a detailed document on motorcycle safety that showed how many accidents happened at different times of the day and night. The speaker appealed to those audience members who learned best by listening, those who learned best by seeing, and those who learned best by reading.

You, too, can find a variety of methods of communicating your message to an audience that learns in diverse ways. Some material in an informative speech is simply too detailed and complex to present orally. You might be able to get more of the message across by presenting these complex materials to the audience at the conclusion of your speech. Other complex data may be easier to understand through a graph, a picture, an object, a model, or a person. Consider using every means necessary to get your informative message to the audience.

A fourth principle of learning is to organize your information for easier understanding. Organization of a speech is more than outlining. Outlining is simply the skeleton macro-organization of a speech. In an informative speech you should consider other organizational possibilities. How often should you repeat your main point? Where is the best place to repeat it? Where do you try to create a proper setting for learning to take place? Where in the speech should you reveal what you expect the audience to remember? Do you place your most important information early or late in the speech?

Relate Your Information to Your Organization

There are probably no indisputable answers to these questions, but speech communication research at least hints at some answers.[10] How often should you repeat your main points? The evidence indicates that two distributed repetitions made little difference in the audience's ability to answer questions about the information. By the time the speaker got to four distributed repetitions, the effectiveness of the technique was beginning to fade. A single statement early in the speech and three distributed repetitions seem to work best. Where in your speech should you try to create an appropriate setting for learning? The earlier the better. Make clear to your audience early in the speech exactly what you expect them to learn from all of the information you intend to present. Where should you place the most important information? The evidence indicates audiences tend to remember information that they hear early and late in the speech better than the information in the middle.

A final point about relating your information to your organization: learn how to indicate orally which parts of your speech are main points and which are subordinate or supporting. In writing, subordination is easy to indicate by levels of headings, but people listening to a speech cannot necessarily visualize the structure of your speech, which is why the effective informative speaker indicates early in the speech what is going to be covered. This forecast sets up the audience's expectations; they will know what you are going to talk about and for approximately how long. Similarly, as you proceed through your speech, you may wish to signal your progress by indicating where you are in your organization through transitions. Among organizational indicators are the following:

"My second point is . . ."
"Now that I have carefully explained the problem, I will turn to my
    solution."
"This story about what happened to me in the service will illustrate my
    point about obeying orders."

In each case the speaker is signaling whether the next item is a main or subordinate point in the informative speech.

Relate Information to Reinforcement

A fifth principle of learning is that audiences are more likely to respond to information if it is rewarding for them, i.e., if they receive **reinforcement** for listening. One of the audience's concerns about an informative speech is "What's in it for me?" The effective informative speaker answers this question not only in the introduction, where the need for the information is formally explained, but also throughout the speech. By the time a speaker is in the middle of the presentation, the audience may have forgotten much of the earlier motivating information presented; so the speaker continually needs to remind the audience how the information meets its needs.

A student speaker, talking to his audience about major first-aid methods, made this statement in his informative speech:

Imagine being home from school for the weekend,
having a nice, relaxing visit with your family.
Suddenly your father clutches his chest and
crumbles to the floor. What would you do to help
him?

The student reminded the audience throughout the speech how each first-aid technique could be applied to victims with heart attacks, serious bleeding, and poisoning. The benefit for the audience was in knowing what to do in each case. Another student began her speech by saying,

Did you realize that at this very moment, each
and every one of you could be, and probably are,
suffering from America's most widespread

ailment? It is not V.D., cancer, or heart
disease, but a problem that is commonly ignored
by most Americans--the problem of being
overweight.

As the speaker proceeded through her information on low-calorie and low-car-
bohydrate diets, she kept reassuring the audience that they could overcome the
problem in part by knowing which foods to eat and which to avoid. The audience
benefited by learning the names of foods that could help or hinder their health.

Reinforcement comes in many forms. In the preceding examples, the reinforcement was in the form of readily usable information that the audience could
apply. A speaker can use other, more psychological forms of reinforcement. "Do
you want to be among the ignorant who do not know what a 'value added tax'
is?" The speaker who confidentially tells you about it is doing you a service because you will no longer be ignorant. A student from Chicago found that most
of her classmates thought first of muggings when someone mentioned Chicago
in conversation. She devoted her informative speech to the positive aspects of
living in that city. The result was that the students in the audience had many
more positive associations about Chicago, including the fact that one of their
fellow students, who looked not at all like a mugger, was from Chicago, and *she*
thought it was a good place to live.

Write down a topic for an informative speech that you have not used in previous application exercises. Explain in the spaces provided how you could apply each of the principles of learning to that topic.

Application Exercise 3: Applying Principles of Learning

Topic: _____

One way that I could relate this topic to what the audience already knows is _____

_____.

One way that I could relate wit to wisdom in an informative speech on this topic is by

_____.

One way that I could use several channels to get my message across on this topic is by

_____.

One way that I could organize my speech to help the audience learn my information is by

_____.

One way that I could provide reinforcement to my audience for listening to my informative

speech on this topic is by _____

_____.

Informative Speaking

The Speech to Inform

We have considered the purposes of informative speaking, the rhetorical principles of informative speaking, and principles of learning. We are now prepared to consider some specific types of informative speeches. Before we begin that process, we will summarize our understanding thus far. Checklist 6 is a simple guide to the informative speech. As you prepare your informative speech and after it is ready for presentation, check each item to see if you have considered it in your speech. A brief speech is unlikely to include all of these points, but they may spark additional ideas that you can apply in your presentation.

The introduction for a speech to inform is particularly important because you must (1) establish your credibility by relating yourself to the topic, (2) establish relevance by relating the topic to the audience, (3) gain the audience's attention and interest in the topic by stating it in such a way that you arouse audience curiosity, (4) forecast the content of your speech, and (5) state specifically what you want the audience to learn from your speech. An overall objective in the introduction is to create an atmosphere for learning, in which the audience will be stimulated to comprehend and remember the important parts of your speech. Figures 9.1 and 9.2 shows students' introductions to informative speeches. The side notes indicate the functions that are being fulfilled.

**Checklist 6:
A Checklist for
the Informative
Speech**

_____ 1. What have you done early in your speech to generate information hunger? Sometime early in the speech, preferably in the introduction, provoke further interest in your topic so that the audience's appetite is aroused and ready for the morsels you are about to present. How is the speech going to meet the audience's needs?

_____ 2. What have you done with the information in your speech to make it easier for the audience to comprehend? Present a limited number of generalizations in simple, concrete language. Also, determine ways to make the audience participate in your message through their actions.

_____ 3. What have you done to help your audience remember your information? State explicitly what you want the audience to learn and remember from your speech. No one can remember all that you say. Have you indicated at the beginning and throughout the speech which items they should remember?

_____ 4. Have you told your audience how they can apply the information that they heard in your speech? People tend to forget quickly information that they have heard unless they can use it in their own lives. Can you inspire the audience to talk about your topic, ask questions about it, or apply the information soon after the speech?

_____ 5. Have you told the audience how you, the speaker, relate to the topic? The audience may comprehend what you say regardless of your credibility, but they are more likely to apply the information if they are convinced that you have special authority or expertise on the topic.

_____ 6. Have you related the topic to the audience? You can ensure both interest and comprehension if you show the audience early in the speech how the information will enrich their lives, enliven their minds, or reduce their ignorance.

_____ 7. Have you determined any ways to add wit to wisdom? Consider using alliterative language, humor, clever wording, amusing anecdotes, illustrative stories, and surprising examples. Make your information palatable to the audience.

_____ 8. Have you related your new information to what the audience already knows? Have you related the strange to the familiar, the unknown to the known? Novel or new information has more impact than old information. Check your information to make sure that you have included ample data that most people in your audience are unlikely to know.

_____ 9. Have you related what you say to what the audience sees? Provide information through several channels of learning. Consider using short films, slides, pictures, posters, graphs, audio tapes, video tapes, objects, people, and handouts.

_____ 10. Have you related your information to your organization? Place important information strategically for maximum impact, repeat or paraphrase your important points in distributed repetitions, and early in the speech establish an atmosphere for learning and specific goals for the audience. The organization of your informative speech should reflect your intent to inform by signaling main ideas, subordinate ideas, and supporting materials.

_____ 11. Have you related your information to reinforcement? What can you do to make your information rewarding or beneficial to your audience? Consider specific ways to reward the audience by making them pleased to know more. Thus, they should apply the information and enrich their lives.

_____ 12. Have you reviewed the chapters on audience analysis, organization, visual aids, introductions and conclusions, topic selection, delivery, and purpose for additional suggestions for developing your informative speech?

The introduction to an informative speech in figure 9.1 fulfills all the functions of an introduction that were discussed in the chapter on introductions.[11] Even though it is a fine introduction, it does have a major flaw: the audience consisted mainly of college sophomores who were not in a good position to apply or use the information in the immediate future.

Another example of an introduction to an informative speech appears in figure 9.2.[12] This introduction fulfills most of the functions of an introduction and students who heard the speech reported high interest in it even though a number of them had no prior knowledge or experience with aviation or aeronautics. How would you improve this introduction?

Example of an Introduction to an Informative Speech

THE UNDERGROUND MOVEMENT

Sets up expectations for a short speech. Gains audience attention. Builds in reward for the audience.

If you listen to me for a few minutes today, I may be able to save you thousands of dollars in the near future. That's right, because of our new technology in the field of architecture, we are now constructing underground homes. The basic difference between this type of building and the old is that instead of building above the ground where frequently changing weather will affect it, the dwelling is now built underground, where the earth acts as natural insulation.

States topic explicitly.

Relates old information to new with a novel idea.

Introduces idea consistent with audience analysis showing an interest in conserving energy.

Relates speaker to topic to establish credibility.

Arouses curiosity by presenting new information.

Reinforces audience interest by stating financial gain.

Forecasts content.

I first learned about this building technique while working with an architectural firm by the name of Brown, Healey and Bock. It was during this time that I found out that I could cut my overall utility bill by 60% in the northern states and as much as 100% in the southern states. This fact is very important because energy costs have gone up over 100% in the last six years. In just a few years, this savings would amount to thousands of dollars.

Creates an atmosphere for learning. States specifically what the audience is expected to comprehend and remember.

Arouses curiosity about facts, figures, and designs to be presented in the body of the speech.

Today, I will share with you some of the facts, figures, and a variety of building designs that I have discovered in my work. By the end of the speech you should be able to remember at least one fact about underground housing, one figure about the savings in this state, and one design that is most likely to work in our area.

Figure 9.1 An example of an introduction to an informative speech.

Figure 9.2 An example of an introduction to an informative speech.

An Example of an Introduction to an Informative Speech

THE KITTY HAWK EXPERIENCE

Gains audience attention. Relates wit to wisdom through descriptive language.

The beach was desolate and barren. A stiff, steady breeze sprayed sand among the dunes below an overcast sky of endless gray. Yet a certain energy or electricity filled the air surrounding a small gathering of men. They were there for a purpose, a reason. Something spectacular was to take place on that cold December day. It was 1903, and two brothers from Dayton were attempting powered flight for the first time. A few witnesses mumbled disbelief and complained of the bitter temperature. Seagulls laughed overhead. It didn't seem possible, but Orville Wright flung his ungainly craft skyward for a brief twelve second flight. Powered flight had become a reality. This was the Kitty Hawk Experience. Two bicycle repairers had discovered the secret. Two brothers from Dayton, Ohio, proved to the world it was possible to fly in a craft heavier than air. It is amazing to realize how their first flight has lead to modern aviation as we know it today.

Relates known to unknown. Arouses interest.

Relates speaker to topic to establish credibility.

Creates an atmosphere for learning. Relates information to organization. Forecasts organization. Relates information to reinforcement.

I myself have been fascinated by flying since early childhood and have spent most of my life involving myself with it in as many ways as possible. Currently I am working towards an Associate's Degree in Aviation Technology which, upon completion, includes a private, commercial, and instrument rating. What took place in South Carolina on that December day in 1903 is incredible, not only to the aviation buff but to all those who have experienced the thrill of flying. From the early experiments with scale models in a homemade wind tunnel right up to the manned glider tests and that first history-making powered flight in December, the story of the Wright brothers is absolutely fascinating.

The body of an informative speech should consist of three to five main points supported by illustrations and examples. In the speech outline shown in Figure 9.3, the speaker included only two main points in his outline, but each included a great deal of information.[13] The outline that is presented suggests that the speech was somewhat dry and uninteresting. When the speaker delivered the speech, he added humorous stories and anecdotal material from an internship in which he was involved and in which he conducted patterned exit interviews for a company. He related himself to the topic because of his experience and related the topic to the audience by asking them questions about their own past employment. His speech could have been improved by generating more information hunger in the audience.

Figure 9.3 An example of an outline for an informative speech.

Example of an Outline for an Informative Speech

THE PATTERNED EXIT INTERVIEW: MAKE IT WORK FOR YOU!

Introduction

I. A high turnover rate means trouble for any company.
  A. The brightest and best educated people frequently leave.
  B. An exit interview can assist management in determining problems that may exist.

II. Three types of exit interviewing exist.
  A. The structured technique.
    1. The employee answers "yes" or "no" to a list of questions.
    2. The primary disadvantage is that there is no time to discuss the rationale for leaving.
  B. The unstructured technique.
    1. This type relies on broad, open-ended questions.
    2. The employee may ramble on, and the interviewer may never receive answers to his or her questions.
  C. The patterned exit interview.
    1. This is the best type of the three possibilities.
    2. I will explain it in complete detail in my speech today.

Body

III. There are four steps in conducting a patterned exit interview.
    A. Determine who is to conduct the interview.
    B. Set up a system that moves an interviewee from termination to an exit interview routinely.
    C. Develop an appropriate interview climate.
    D. Conduct the interview.
        1. Try to establish rapport.
        2. State the purpose of the interview.
        3. Focus on the characteristics and attitudes that are commensurate with the previously held position.
        4. Discuss the reasons for leaving the job.
        5. Compare the old and the new positions.

IV. Guidelines that will result in improved exit interviews exist.
    A. Stress confidentiality in the interview.
    B. The interview should not occur on the last day of employment.
    C. One hour is sufficient time in which to conduct the interview.
    D. Avoid closed questions in the body of the interview.
    E. Avoid provoking hostility in the interviewee.

Conclusion

V. This type of interview has many benefits.
    A. Managerial deficiencies may be identified.
    B. The basis for improved working conditions can be identified.
    C. Satisfactory programs for compensation and benefits can be developed.
    D. Training and development, employee and labor relations, and personnel research can be improved.

VI. One large corporation in the Southwest reduced its turnover by 90% by implementing the patterned exit interview.

Bibliography

Dixon, Andrew L. "The Long Goodbye," *Supervisory Management* 27(January 1982), pp. 26-29.
Embrey, Mondy, and Noe. "Exit Interview: A Tool For Personnel Development," *The Personnel Administrator* (May 1979), pp. 43-48.
"Exit Interviews of Departing Employees Can Provide Valuable Management Information," *Practical Accountant* 14(June 1981), pp. 65-69.

Types of
Informative
Speeches

The category of informative speeches includes a wide variety of different kinds of speeches. In chapter 7, the speech of definition and the speech of description were briefly discussed. They are two types of informative speeches. In this section we will further explain the speech of definition and the speech of description, and we will introduce the speech of explanation, the speech of demonstration, and the speech of investigation. As you will observe, these speeches all fall under the general rubric of informative speeches, but each has unique characteristics which allow it to be differentiated from the others.

Speech of
Definition

The speech of definition sounds fairly simple and straightforward. You may even be wondering how an entire speech can be based upon definition. After all, defining a word is simply the process of supplying a few other words that explain what the word means. However, if you have read chapter 7, or if you have reflected on the number of "communication breakdowns" you have had because of differences in definition, you know that defining words and concepts is far more complex than it might originally appear to be. Supplying definitions for terms may in fact be the basis of all other types of informative speeches, and it could even be suggested that definition is the most important of the lines of argument used by speakers.

A number of methods of defining were offered in chapter 7. Among the methods discussed were comparison, contrast, use of synonyms, use of antonyms, etymology, differentiation, use of operational definitions, and use of experiential definitions. If you have forgotten any of these types of definitions, you may wish to review chapter 7 and to read the example in Appendix D.

A number of speech topics lend themselves to the speech of definition. Listed here are some titles of successful speeches of definition:

1. Is the U.S. a Democracy?
2. What Is the "Electronic Church?"
3. What Is "Self-Disclosure?"
4. The Autokinetic Effect: Why Stationary Objects Are Perceived as though They Were in Motion.
5. What Are "Valley Girls?"
6. Understanding Seriography.
7. "Dieting" Could Mean 6000+ Calories per Day!
8. Parapsychology: The Science of Ghosts and Goblins.
9. Voyeurism: A Sex Disease.
10. The Autistic Child.
11. What Is "Speed Reading?"
12. What Is "Somatotype?"

13. Cholesterol Is Not Just a Disease of the Old.
14. Stockholm Syndrome: Becoming One with Your Kidnapper.
15. S.P. S. S. Is Not Just Another Computer.

These titles should help you think of other topics that would be appropriate for the speech of definition. You may wish to complete the application assignment in chapter 7 on the speech of definition.

The speech of description is an informative speech in which you describe a person, place, object, or experience by telling about its size, weight, color, texture, smell, and/or your feelings about it. This speech was introduced in chapter 7. The speech of description relies on your abilities to use precise, accurate, specific, and concrete language; to demonstrate a diverse vocabulary; to use words that have appropriate connotative and denotative meanings; and to offer necessary definitions. You may wish to review some of these ideas in chapter 7 and read the example in Appendix E.

Speech of Description

A variety of topics lend themselves to the speech of description. Listed here are some titles of speeches that seemed to work particularly well for this type of informative speech.

1. Leo Buscaglia: A Motivating, Loving, and Inspiring Italian.
2. Cincinnati: A City of History.
3. The Perfect Spouse for the 1980s.
4. Life in a Fraternity.
5. Touring America on a Motorcycle.
6. My Mother Is My Best Friend.
7. John F. Kennedy: The Legend Lives On.
8. The Common Cold: Facts vs. Fiction.
9. Behind the Scenes of "Dallas."
10. Oktoberfest in Munich.
11. Fort Lauderdale: A College Student's View of Heaven in March.
12. Double Take: A Portrait of My Twin.
13. Sin City: A Tour of Las Vegas.
14. What Is "Loneliness" for a Senior Citizen?
15. Alaska: Can America's Last Wilderness Survive?

This list of topics should be suggestive, but it is certainly not exhaustive of all of the possible kinds of topics that are appropriate for the speech of description. There is an application assignment in chapter 7 for this informative speech. You may wish to complete that assignment with these suggested topics in mind.

DUNAGIN'S PEOPLE

"WHAT A CLEAR UNSPOILED STREAM!...YOU CAN READ THE LABELS ON THE BEER CANS!"

Speech of Explanation

The speech of explanation is an informative speech in which you tell how something works, why something occurred, or how something should be evaluated. You may explain a social, political, or economic issue; you may describe an historical event; you may discuss a variety of theories, principles, or laws; or you may offer a critical appraisal of art, literature, music, drama, film, or speeches. A wide collection of topics may be included in this category. Some possible speech titles for the speech of explanation follow.

1. Bulemia: The Binge and Purge Compulsion.
2. Understanding Our Political System.
3. Where Have All the Jobs Gone?
4. Horror Movies: Why We Pay to Be Frightened.
5. Is Graduate School in Your Future?
6. Why People Use Alcohol to Socialize.
7. The Evolution of the American Sitcom.
8. Cable Television: Will It Replace the Networks?
9. How to Buy a Good Used Car.
10. The Landslide Election of 1932.
11. The Significance of the Battle of Gettysburg.
12. The Effects of Capital Punishment on the Murder Rate.
13. An Analysis of Martin Luther King's Speeches.
14. President Carter's Foreign Policy Decisions.
15. How Thermodynamics Keeps Us Warm.

The next kind of informative speech, the speech of demonstration is an informative speech in which you show the audience an object, person, or place; in which you show the audience how something works; in which you show the audience how to do something; or in which you show the audience why something occurs. In other words, the speech of demonstration may be similar to the speech of explanation or the speech of description, but the focus in the speech of demonstration is on the visualization of your topic. For instance, one of the suggested topics for the speech of description provided above is a speech about Cincinnati. If you provided overheads with maps of the city, posters with depictions of major attractions, and photographs of points of interest, the speech would be one of demonstration. Similarly, a speech on horror movies, as suggested above, may be a speech of explanation. If, however, you add short excerpts from various movies illustrating the four reasons that people pay to be frightened, the speech becomes one of demonstration. The key to a speech of demonstration is that you are actually showing the audience something of your topic.

As you consider topics that are appropriate for the speech of demonstration, you should not simply recall a speech of explanation or a speech of description and add a few pictures, a poster, or an overhead to it and believe that you have an appropriate speech of demonstration. As you attempt to decide on a topic, you

Speech of Demonstration

should consider those ideas, concepts, or processes that are too complex to be understood through words alone. Similarly, consider the wide variety of items and materials that can be used to demonstrate your topic. You may wish to read chapter 8, in which visual aids such as the chalkboard, posters, movies, slides, opaque and overhead projections, living models and physical objects, handouts, and yourself (as a visual aid) are discussed. Which items will be most useful for your topic? Do not rely on those visual aids that are the simplest to construct or the most obvious; instead, use those items that best illustrate your topic. Listed below are some titles of speeches that were highly effective speeches of demonstration.

1. All It Takes Is Concentration: The Practice of Self-Hypnotism.
2. The Art of Reggae Dancing.
3. The Basic Steps in Learning How to Sail.
4. How to Operate a Personal Computer.
5. Trim the Thighs with Exercise.
6. How to Buy a Fall Wardrobe for Less than $50.00.
7. How to Use Mnemonic Devices to Aid Memory.
8. The Difference between a "C" Paper and an "A" Paper.
9. Let There Be Light: Instruction in Homemade Electricity.
10. Proper Care of Your Direct-Drive Turntable.
11. Strengthening Exercises for the Serious Runner.
12. How Time Flies: A Plan for Budgeting Your Time.
13. The Art of Ear Piercing.
14. How to Grow Your Own Yeast.
15. Solving the Rubik's Cube Revenge.

Speech of Investigation

The final informative speech discussed in this section is the speech of investigation. This informative speech may have many of the same purposes as the speeches of definition, description, or explanation. The unique feature of the speech of investigation is that heavy reliance is placed upon the speaker's investigatory skills. This speech is sometimes called "expository", which means that it relies upon the examination of resource material. You are probably most familiar with the speech of investigation as lectures, oral reports, or public presentations. Some of the types of informative speeches that we have discussed above rely heavily, or exclusively, on knowledge that is gleaned through personal experience. The speech of investigation relies upon knowledge gained from in-depth reading and research. You may wish to re-examine the material in chapter 5 to recall specific sources of information for the speech of investigation. Remember that both primary and secondary sources can be used. Listed below are some speech titles suggestive of appropriate speeches of investigation.

1. Counseling Services Available on U.S. College Campuses.
2. Differences and Similarities between Communism and Socialism.
3. The Effects of Cigarette Smoking on the Unborn.
4. What Employers Look for in the Job Interview.

5. The History of Rock Music.
6. The Basic Principles of Federal Broadcasting Regulations.
7. The Extent of World Hunger.
8. The History of Modern Art.
9. What Is the Truth behind the Nielsen Numbers?
10. What Are the Principles of Satellite Communication?
11. The Influence of the Aging in America.
12. Economic Changes in the U.S. in the Past Fifty Years.
13. Socialization Differences between Women and Men.
14. Sexual Practices in Early Twentieth Century America.
15. Talk to the Animals: Communicating with Other Primates.

Conclusion

In this chapter you learned that the purposes of informative speeches are to generate a desire for information on the part of the audience, to seek audience understanding of the information, and to invite audience retention and application of the information in the speech. Among the important points concerning the purposes of informative speaking, you learned that audiences comprehend generalizations and main ideas better than details; audiences comprehend simple words and concrete ideas better than big words and abstractions; a sense of anticipation can encourage listening and understanding; and audience participation increases comprehension.

Two rhetorical principles function in informative speaking. The first is that the speaker should explicitly state the relationship between himself or herself and the topic. The second is that the audience needs to know its relationship to the topic. These principles can be observed by describing your qualifications to discuss the topic and by demonstrating how the audience will find this information useful.

You learned five principles of learning related to the informative speech. They are (1) relating new ideas to old ideas and strange information to familiar information; (2) employing wit in communicating wisdom; (3) showing the audience what you mean through demonstration or visual aids; (4) organizing your information for easy comprehension; and (5) providing reinforcement for the audience for learning your information.

Finally, you learned about five different types of informative speeches: the speech of definition, the speech of description, the speech of explanation, the speech of demonstration, and the speech of investigation. The speech of definition is based on explaining the meaning of a word or a few words. The speech of description relies upon your ability to offer precise, accurate, and concrete language; to demonstrate a sufficient vocabulary; to use appropriate words; and to offer definitions. The speech of explanation is one in which you tell how something works, why it occurred, or how it should be evaluated. The speech of demonstration includes some object that is actually seen by the audience. The speech of investigation relies upon your research and investigative skills. In the next chapter we will consider the persuasive speech.

Application Assignment

The Speech of Explanation

Deliver a four- to six-minute speech in which you explain how something works, why something occurred, or how something should be evaluated. You are encouraged to rely on sources of information like encyclopedias, textbooks, newspapers, magazines, and professional journals. Chapter 5 cites other sources that might be helpful as you prepare this assignment. You will be evaluated on how well your audience understands what you are explaining. The information on audience analysis presented in chapter 3 may be useful as you consider the most successful manner in which to present your information. Consider information with which your audience is already familiar and demonstrate relationships between the known and the new information that you are offering. Considering how you can translate unfamiliar terms into known quantities. Try to determine how you can motivate your audience to be interested in what you are attempting to explain. *Note:* An example of a speech of explanation can be found in Appendix F; it can serve as a model for this assignment.

The Speech of Demonstration

Write an outline for a speech of demonstration that is to be about four to six minutes in length. Include in your outline a title, a purpose statement, an introduction, a body, and a conclusion. On the left-hand side of the sheet, specify the visual aids that will be used and the purpose of each visual aid. Examine your outline to determine if the visual aids are really necessary for understanding of if they are merely "props;" try to insure that no additional visual aids are necessary for the audience to understand your message. You will be evaluated on your ability to identify creative and appropriate visual aids for your topic and on your ability to use visual aids when necessary and useful for understanding. *Note:* An example of a speech of demonstration can be found in Appendix G; it can serve as a model for this assignment.

The Speech of Investigation

Try to determine some topics that would be appropriate for the speech of investigation. Brainstorm and identify at least five topics for each of the following categories: (1) political, economic, or social issues; (2) communication-related topics; (3) topics about specific people, or people in general; (4) topics about art, music, literature, theatre, or dance; and (5) historical events. After you have written at least twenty-five topics (five for each of the five categories), identify three that have particular interest for you. For each of the three, suggest the resources that you might rely upon to gain the information you need. Your evaluation on this assignment is dependent upon your creativity in identifying interesting topics for yourself and a potential audience and upon your ability to determine sufficient and appropriate sources of information. *Note:* An example of a speech of investigation can be found in Appendix H; it can serve as a model for this assignment.

Vocabulary

behavioral change An objective of public speaking by which the audience talks or acts differently as a result of the speech.

comprehension A synonym for understanding, often "tested" by asking for restatement, paraphrase, or application of the information.

desire for information A need the speaker creates in an audience so that they are motivated to learn from the speech.

principles of learning Principles that relate to what governs audience understanding and comprehension.

reinforcement A psychological or physical reward to increase an audience's response to information given in a speech.

rhetorical principles Two principles of public speaking that focus on the relationship between the speaker and the topic and on the relationship between the topic and the audience.

subordination Showing that one piece of information is less important than or merely supports another.

Endnotes

1. Charles R. Petrie, Jr., "Informative Speaking: A Summary and Bibliography of Related Research," *Speech Monographs* 30 (1963): 79–91.
2. Ibid., p. 80.
3. Carole Ernest, "Listening Comprehension as a Function of Type of Material and Rate of Presentation," *Speech Monographs* 35 (1968): 154–58. See also John A. Baird, "The Effects of Speech Summaries upon Audience Comprehension of Expository Speeches of Varying Quality and Complexity," *Central States Speech Journal* 25 (1974): 119–27.
4. Petrie, p. 84.
5. Elena P. Zayas-Baya, "Instructional Media in the Total Language Picture," *International Journal of Instructional Media* 5 (1977–78): 145–50.
6. R. Ehrensberger, "An Experimental Study of the Relative Effectiveness of Certain Forms of Emphasis in Public Speaking," *Speech Monographs* 12 (1945): 94–111.
7. Ibid.
8. Kenneth Andersen and Theodore Clevenger, Jr., "A Summary of Experimental Research in Ethos," *Speech Monographs* 30 (1963): 59–78.
9. "Household Insecticides," *Consumer Reports* 44 (1979): 362–67.
10. Ehrensberger, pp. 94–111.
11. From a paper submitted by Michael Grahek in Fundamentals of Public Speaking, Iowa State University.
12. Based on a paper submitted by John Messer in Fundamentals of Human Communication, Ohio University.
13. Based on a paper submitted by Robert Fott in Fundamentals of Human Communication, Ohio University.

Chapter 10

Outline

Introduction: Rationale for persuasive speaking.
- I. Defining persuasive speaking.
- II. Three purposes of persuasive speaking.
    - A. Shaping responses.
    - B. Reinforcing responses.
    - C. Changing responses.
- III. Five principles of persuasion.
    - A. Consistency persuades.
    - B. Small changes persuade.
    - C. Benefits persuade.
    - D. Fulfilling needs persuades.
    - E. Gradual approaches persuade.
- IV. Reasoning in persuasive speaking.
    - A. Inductive reasoning.
    - B. Deductive reasoning.
    - C. Tests of reasoning.
- V. Evaluating evidence.
    - A. Tests of types of evidence.
        - 1. Testimony.
        - 2. Statistics.
        - 3. Example.
        - 4. Comparison.
        - 5. Analogy.
        - 6. General questions.
    - B. Believability of evidence.
- VI. Appeals to the emotions.
    - A. *Ad hominem* argument.
    - B. Illegitimate authority.
    - C. Oversimplification.
    - D. Distraction.
    - E. Fear appeals.
    - F. Narrative.
- VII. Presenting sides, citing sources, and putting together a persuasive speech.
- VIII. Types of persuasive speeches.
    - A. The speech of reasons.
    - B. The speech of opposition.
    - C. The speech of action.

Conclusion: A review of the purposes and principles of persuasive speaking.

Objectives

When you have completed chapter 10, you should be able to answer the following questions:

1. What are the main purposes of persuasive speaking?
2. What are five principles of persuasion that can be used in persuasive speaking?
3. What are induction, deduction, and the tests of evidence?
4. Where should your best argument be placed, when should you use a one-sided approach, and when should you argue pro-con?
5. What are some problems with emotional appeals?
6. What are three types of persuasive speeches?

When you have completed chapter 10, you should have utilized skills in

1. Determining a purpose for your persuasive speech;
2. Applying the principles of persuasion in a speech;
3. Using reasoning and the tests of evidence; and
4. Delivering a persuasive speech.

Application Exercises

1. What is persuasion?
2. Shaping, reinforcing, and changing.
3. Student hierarchy of needs.
4. Principles of persuasion.
5. Inductive and deductive reasoning.

Persuasive Speaking

. . . I am convinced that intelligence, patience, and eloquence can, sooner or later, lead the human race out of its self-imposed tortures provided it does not exterminate itself in the meantime.

Bertrand Russell

Introduction

The persuasive speech is often the last speech delivered in a beginning speech communication course. The persuasive speech comes last because it is complex: you not only have to convey information, you must also try to change the audience's mind or move it to action. The persuasive speech comes last because it is the culmination of everything that you have learned about preparing and delivering a speech. Defining, explaining, describing—which proved so valuable in communicating information—are evident also in the persuasive speech. The skills that you have developed in delivery are called into play again. The persuasive speech is your final performance, in which you should demonstrate that you have begun to master all aspects of public speaking.

What will you learn in this chapter on persuasive speaking? First, you will discover how to distinguish persuasion from purely informational discourse, on the one hand, and from highly coercive methods on the other. Next, you will explore some principles of persuasion that you can apply in your speeches. A third area of concern will be the role of reason and emotion in persuasive speeches. By the end of chapter 10 you will be familiar with three types of persuasive speeches: the speech of reasons, the speech of opposition, and the speech of action.

Defining Persuasive Speaking

A persuasive speech is distinguished from other types of speeches by its intent, its purpose, and its effects. The informative speech defines, explains, demonstrates, describes, or investigates. Its central purpose is to increase an audience's understanding or knowledge about a topic. The topics for informative speeches underline that purpose: "Understanding Classical Music," "How to Make Draft Beer", or "What is Recession?" The speaker increases your knowledge without necessarily expecting a change of mind or action. The **intent** of a persuasive speech goes further: it seeks a predetermined change in the audience's mind and/or its actions.

One final characteristic helps define persuasive speaking: it is persuasion only if the audience is in a position to *choose* compliance. If the "persuader" is in a position to order, force, or coerce the audience, so that the audience or receiver perceives no real **choice**, then we say that this communication is outside the province of persuasion. Of course, some persuasive speeches may imply some modest levels of coercion, but if the receiver perceives obedience, jail, joblessness, or some other no-choice situation arising from non-compliance, then the message has passed beyond persuasion into coercion.

What then, is persuasive speaking? *Persuasive speaking is a message delivered to an audience by a speaker who intends to influence their choice by shaping, reinforcing, or changing their responses toward an idea, issue, concept, or*

HOWIE

By Glasbergen

1 - 28

"Cigarettes, diet soda, bacon . . . what is this,
a grocery list or a suicide note?"

*product. The attempt at persuasion is successful only if the message has its
intended effect; that is, the message does* in some *measure affect the audience's
choices.* Since the definition of persuasive speaking hinges heavily on the three
main purposes of persuasive speaking, you will find a fuller explanation of each
in the next section.

Application Exercise 1: What Is Persuasion?

In each of the items below, consider what you know about persuasive speaking. Write "yes" before those items that describe persuasion and "no" before those that do not.

_____ 1. An audience listening to a speech on investments learns, from seeing collar bars and tie tacs on the speaker's clothing, that they are in style, and many persons in the audience subsequently start wearing these accessories.

_____ 2. The speaker delivers a speech designed to increase what the audience knows about FCC regulations.

_____ 3. After the briefing, the major orders the soldiers to disperse immediately and return to barracks.

_____ 4. The speaker wanted his audience to run out and buy his new book after his speech on the contents, but the audience was so repulsed by the speech that no one bought the book.

_____ 5. The boss gives a management pep talk to her employees and mentions at the end that anyone who does not increase sales by the end of the month will find himself or herself without a job.

Answers: None of the examples above are persuasion. In item 1 the speaker did not intend to influence the audience's use of accessories; in 2 the speaker was not shaping, reinforcing, or changing the audience; in 3 and 5 the audience did not perceive choice; and in 4 the intended goal was not realized.

Three Purposes of Persuasive Speaking

You may have noted the main distinction between informative and persuasive speaking: the informative speaker has a cognitive goal—to increase an audience's understanding or knowledge concerning a topic—while the persuasive speaker intends to go beyond understanding and clarifying to try to *change* the audience in some way. The three purposes of persuasive speaking, or the three ways in which the persuasive speaker attempts to change the audience, are through shaping, reinforcing, and changing audience responses toward some idea, product, issue, or concept.[1] The persuasive speaker ultimately seeks some action or some behavioral change on the part of the receiver.

Purposes of Persuasive Speaking

1. Shaping responses
2. Reinforcing responses
3. Changing responses

One purpose of persuasive speaking is to shape the way the audience responds. **Shaping** can be accomplished whether the audience knows a great deal about a topic or not, but the effects of shaping are most apparent when the audience knows very little about the topic.

A good example is the public response to personal computers in the early 1980s. At the turn of the decade computers were mostly too large or expensive for home use. The people who really knew computers were mainly in the military, large institutions, and big business. By 1982, however, the computer had been miniaturized and mass produced, making it readily accessible to small businesses and even middle-class individuals. Promoters of the new technology used workshops, speeches, ads, specialized magazines, and many other means to sell their new home computers. On the eve of 1983, *Time* magazine named the computer the "Man of the Year" because of its profound effects on the lives of Americans. All of this promoting of home computers was shaping people's responses toward the product. People who in 1981 did not know a daisy wheel from a turnip were by 1983 talking glibly about modems, cps, megabytes, and memory. Shaping of responses was taking place through conversations, displays in stores, and considerable publicity.

The shaping of new responses in an audience is nearly always linked to established values. Daryl Bem describes a **value** as a "a primitive preference for or a positive attitude toward certain end states of existence (like equality, salvation, self-fulfillment, or freedom) or certain broad modes of conduct (like courage, honesty, friendship, or chastity)."[2] The persuasive speaker links the new idea or product to values already inherent in the audience. In the case of the home computer, the persuaders linked them to efficiency, progress, and competition. If you or your business did not have one, then you were behind the times, slower to produce, and behind the competition. People whose notion of home computers was being shaped were found to change their vocabulary, their reading habits, and even their everyday talk. Thus, you should remember that shaping responses is the process of linking the new and the novel to established values in the audience, and that it results in behavioral change.

A second purpose of persuasive speaking is the **reinforcing** of responses in an audience, to invite their continuing current behavior toward some product, idea, or issue. Wallace Fotheringham, in his book on persuasion, describes this action goal of persuasion as continuance: to keep an audience doing what they already do.[3] At first glance, this purpose of persuasion would appear to be a minor one; in fact, however, it is responsible for much of the persuasion around us. Radio and television stations, networks, and cable systems try to keep us loyal to their stations and programs; clothing, cosmetic, tobacco, and liquor companies seek our continued patronage; and educational, religious, and political organizations strive to keep us in their camp.

How can reinforcing responses—keeping us doing what we already do—be called persuasion when it results in no effective change in behavior? The answer is that encouraging such continuing behavior is persuasion because it still affects

"After my little talk, no doubt, all of you will rush right out to join 'Uncle Burpy's Foosbonger Cadets.' "

our choices. For example, you have the right to choose whether or not you practice a given religion. To the extent that the priest, rabbi, or minister can keep you coming to religious services on a regular basis, he can continue to influence your choice in the matter. As soon as you stop that behavior, other influences are likely to capture your attention. Reinforcing or rewarding an audience for being virtuous, for staying with the company, for working hard, or for doing what parents and teachers say, does influence your choices and your behavior.

The shaping of responses is linked to established values in the audience. The reinforcing of responses is related both to values and attitudes. **Attitudes** are more fragile than values. They are described by Bem as "likes or dislikes" toward people, ideas, policies, and situations.[4] They are characterized by favorability, strength, and importance. For instance, your attitude toward politics might be favorable, but weak and unimportant; so you might think kindly of political contests without ever voting. Your attitude toward your mother, on the other hand, might be favorable, strong, and important. Attitudes, because they are fragile, seem to need constant care. That care comes, in part, from persuasive messages designed to influence your responses through reinforcement.

Changing Responses

The third purpose of persuasive speaking is the **changing** of responses in an audience, to alter their behavior toward a product, concept, or idea. Typically, the persuasive speaker attempting to change responses asks the audience to start and/or stop some behavior: stop smoking, start using mass transportation, use acupuncture, have cosmetic surgery, eat low cholesterol foods, or drink Pepsi instead of Coke. In many ways changing responses can be a difficult task. You can shape someone's responses toward the new and novel without seriously upsetting their lives; you can take advantage of the inertia of everyday living when you reinforce responses; but change often comes hard for human beings if it requires any serious altering of well-established habits or ideas. In the past, shaping has been closely associated with learning; reinforcing has been largely ignored as a persuasive purpose; but changing responses has been the main focus of persuasive speaking for two millennia; so it needs no further justification here.

Now that you have read about these three goals of persuasive speaking, try to identify in the purposes below which of the three is being described. Place an S in the blank for shaping responses, an R in the blank for reinforcing, and a C in the blank for changing responses.

Application Exercise 2: Shaping, Reinforcing, and Changing

_____ 1. To secure twelve signatures on this petition against nuclear armament.

_____ 2. To thank the audience for their participation in my campaign for auditor of Franklin County

_____ 3. To encourage the audience to start thinking like Republicans on some of the major issues

_____ 4. To get at least three of my classmates to stand up and state that I have changed their minds about donating blood

_____ 5. To drop in and talk to the management analysts at InCo Corporation (who bought a computer from me a few months ago) just to make sure that everything is still satisfactory

Answers: 1-C, 2-R, 3-S, 4-C, 5-R.

Now that you have a better idea of how the three purposes of persuasive speaking work, we can turn to some principles of persuasion that you can apply in your persuasive speeches.

Just as in the chapter on informative speaking we examined some principles of learning that can be used in informative speaking, so in this chapter we will examine some principles of persuasion that you may use in your persuasive message. Following are five principles of persuasion that you should keep in mind as you prepare your persuasive speeches.

Five Principles of Persuasion

Principles of Persuasion

1. Consistency persuades
2. Small changes persuade
3. Benefits persuade
4. Fulfilling needs persuades
5. Gradual approaches persuade

Consistency Persuades

The first principle of persuasion is that audiences are more likely to change their behavior if the suggested change is *consistent* with their present beliefs, attitudes, and values. Attitudes have already been defined as predispositions to like or dislike, and values have been defined earlier as more enduring end-states of existence or broad modes of behavior. **Beliefs** are explained most succinctly by Martin Fishbein:

> Two persons who are equally opposed to segregation may have quite different conceptions of its nature, causes, and consequences and may hold different views concerning the actions that should be taken to eliminate segregation. . . . These two persons are said to have the same attitudes toward segregation but to hold different beliefs about it. Attitudes are learned predispositions to respond to an object or class of objects in a favorable or unfavorable way. Beliefs, on the other hand, are hypotheses concerning the nature of these objects and the types of actions that should be taken with respect to them.[5]

These beliefs may be taken for granted (an object exists even when we are not looking at it), or based on our senses (I can feel and see that a bowling ball is round), or based on external authority (my father told me never to trust a salesperson).[6]

The person who tries to persuade another person needs to recognize that values, attitudes, and beliefs reflect different levels of conviction, with values being the most difficult to alter and beliefs the least difficult. It is also necessary to recognize that whatever is suggested as a behavioral change will be more likely to succeed if it is consistent with some value, attitude, or belief that the audience already holds. Finally, the persuader needs to recognize that people's attitudes, beliefs, and values are sometimes in conflict with each other. For example, a person may believe in the general proposition that all persons are created equal (a value) but still hold quite strongly to the notion that neighborhood schools should be all black or all white (a belief) and dislike persons who are not very much like himself or herself (an attitude). On the other hand, the person may consistently hang onto these attitudes, beliefs, and values with little variation over a lifetime.

The persuasive speaker uses this **consistency** over time by assessing the chances for shaping, reinforcing, or changing the audience, and by measuring the message against the audience's present position. People who have already given money toward a certain cause are the most likely to give more to the same and similar causes. That behavior is consistent. People who value competition are the most likely candidates to enter into still another competitive situation; people who believe in segregating old people into communities or institutions of their own (a belief) will be the most likely to accept or even promote a bond issue for more separate housing for the aged; and persons who dislike immigrants (an attitude) will openly discourage their movement into the neighborhood. The effective persuader uses audience consistency to shape, reinforce, or change.

The second principle of persuasion is that audiences are more likely to alter their behavior if the suggested change will require small rather than large changes in their behavior. A common error of beginning speakers is that they ask for too much change too soon for too little reason. Audiences are reluctant to change, and any changes they do make are likely to be small ones. Nonetheless, the successful persuasive speaker determines what small changes an audience would be willing to accept consistent with the persuasive purpose.

Small Changes Persuade

What if you, as a persuader, are faced with an audience of overweight Americans who are loath to exercise and resistant to reduced eating? Your temptation might be to ask for too much too soon: quit eating so much and start losing weight. The message would likely fall on unreceptive ears, because it is both inconsistent with present behavior and asking for too much change too soon. You could limit your persuasive message by encouraging the audience to give up specific foods, or a specific food that is part of their problem. However, an even better example of a small change consistent with the audience's present behavior would be to have them switch from regular to dietetic ice cream. An audience that would reject a weight-loss program might be more willing simply to switch from one form of food to another, because that change would be minimally upsetting to their present life patterns.

Are there any qualifications or limitations on this second principle of persuasion? One factor that needs to be considered in deciding how much to ask of an audience is their commitment level. Studies in social judgment show that highly committed persons, people who believe most intensely or strongly about an issue, are highly resistant to any positions on the issue except their own or ones very close to it. To such an audience, reinforcement would be welcome, shaping would be a challenge, and change would be very difficult indeed. On the other hand, audience members who do not feel strongly about an issue are susceptible to larger changes than are those who already have established positions to which they are committed.

To state the principle more concretely: a speaker addressing a religious rally of persons who abhor drinking, dancing, and smoking can get warm acceptance for a persuasive message that reinforces or rewards those ideas; he would be greeted with cautious skepticism with a speech attempting to shape any responses different from those already established; and he would be met with outright rejection if he requested changes in behavior that run counter to those already embraced. On the other hand, a heterogeneous audience of persons uncommitted on the issue of regular exercise would be susceptible to considerable response shaping, and an audience of the already committed would receive reinforcement and would at least consider adopting some small changes in behavior. The successful persuader is skilled at discerning which small changes, consistent with the persuasive purpose, can be asked of an audience.

Benefits Persuade

The third principle of persuasion is that audiences are more likely to change their behavior if the suggested change will benefit them more than it will cost them. **Cost-benefit analysis,** for example, is considered every time we buy something: "Do I want this new jacket even though it means I must spend $50.00 plus tax? The benefits are that I will be warm and will look nice. The cost is that I will not be able to get my shoes resoled or buy a new watch." The persuader frequently demonstrates to an audience that the benefits are worth the cost.

A student who sold vacuum cleaners told of a fellow sales representative who donned white gloves and a surgical mask when he looked at the customer's old vacuum cleaner. By the time he had inspected the brush and changed the bag, he was filthy. He would then demonstrate that the old vacuum threw dust all over the house as it dragged across the carpet. By the end of his sales pitch, the sales representative was going to try to convince the customer that the old vacuum was not only ineffective, but also increased the amount of dirt flying around the house. The cost of the new vacuum would, according to this sales representative, be worth the benefit of owning a cleaning machine that picked up dirt instead of spreading it around. Remember that you need to reveal to your audience the benefits that make your proposal worth the cost.

How can you use cost-benefit analysis in your classroom speech? Consider the costs to the audience of doing as you ask. What are the costs in money, time, commitment, energy, skill, or talent? Consider one of the most common requests in student speeches: write to your representative or senator. Many student speakers make that request without considering the probability that nobody in class has ever written to a senator or representative. Even if the speaker includes an address, the letter writing will take commitment, time, and even a little money. Few students are willing to pay those costs. On the other hand, if the speaker comes to class with an already written letter and simply asks for signatures from the class, then the cost is a few seconds of time, and the speaker is more likely to gain audience cooperation. Whenever you deliver a persuasive speech, consider the costs and how you can reduce them so the audience will feel they are worth your proposed benefits.

Fulfilling Needs Persuades

The fourth principle of persuasion is that audiences are more likely to change their behavior if the suggested change meets their needs. Abraham Maslow has provided an often quoted **hierarchy of needs.**[7] His hierarchy includes physiological needs like oxygen, food, water, and rest; safety needs like security from physical and psychological harm; love needs like approval and acceptance; esteem

needs like recognition and self-respect; and self-actualization needs like self-fulfillment. The order of these needs is important. The first must be met before the second comes into play, and so on down the line.

Maslow's hierarchy of needs makes sense: you need oxygen to breathe more than you need money for tuition. However, you may find the concept of needs more useful in classroom speeches if you analyze your own class for specific needs that are relevant to your community, your college, and your class. For example, the biggest unmet need of the majority in your class may be a need to earn higher grades, to secure work, to find time for study, or to find a place to park. See if you can assess the important unmet needs of your classmates by completing Application Exercise 3.

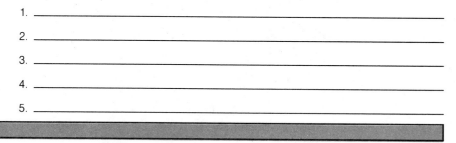

Application Exercise 3: Student Hierarchy of Needs

Persuasive speeches often appeal to an audience's unmet needs. Since needs vary in different communities, colleges, classes, and individuals, you can make yourself more sensitive to audience needs by rank ordering five unmet needs that you believe are important to your audience.

1. _____
2. _____
3. _____
4. _____
5. _____

Gradual Approaches Persuade

The effectiveness of a persuasive speech hinges on audience acceptance of the speaker's suggested changes in their lives. The principle explained in this section suggests that a gradual approach is more likely to work than one in which the audience is asked too soon for the behavioral change. The effective persuader often begins with common ground and coorientation to demonstrate his or her similarities to the audience in background and ideas. The successful persuader frequently moves from the arguments and evidence that the audience finds most acceptable to those that the audience will find harder to accept. Persuasion is a kind of seduction in which the audience is more likely to cooperate after courtship than after a brash proposition.

Consider what you would do if you found yourself in the embarrassing position of wanting to borrow $25.00 from someone you did not know well. You probably would not start by saying "Give me $25.00." Instead, you might begin with harmless conversation about the weather, the room you are in, or the way each of you looks. Eventually, you would get around to the hard luck story that brought you to the predicament of needing money. You might hint that you wish you could find someone to lend you some money until the following week. Ultimately, you might ask if the other person could help you by lending you the money.

Similarly, in a persuasive speech you do not start by saying, "I want you to donate your eyes to the eye bank." Instead, you start gently with "safe" information about how many people have been saved from blindness by cornea transplants. You mention that the program is sponsored by the local Lion's Club. You reveal how many other people in the community, students in particular, have signed papers to allow their eyes to be used to help another person. Only after this careful courtship do you reveal that you have pledge cards for them to sign if they have compassion for their fellow human beings. The behavioral change—the signing of a commitment card—is the end result of a gradual approach.

Remember, as you prepare your persuasive speech, that audiences are more likely to change their behavior if the suggested change is consistent with their present beliefs, attitudes, and values; if it requires small rather than large changes in their lives; if it benefits them more than it costs them; if it meets their needs; and if it is a culmination of acceptable ideas. With these principles to apply in your persuasive speeches, you can move now to the matter of content in the persuasive speech.

After reading the section on principles of persuasion, you should be able to identify cases in which they are correctly used. Examine the cases below and indicate in the margin which of the following principles is being observed:

C = consistency persuades
S = small changes persuade
B = benefits persuade
N = fulfilling needs persuades
G = gradual approaches persuade

Application Exercise 4: Principles of Persuasion

_____ 1. To save my audience considerable time and effort, I am going to provide them with a form letter which they can sign and send to the administration.

_____ 2. Because I know that most of my classmates are short of cash, I am going to tell them how to make some quick money with on-campus jobs.

_____ 3. I plan to wait until the very end of the speech to tell the audience that the organization I want them to join will require two hours of driving per week.

_____ 4. My audience of international students already believes in the values of learning public speaking; so I think they will respond favorably to my recommendation for a course in voice and articulation.

_____ 5. I really want my audience to believe in Jesus Christ the way I do, but I'll try today to simply get them to consider going to church while they are in college.

Answers: 1-B, 2-N, 3-G, 4-C, 5-S.

Reasoning in Persuasive Speaking	How can you convince an audience that your idea meets their needs? How can you demonstrate the benefits of your plan? How can you show that your idea is consistent with the audience's present beliefs, attitudes, and values? One of the two primary methods of persuading an audience is through reasoning—through the use of arguments with reasons, evidence, and inferences. To begin to understand reasoning, you will need to know the difference between inductive and deductive reasoning, the two categories into which reasoning can be divided.[8]

Inductive Reasoning	**Inductive reasoning** consists of reasons, usually in the form of evidence, that lead to a generalization. The following example illustrates the form of inductive reasoning:

> Professor X gave me a D in history.
> Professor X gave Fs to two of my friends in the same course.
> Professor X posted a grade distribution with many Ds and Fs.
> Professor X boasts about his rigorous grading standards. Therefore,
> Professor X is a hard grader [generalization].

Inductive reasoning, then, provides evidence that gives you an "inferential lead" to the generalization. Inductive reasoning requires an inference because a generalization is drawn that is probably, but not unquestionably, true—based on the evidence.

In the argument above, the **generalization** that Professor X is a hard grader remains only a probability, even with the evidence presented. What if both you and your friends are poor history students, and the posted distribution was for a "bonehead" history course open only to students with poor academic records? You need to remember that in inductive reasoning, the persuader gathers evidence that leads to a *probable* generalization, but that generalization can always be questioned by reinterpretation of old evidence or the introduction of contrary evidence.

Deductive Reasoning	**Deductive reasoning** is a second way to apply logic to your argument. In inductive reasoning you have a generalization supported by or induced from the evidence; in deductive reasoning you have a **conclusion** deduced from a major and a minor premise. Instead of resulting in a probability, as inductive reasoning does, the deductive argument results in a conclusion that necessarily follows from the two premises. A deductive argument looks like this:

> Major premise: All insects have six legs;
> Minor premise: ants are insects;
> Conclusion: therefore, ants have six legs.

Notice that if the premises are true, then the conclusion must necessarily be true also, because in a sense the two premises are the same thing as the conclusion.

PEANUTS • By Charles M. Schulz

In conversation and even in most speeches, a deductive argument usually does not sound or look quite as formal as it appears above. In fact, the argument cited above would more likely appear in a speech like this: "Since all insects have six legs, ants must too." The reasoning is still deductive, except that the minor premise is implied rather than openly stated. This can make deductive arguments difficult to analyze—or even detect—in actual speeches. For this reason, it is necessary to listen closely to the reasoning in speeches, in order to determine what has been implied—or *seemed* to be implied, but actually wasn't—in addition to what has been stated openly.

On the other hand, if you feel you have particularly strong deductive arguments in your own speech, you should take the time to state them clearly and completely. Well-reasoned deductive arguments can have great persuasive power because, once the audience has accepted the validity of the premises, *the conclusion is inescapable*. Mathematical proofs commonly take the form of deductive arguments, and the reasoning in your own speech should have all the clarity and impact of such proofs: if A equals B, and if B equals C, then A equals C.

Tests of Reasoning

You can apply several "tests" to correctly identify inductive and deductive reasoning. One test is to observe if the argument moves from the general to the particular ("All adolescents have skin problems; therefore, since Amanda is an adolescent, she must have skin problems"). If so, the argument is probably deductive. A second test is to see if the argument moves from a big category to a small or individual one ("All people have fears; so our enemies must have fears also"). If so, the argument is probably deductive. A third test is to observe if the argument moves from a small group or collection of individuals to a large one ("Randy drinks beer, Cindy drinks beer, and Rod drinks beer; so they must be alcoholics"). If so, then the argument is probably inductive.[9]

Try application exercise 5 to test your own skill at identifying inductive and deductive reasoning.

Application Exercise 5: Inductive and Deductive Reasoning

Using the "tests" described above and the descriptions of inductive and deductive reasoning, identify each of the following arguments, with I for Inductive or D for Deductive, by placing the appropriate letter in the blank on the left.

_____ 1. Sam, Fred, and Joan are all rich; therefore, most people in this community must be rich.

_____ 2. College students always cause mischief; so Andy must be a college student.

_____ 3. Other states have raised the drinking age to reduce accidents; therefore, this state should raise the drinking age also.

_____ 4. Americans practice freedom of speech; so those students in the public speaking class must be Americans.

_____ 5. Every time I drink milk I break out with hives; so I must have an allergy.

Answers: 1-I, 2,3-I, 4-D, 5-I.

Evaluating Evidence

We have examined inductive and deductive reasoning. In order to be effective persuaders, we must also understand what evidence is and how to evaluate it. What is evidence? **Evidence** consists of the reasons why a claim should be accepted or believed. Evidence can be physical: in a trial, a gun, a blood sample, or a fingerprint can be used as evidence that a particular person murdered another person. In speeches, evidence often is presented through language and numbers. Statistics, testimony of experts, and results of surveys and studies can provide evidence to back a claim. Examples, illustrations, comparisons, and analogies can serve as supporting material and clarifiers but are not considered strong when used as evidence or proof. In inductive reasoning, however, the quantity and quality of the evidence can make the resulting generalization more or less probable; so the person who wants to persuade needs to know about evidence and how it can be evaluated.

Tests of Types of Evidence

Evidence takes various forms. Evidence used in speeches consists of (1) testimony, (2) statistics, (3) example, (4) comparison, and (5) analogy. This section will explain the forms and tell you how to evaluate each kind.

Forms of Evidence

1. Testimony
2. Statistics
3. Example
4. Comparison
5. Analogy

We will start our exploration of the **tests of evidence** with the kind of evidence that occurs frequently in classroom speeches: testimonial evidence. **Testimonial evidence** is an opinion, usually by an expert, that lends authority to whatever you are claiming in your speech. For example, I might quote the U.S. Surgeon General as an authority on some aspect of health because I know my audience is more likely to believe that person than me on that subject.

Testimony

Testimonial evidence needs to be evaluated on five grounds: expertise, proximity, time, tension, and freedom.[10] The person giving the opinion must be qualified—by education, experience, rank or office—to speak on the issue, in order to meet the criterion of **expertise.** The person giving the opinion must have been close enough to the issue, figuratively or literally, to meet the criterion of **proximity.** The person must provide the opinion as soon as possible after an observation or event, so that it does not get distorted by other events or memory decay, in order to meet the criterion of **time.** The person must express the opinion in a milieu as free of **tension** and trauma as possible, lest the upheaval of the moment (e.g., witnesses to an accident) distort the testimony. And finally, the testimony should come from someone who has the **freedom** to present an unbiased opinion, unhampered by written or unwritten rules of an employer, a government, or a culture. For example, an employee of IBM is in an awkward position to denigrate an IBM product or praise a competitor's product. Evaluating testimonial evidence becomes largely a matter of whom you and your audience trust. Close examination of these five dimensions of testimonial evidence may give you a better understanding of why you do or do not trust a source of evidence.

Statistics

A second kind of evidence that the persuader needs to evaluate is **statistical evidence.** Statistics can be a strong form of evidence if they are gathered under rigorous procedures, used with sufficient context to help the audience interpret them, and are pertinent to the claim. As a speaker you must understand what an average, a percentage, and other statistical measures mean. As in the case of testimonial evidence, where you got the statistics or who provided them can increase or decrease their credibility.

Some specific considerations in evaluating statistics include the following: Who made up the subject pool from which the statistics were drawn? Was the number of people in the study large enough to allow you to generalize to the population? And is there a causal link between your evidence and your conclusion? In general, the best subject pool is a random sample of the group being studied. If everyone has an equal chance of being selected, the resulting statistics will be stronger than if some persons have a better chance of being selected than others. The number of persons participating in a study also makes a difference. Sometimes very few of the persons randomly selected to participate actually return questionnaires, show up for the experiment, or complete the activity for which they were selected. The more the people who were selected actually participate, the stronger the statistics based on the sample. Finally, if you can show that one thing causes another (a temperature of 32 degrees Fahrenheit causes freezing of water), then you have stronger evidence than you would have with a correlation (increased obesity correlates positively with increased instances of diabetes). Statistics are only as strong as the methods by which they are derived; so the persuader needs to provide information that will enable the audience to interpret and understand the figures.

A third form of evidence that can be a powerful persuader—even if it is regarded *Example*
as a relatively weak form of proof—is the **example.** The persuader evaluates the
example by asking how typical it is in the general population or in the group
being examined. To point out that one bank clerk embezzeled $50,000.00 is an
interesting example of white collar crime, but it does not permit you to generalize
about bank clerks—unless you can show that the clerk's behavior was typical.
The more typical the example, the stronger it stands as evidence in support of a
claim.

A fourth kind of evidence that can be used in support of a claim is the **compar-** *Comparison*
ison. Basically, a comparison argument states that when two items are very much
alike, an idea that has worked for one will probably work for the other. Mary
and Beth are both 13 year-old females who go to the same school, share the same
friends, and even live in the same suburb; therefore, the bedtime policy that has
worked so successfully for Mary's parents should be tried by Beth's. The best
way to evaluate a comparison is to recognize that the more you can demonstrate
that the compared items are alike, the greater are the chances that what is good
or bad for one is good or bad for the other. In short, you need to ask of comparison
evidence: how much are the compared items alike?

A fifth type of evidence, which is perhaps weakest of all as proof but can help *Analogy*
increase clarity, is the **analogy.** Remember from the earlier chapter on supporting
material that the analogy compares two items that are basically different: People
are similar to their canine friends—the more you stroke them, the better they
like you. The analogy used as proof is relatively easy to attack; all you have to
do is demonstrate all the ways the compared objects are different from each other
to show that they are probably also unlike in the way proposed.

In addition to these specific inquiries that you can use to evaluate different types *General Questions*
of evidence, there are some general questions that you can ask about evidence.
Among them: Is your evidence consistent with other known evidence? Is there
any evidence to the contrary? And does your generalization go beyond your evidence? The more your evidence is consistent with other known evidence, the
stronger it is likely to be perceived. Conversely, the less consistent your evidence
is with other known facts, the less likely it is to be believed. The existence of any
evidence to the contrary can challenge your generalization. The person who says
that no one has ever died from using aspirin can have multiple millions of cases
in support, but a single death can render the generalization untrue.

Finally, there is another feature of evidence and its use in reasoning that makes **Believability**
a big difference to the speaker as persuader. The questions to ask in evaluating **of Evidence**
evidence are just one aspect of how evidence works. The other, equally important,
aspect is whether or not the evidence is believable to your audience. Human beings
tend to doubt statements about which they disagree: smokers deny the negative

effects of smoke on their lungs; overweight people blame their condition on metabolism or glands; and poor students often portray themselves as victims of teacher abuse. Evidence that counters what a person already believes will be met by resistance, rejection, and disbelief. Effective evidence, then, needs to meet two kinds of tests: the tests of evidence and the test of **believability.**

Appeals to the Emotions

Thus far in this chapter, we have considered reasoning and logical appeals. However, the persuasive speaker needs to recognize that reasoning is not the only means of securing change in an audience's mind or actions. As one writer put it:

> The creature man is best persuaded
> When heart, not mind, is inundated;
> Affect is what drives the will;
> Rationality keeps it still.[11]

Among the multitude of ways that a persuader can persuade, the use of reason has the highest regard. Appeals to an audience's emotions, on the other hand, are often treated as a less reputable means of achieving a persuasive purpose. We examine them in this book not because we encourage their unqualified use, but because you will have occasion to hear and use them. We will move first through some of the **emotional appeals** that are regarded as a bit questionable and end up with one that we advocate for your persuasive speeches.

Monroe Beardsley, in his book *Thinking Straight,*[12] provides over 300 pages of information on how reasoning and logic can be applied in everyday circumstances. Among the emotional appeals that he discusses are: (1) appeal to pity, (2) alarm, (3) flattery, (4) identification with the audience, (5) *ad hominem* argument, (6) argument from illegitimate authority, (7) oversimplification, and (8) distraction. Some of these emotional appeals have not been carefully examined by serious researchers, so their actual effectiveness is unknown. Nonetheless, we will examine some that invite further clarification and examine closely any that have been systematically analyzed for their effectiveness.

Types of Emotional Appeals

1. Pity
2. Alarm
3. Flattery
4. Identification with the audience
5. *Ad hominem* argument
6. Argument from illegitimate authority
7. Oversimplification
8. Distraction

Persuasive Speaking

Emotional appeals are unsatisfactory because they can distract from the "real issue" that can best be addressed by reason. To flatter an audience or to evoke their pity, for example, is to seek behavioral change through affection or avoidance instead of through reasons and evidence. The use of "identification with the audience"—advocated elsewhere in this text—is portrayed in Beardsley's book as an attempt to get the audience to do something simply because the speaker has many similarities with the audience, not because there is a logical reason for doing so.

The **ad hominem** (add hom-ah-nim) **argument** is one that attacks another speaker as a person, for reasons that have little or nothing to do with the issue. For example, the speaker, unable to think of reasons why the audience should not listen to the opponent, starts attacking him on grounds that are unrelated to the issue: "He is an arrogant snob who is not even from this city!" *Ad hominem* means literally "to the man," that is, the argument goes to the speaker instead of "to the thing" *(ad rem)* or the issue.[13] The use of *ad hominem* arguments in persuasive speeches is not recommended, but the persuasive speaker should learn to recognize why it is discouraged in rational argument.

Ad Hominem
Argument

Illegitimate Authority	The argument from **illegitimate authority** is one in which the speaker states opinions beyond his or her area of expertise. Television personalities, movie stars, popular authors, and even political and religious leaders sometimes are asked for opinions on topics for which their level of expertise is no greater than your own. You need to ask yourself if the person with the latest hit record is an authority on the economy, if the atomic scientist is an expert on nutrition, or if the talk show host is an expert on anything. To be well-known is not the same as knowing something about an issue.
Oversimplification	**Oversimplification** means reducing the issue until it no longer represents the real complexity of the problem. Lowering interest rates will fix the economy, finding welfare cheats will solve our financial problems, and better communication will eliminate the problem of divorce—these are all examples of oversimplification. Oversimplification can also mean the omission of contrary evidence. A speaker might be able to make an apparently strong case for the electric chair by leaving out any evidence against it. Most controversial issues in our society reflect complex problems that demand complex solutions; oversimplification can be the enemy of reasoned discourse.
Distraction	**Distraction** is the shift of attention from the main issue to a side issue. One method of distraction, used all too often in the courtroom, is to amass so much evidence—some relevant and some not—that neither judge nor jury can reach a reasonable conclusion. Another method of distraction is to bring up a side issue about which people feel strongly. The speech about why we should have a national health policy that emphasizes prevention can be distracted quickly by the opponent who gets people arguing about whether this is a communist or socialist solution to our national health problems.
Fear Appeals	The only category of emotional appeals that has been studied extensively is the use of alarm or **fear appeals**. Janis and Feshbach examined three levels of fear appeals in dental hygiene communication and found that the least threatening appeal worked better than the moderate fear appeal, which in turn worked better than the strong fear appeal.[14] Powell, on the other hand, found that a strong fear appeal worked better than weak fear appeals in civil defense messages.[15] Apparently there is no agreement that one kind of fear appeal will work better than another, but people do seem to be more persuaded when a loved one is threatened than when they themselves are.[16]
	The most solid conclusion to emerge from the research on fear appeals is that the persuader should include reassurance in the message. Apparently, when the persuader simply generates a high degree of fear, the audience protects itself by means of avoidance, by rejecting the message. The presence of reassuring recommendations—some way to avoid the threat—results in greater shifts of opinion and more positive evaluations of the speaker.[17] If you use alarm or fear appeals, then, they should be accompanied by recommendations for avoiding or overcoming the fear.

Many of the emotional appeals reviewed so far are discouraged in public speaking because appeals to hate or prejudice are seen as negative in our society and because appeals to sympathy, pity, and even love are often seen as inappropriate. No self-respecting persuader endorses the use of the *ad hominem* argument or appeals to illegitimate authority, oversimplification, distraction, or fear. Nonetheless, there is one persuasive technique that is basically emotional in its impact but that has not received the negative ratings shared by the others. That is the narrative or story.

The narrative or story can include many appeals to the emotions, but it escapes the harsh judgment of the appeals cited above because it rarely poses as evidence or argument; instead, it adds interest value and dramatic impact to the persuasive speech. The narrative may have avoided negative criticism because of the company it keeps. Most of the world's holy books—the Bible, the Koran, and the Book of Mormon, to name a few—are full of stories, allegories, and parables. Well-known evangelists like Oral Roberts and Billy Graham persuade through dramatic stories. You can learn from them that the use of narratives or stories can persuade. Sometimes a speech full of statistics about the poor can have less impact on an audience than one story about an actual family that had to resort to eating dogfood and garbage because of their plight.

Narrative

Now that you have an argument that meets the tests of evidence and the requirement of believability—and now that you are at least familiar with the basic emotional appeals—what are you supposed to do? This section answers these questions: When should you present only arguments in favor of your case? When should you present both sides of an issue? What does the educational level of your audience have to do with presenting a one-sided or two-sided treatment of the issue? Why should you be careful not to omit important arguments in your presentation? And what other factors should you keep in mind as you put together your persuasive speech?

Presenting Sides, Citing Sources, and Putting Together a Persuasive Speech

First, when should you present a **one-sided approach**—that is, only arguments and evidence in favor of your position on an issue? Research seems to indicate that pro-arguments and evidence are more effective when the audience already agrees with your position; in fact, a two-sided approach appears to work less well for such an audience. A **two-sided approach** tends to work better when the audience is basically opposed to your point of view. An educated audience, like your classmates, are also usually more favorably disposed to a two-sided approach, while less-educated persons tend to favor only a one-sided presentation with supporting arguments. Why should you be careful to include relevant arguments that the audience knows? The absence of a relevant argument is more noticeable to an audience in a two-sided approach than in a one-sided approach with supporting arguments only.[18] Finally, if your audience is likely to hear arguments against your position from others, you can reduce the impact of those counterarguments by mentioning them openly in your own persuasive speech.[19]

A caution also is in order concerning your use of facts, statistics, testimony, and studies in your persuasive speech. You are expected to use oral footnotes to indicate where you found your information, whether it was from a written source, a person you interviewed, or a television program. Verifying information with oral footnotes allows the audience to check on the information. One research study indicated that an authority-based claim, in which you state who said what, may slightly improve your own credibility. However, using a claim made by an authority was only slightly better than a claim not made by an authority in changing the audience's attitude.[20] Standard classroom practice, the rules of scholarly research, and the ethics of persuasive speaking all support the idea that the persuasive speaker should reveal the sources of information to the audience.

As you begin to put together your persuasive speech, you will want to be sure that your speech observes the principles of persuasion as stated in this chapter. Be sure that your speech includes audience analysis to determine what the audience needs, includes tests of evidence to determine the soundness of your arguments and evidence, and includes audience analysis to determine the requirement of believability. See that the speech's message suggests some change in the audience's perceptions of the issue (i.e., shaping of responses). You should exercise care in deciding on a one-sided or two-sided approach, recognize the educational level of your audience, and include any arguments that your audience will deem relevant. You should examine your arguments to make sure that your generalizations follow from the evidence, that the evidence is relevant to the generalization, and that it is verifiable through an oral footnote for anyone who may choose to check. Keeping these things in mind, we are now prepared to consider the different types of persuasive speeches in which they occur (just as we discussed the various types of informative speeches in the last chapter).

Types of Persuasive Speeches

The main distinction between the informative and the persuasive speech is its purpose: the informative speech attempts to increase what an audience *knows;* the persuasive speech attempts to change what an audience *does* by shaping, reinforcing, or altering their behavior. The three types of persuasive speeches that we will examine here are the speech of reasons, the speech of opposition, and the speech of action.

The Speech of Reasons

The primary persuasive purpose of the speech of reasons is to change the audience's mind on an issue by reasoning to shape their responses to it. This speech uses logic, evidence, inferences, generalizations, and conclusions to convince the audience to respond favorably to a specific position on an issue. It might result in a measurable shift of opinion, which one could record on a questionnaire or determine from responses from an audience, showing that they now see the issue differently. People who already believe as the speaker advocates hear a speech that reinforces their responses on the issue. They might register their agreement on the evaluation form or in the question and answer period. However, the majority of persons in the audience should not already agree with the position; otherwise, it would simply be a speech to reinforce rather than to shape an audience's responses.

As you approach your assignment, one of your first problems will be to select a topic. You can brainstorm or draw on your education and experience to find a suitable topic for you and for your audience. To give you a few ideas for speeches that are designed to shape the audience's responses, the following list is provided.

1. The Drinking Age Should Be Raised to Twenty-five.
2. Tuition Should Be Raised.
3. Computer Courses Should Be Required in College.
4. Hearing Loss: A Reason to Avoid Live Bands.
5. Why Speaking and Writing Should Be Required in College Courses.
6. Reading Newspapers: A Lost Art among College Students.
7. Why College Youth Should Oppose Social Security.
8. A Regular Program of Exercise Can Harm You.
9. Why Students Should Avoid Law and Medicine.
10. Five Reasons Why You Should Not Be a Business Major.

One characteristic that all ten topics have in common is that the majority of students in the audience probably would not agree. If they were to agree, then the topic is probably inappropriate for this assignment. Use the list to generate some ideas of your own on topics for the assignment described below.

A second type of persuasive speech, the speech of opposition, is one in which you oppose ideas that are commonly believed or that have been presented by someone else. Let us say that you heard a classmate take a position in her speech of reasons that you profoundly disagree with. You want to prove her wrong; so you proceed to research the issue and make your counterargument in the speech of opposition. You state your disagreement; point out any flaws in the other person's arguments, reasoning, evidence, inferences, generalizations, and conclusions; and try to shape the audience's responses in another direction.

The Speech of Opposition

A second approach to the speech of opposition is to deliver a speech that attacks society's "sacred cows": the ideas, concepts, and practices that go largely unquestioned because they are so widely obeyed or accepted. Some examples of speeches of opposition that will oppose what another student said or attack some commonly held belief are illustrated below:

1. The Case for Nuclear War.
2. Why Fight Extinction of Rare Animals and Birds?
3. Some Major Reforms Needed in Higher Education.
4. Why the Government Should Operate the Steel, Gas, and Oil Industries.
5. Speech Anxiety: the Case against Public Speaking.

6. Negative Aspects of Organized Religion in America.
7. The Effect of Computers on Families.
8. Why America Should Eliminate Automobiles.
9. How to Wean Yourself from Your Television.
10. Why Reading and Writing Are Unnecessary Today.

The purpose of the speech of opposition is to help the speaker and the audience recognize that there are usually reasonable arguments on both sides of issues that go undiscussed. The speech of opposition encourages skills in analysis of argument, researching for additional evidence, and selecting arguments that an audience will find persuasive.

What exactly are you to do in rebutting someone else's ideas? A careful look at the section on reasoning in this chapter suggests these important questions: Did the speaker reveal the source of evidence through oral footnotes? Were those sources expert, objective, and legitimate? Did the generalization go beyond the evidence? Did the reasons and the evidence lead to the generalization? Was there any unmentioned contradictory evidence? In addition to these general inquiries about someone else's position on an issue, you may want to keep alert for any fallacies that you can detect in your opponent's speech.

Fallacies are violations of the rules of inference.[21] Listed are some of the more common fallacies, with an example of each to help you recognize them.

Common Fallacies

1. Hasty generalization
2. *Post hoc, ergo propter hoc*
3. Cross-ranking
4. Equivocation
5. Argument from analogy

The **hasty generalization** violates the rules of inference by drawing a generalization based on too little evidence. Example: I have in the past employed two white, male workers. Both proved to be poor employees. Therefore, I have vowed never again to hire a white, male employee. Problem: the sample—two persons— was too small and not random; also, the generalization does not account for the many other reasons why the employees may have been inadequate.

The **post hoc, ergo propter hoc** ("after this; therefore, because of this") fallacy confuses correlation with causation. Just because one thing happens *after* another does not necessarily mean that it was *caused* by it. Example: I found that I was pregnant right after our trip; therefore, going on a trip must cause pregnancy. Problem: the trip may have correlated (occurred at the same time) with the onset of pregnancy, but the trip is not necessarily the cause.

The **cross-ranking fallacy** violates the rules of inference by using more than one basis of comparison at the same time. Example: I want to classify the basketball players in the NBA into (a) tall players, (b) black players, and (c) high-scoring players and then compare their performances. Problem: height, color, and skill are three different bases of comparison; so a tall, black, high-scoring player fits in all three categories and so in a sense is merely being compared with himself.

The **equivocation fallacy** means that a word is used in several different ways to make it appear more relevant than it is. Example: Johnny is a juvenile delinquent for talking to his mother that way. Problem: the term *juvenile delinquent* is a legal term for under-aged children who commit serious crimes; verbal abuse to one's mother is not such a crime.

The **argument from analogy fallacy** means that an analogy compares two unlike things, asserts that they have something in common, but then goes too far by suggesting that still another characteristic is common to both. Example: Both England and the United States have democratic governments, both have laws that spring from "common law," and both have problems with crime. England has fewer deaths from police bullets because their police, the bobbies, do not carry guns. Therefore, we should disarm our police to reduce the problem of police killing citizens. An argument from analogy necessarily omits important differences (fewer English criminals are armed), making the argument from analogy a weak form of argument.

Add to these five fallacies the two that you learned earlier—oversimplification and distraction—and you have seven fallacies to add to the general criticisms that you can make about another person's reasoning in your speech of opposition.

The Speech of Action

This last type of persuasive speech is a culmination of all that you have learned about public speaking. You can and should use the defining, describing, explaining, demonstrating, and investigating that you learned in the informative speech. You should include the reinforcing of responses among those who already believe as you do, the shaping of responses for those whose perceptions you wish to alter, and the changing of responses for those who do not believe as you do. The most important aspect of the speech of action is that its purpose is to induce an overt change in the audience, to get them to do something in response to your speech.

The speech of action should use the principles of persuasion. It should (1) suggest change that is consistent with present beliefs, attitudes, and values; (2) suggest change that will require small rather than large changes in their lives; (3) suggest changes that will benefit the audience more than it will cost them; (4) suggest changes that meet the audience's needs; and (5) approach the change gradually in the speech.

Because the speech of action is successful only if the audience is actually moved to action, the speech can use a mixture of rational and emotional appeals. You may wish to show the audience that you share their concern because of what you have in common with them; you may wish to use fear appeals with reassurance; or you may wish to include narrations or stories that give your speech dramatic

impact. You should avoid the use of arguments and evidence or emotional appeals that are unethical, such as appeals to hate, prejudice, sexism, or racism. And you should avoid appeals based on flattery, *ad hominem,* oversimplification, distraction, or distortion. Use of these types of emotional appeals can result in a *boomerang effect* in which the audience dislikes you and/or your topic more after the speech than they did before the speech.

The speech of action allows you to express your own feeling and opinions based on your own experience, but the best speeches of this type rely heavily on expert testimony, careful reasoning, and the use of good evidence that meets the tests of quality and believability. A review of inductive and deductive reasoning and the tests of evidence and generalization are in order.

Two research findings are relevant to the speech of action. The first research finding is that a highly credible speaker can ask for more change in an audience—and get it—than can a speaker who is perceived as low or moderate in credibility.[22] The speech of action is likely to be one of the last that you deliver in your public speaking class. By now you should know more about your credibility with your classmates. If you sense that you are perceived as highly credible by your classmates, then perhaps you can ask for more change from your audience and get it. The second research finding relevant to the speech of action is that the speaker who explicitly asks for an audience's overt response is more likely to get it than will the speaker who only hints, implies, or suggests that the audience take some action.[23] You can improve your chance of gaining audience compliance by asking for the specific action.

In speeches of action, you should consider building your speech toward a request for action, rather than stating the action you seek at the beginning of the speech. In most of the other types of speeches considered in this text, you have been encouraged to be as clear as possible about your purpose by stating it in the introduction. Indeed, that works well in an informative speech, where the objective is clarity. However, asking an audience to do something, without proper preparation, can result in failure in a speech of action. For example, a speech that begins with "I want you to donate your body to science," could be met with revulsion, but a speech that builds a sound case for that goal by reviewing its humanitarian purpose can lead the audience to accept the idea.

What are some possible topics appropriate for the speech of action? Below is a brief list that you can use to help you find others.

1. Start an Exercise Program.
2. Stop Eating Meat.
3. Vote This Week.
4. Tell Others about Lobbyists.
5. Study Creatures of the Deep.
6. Learning through Public Television.
7. Avoiding Venereal Diseases.
8. Budgeting Your Time.
9. A Method of Decision-Making.
10. Preparing for the LSAT.

Checklist 7: A Checklist for the Persuasive Speech

_____ 1. Have you determined if your intent is to shape, reinforce or change your audience's responses?

_____ 2. Have you shown how the change you are suggesting for the audience is consistent with their past behavior?

_____ 3. Have you kept your requested changes modest so that the audience does not perceive your request as too much to ask of them?

_____ 4. Have you demonstrated for the audience the benefits they will receive if they do as you request?

_____ 5. Have you shown the audience ways that your request will fulfill their needs?

_____ 6. Have you approached your suggested change gradually so the audience does not perceive that they are being asked to change without sufficient preparation?

_____ 7. Have you employed inductive and deductive reasoning with evidence that meets the tests?

_____ 8. Have you placed your arguments for maximum effect, consciously presented one side or two, and cited sources to verify your evidence and arguments?

_____ 9. Have you avoided fallacies and evaluated your emotional appeals for appropriateness?

_____ 10. Have you composed your speech so that it fits predominantly into the classification of reason, opposition, or action?

Conclusion

This chapter began with a definition of persuasive speaking which indicated that the persuader intends to change the audience's behavior through reinforcing, shaping, and changing its responses on an issue. Five principles of persuasion were explained: (1) the role of consistency in persuasion, (2) the need to break down big proposed changes into smaller ones, (3) the necessity of showing benefits that are greater than the costs to the audience, (4) the importance of meeting audience needs in the speech, and (5) the suggestion that a gradual approach to change works better than asking for too much too early in the speech.

Next we explored inductive and deductive reasoning, the tests of evidence, and the requirement of believability. We discussed when to use a one-sided or a two-sided message, especially in relation to audiences of different educational levels. Citing sources with oral footnotes was reviewed as a means of allowing the audience to verify evidence.

Our discussion of reasoning in persuasive speeches was followed by a consideration of emotional appeals. Among them were appeals to pity, flattery, identification, fear, the *ad hominem,* illegitimate authority, oversimplification, and distraction. Some of these appeals were discounted as unethical, and others were recommended only with caution because they detract from reason. One that *was* recommended, because of its common use in our society and its effectiveness, was the narrative or story used for dramatic impact and interest value.

Finally, we explored three basic types of persuasive speeches: (1) the speech of reasons, with its emphasis on shaping an audience's response through arguments and evidence; (2) the speech of opposition, with its emphasis on presenting a case against a commonly-held practice or belief; and (3) the speech of action, with its mixture of rational and emotional appeals aimed at changing the audience's behavior.

Application Assignment

The Speech of Reasons

Deliver a five- to eight-minute speech in which you attempt to shape the audience's response toward some idea, issue, or project. This assignment goes beyond the speech of explanation in chapter 9, where the main purpose was to clarify the audience's understanding. In the speech of reasons the main purpose is to *shape* the audience's responses by employing reasoning with evidence that meets the tests of quality and believability, with sound generalizations or conclusions that follow from evidence. As in the speech of investigation, you will be expected to use evidence gained from reading and research on the topic, with oral footnotes to reveal where you found the information. *Note:* An example of a speech of reasons can be found in Appendix I; it can serve as a model for this assignment.

The Speech of Opposition

In a five- to eight-minute speech, you should oppose the ideas of someone else or a "sacred cow" (an unquestioned behavior or idea in our society) through an enlightened criticism of the other person's sources of information, citation of sources, reasoning, uses of evidence, soundness of generalizations and conclusions, and violations of the rules of inference (fallacies). To expose fallacies or to provide proof for another point of view, the speech should employ oral footnotes, research, and the results of reading and/or interviews to provide evidence. In the end, the speech of opposition should draw a different conclusion from the one being opposed. The speech of opposition should seriously challenge the other person's message in such a way that the audience no longer accepts unqualified endorsement of the earlier message. Your speech should induce doubt (shaping of response) and even change people's minds about the issue. *Note:* An example of a speech of opposition can be found in Appendix J; it can serve as a model for this assignment.

The Speech of Action

Deliver a six- to eight-minute speech in which you persuade your classmates to take some action that you recommend. The action should be appropriate for you and for your audience. The means of gaining the action should include both reasoning and emotional appeals. In addition to inductive and/or deductive reasoning, you can seek identification with your audience, employ alarm or fear appeals with reassurance, or tell a dramatic story to illustrate your point. Be wary about selecting a purpose that is too easy (e.g., persuade your audience to eat candy) or too difficult (e.g., join my offbeat religious group). Instead, select a serious topic concerning which your audience can make an important contribution through their actions. Try to reinforce those already convinced, to shape those who are doubtful, and to change most of them in the direction you suggest. *Note:* An example of a speech of action can be found in Appendix K; it can serve as a model for this assignment.

Vocabulary

ad hominem **argument** A situation in which the speaker is attacked for something that lies outside the realm of the issue; literally, an attack on the person rather than the issue.

argument from analogy fallacy A fallacy in which similarities between items are assumed even though they have not been clearly established.

attitude A tendency to like or dislike something or somebody; a learned predisposition to respond favorably or unfavorably toward something.

belief Based on attitudes, beliefs are our hypotheses about the nature of things and what we should do about them, e.g., I might have the belief that good works will lead to salvation (value).

believability Besides meeting the tests of evidence, evidence must be acceptable to the audience before they are likely to be persuaded.

changing One of the three behavioral purposes of persuasive speaking, in which the audience alters overt behavior as a result of a persuasive message.

choice One of the criteria for determining whether or not a speech is persuasive is that the audience must perceive choice, that is, must feel free to choose what the speaker recommends; when an audience does not perceive choice, the message is classified as coercion, not persuasion.

conclusion The logical deduction in deductive reasoning, a conclusion is true if its major and minor premises are true and correctly arranged (valid).

consistency The idea that people are more likely to be persuaded by that which is in line with or consistent with what they already believe and do.

cost-benefit analysis The idea that an audience is more likely to do as the persuader suggests if its costs in time, money, or effort are lower than the expected benefits or advantages.

cross-ranking fallacy A fallacy based on using more than one basis of comparison, such as using height, race, and skill to classify basketball players.

deductive reasoning One of two kinds of reasoning, deductive reasoning uses a major and minor premise that necessarily lead to a conclusion.

distraction To draw attention away from the issue at hand by bringing in a topic that will get everyone upset; also includes massing relevant and irrelevant data in such quantity that the audience can no longer discern the difference.

emotional appeals Attempts to persuade an audience by using human emotions (love, hate, fear, prejudice, and so on) to secure change. These appeals are discredited when they distract from the issue at hand.

equivocation fallacy A fallacy in which a word with several meanings is used in a sense that is improper for the argument.

evidence The reasons why a generalization should be believed in inductive reasoning.

expertise One of the tests of testimonial evidence (opinion), in which you evaluate the source's capacity to know something about the subject on which he or she has stated an opinion.

fallacies Violations of the rules of inference, such as hasty generalizations, equivocation, cross-ranking.

fear appeals Emotional appeals that threaten you or your loved ones; linked with reassurance, they tend to work better than they would if you did not indicate to the audience a way to escape the threat.

freedom One of the tests of testimonial evidence (opinion), in which you determine whether or not the source was in a position to state the opinion without being influenced by outside forces such as the government, an employer, and so on.

generalization The inferred result of inductive reasoning, this broad statement is a probability that encompasses the evidence presented to support it.

hasty generalization A generalization that is drawn on insufficient evidence.

hierarchy of needs A rank-ordered list of physical and psychological requirements needed to keep body and mind healthy. It forms the basis of making persuasive appeals.

illegitimate authority Securing opinions about an issue or subject that is outside a person's area of expertise, e.g., to ask the opinion of Miss America about the state of the economy.

inductive reasoning One of two kinds of reasoning, inductive reasoning employs evidence that leads to a generalization that is probably true.

intent One of the criteria for determining whether or not a speech is persuasive is the speaker's intention to change the audience; unintended effects of a message are not classified as the result of persuasion.

one-sided approach A situation in which the audience is provided with only the "pro" arguments and evidence on an issue; appears more persuasive with less educated audiences and with those already committed to the position being advocated.

oversimplification To reduce an issue to such simple terms that it overlooks the complexity of the problems; includes leaving out considerable relevant data to state a problem or propose a solution.

post hoc, ergo propter hoc. A fallacy based on confusing correlation with causation; means literally, "after this, therefore because of this."

proximity One of the tests of testimonial evidence (opinion), in which you determine whether or not the source was in a position to know about the subject or topic on which an opinion was stated.

purpose The purpose of a persuasive speech is to change the audience in some way by shaping, reinforcing, or altering their responses concerning some idea or issue.

reinforcing One of the three behavioral purposes of persuasive speaking, in which the audience perceives reward for its present behavior, ideas, or beliefs; reinforcing encourages the audience to persist in its present mode.

shaping One of the three behavioral purposes of persuasive speaking, in which the audience learns from the speaker to change perceptions about an issue or idea.

tension One of the tests of testimonial evidence (opinion), in which you determine whether or not the source could arrive at and state the opinion undistorted by the situation in which it was rendered.

testimonial evidence An opinion, usually by an expert, that lends authority to a claim made in a speech.

tests of evidence The questions that need to be answered about the source and substance of anything submitted in support of a generalization, to determine its quality.

time A criterion for evaluating testimonial evidence; testimony must be obtained soon enough after an event to avoid memory loss or distortion.

two-sided approach A situation in which the audience is provided with both the pro and the con sides of an issue; an approach that appears more persuasive with educated audiences and with persons hostile to the proposed position on the issue.

value A primitive preference for or positive attitude toward a state of existence (justice, freedom, fulfillment) or broad mode of conduct (bravery, integrity, friendship); relatively resistant to change through persuasive messages.

Endnotes

1. An expanded version of the three behavioral effects appears in Gerald R. Miller, "On Being Persuaded: Some Basic Distinctions," in Michael E. Roloff and Gerald R. Miller, *Persuasion: New Directions in Theory and Research* (Beverly Hills, Ca.: Sage Publications, 1980), pp. 16–26.
2. Daryl Bem, *Beliefs, Attitudes and Human Affairs* (Belmont, Ca.: Brooks/Cole, 1970), p. 16.
3. Wallace Fotheringham, *Perspectives on Persuasion* (Boston: Allyn & Bacon, 1966), p. 33.
4. Bem, p. 14.
5. Martin Fishbein, Seminar lecture on attitude change conducted at the University of Illinois, Spring 1965, and quoted in Gary Cronkhite, *Persuasion: Speech and Behavioral Change* (Indianapolis: Bobbs-Merrill, 1969), p. 64.
6. Bem, pp. 4–7.
7. A. H. Maslow, "A Theory of Human Motivation," *Psychological Review* 50(1943): 370–96.
8. Monroe C. Beardsley, *Thinking Straight: Principles of Reasoning for Readers and Writers* (Englewood Cliffs, N.J.: Prentice-Hall, 1956), p. 28.
9. Beardsley, p. 31.
10. More detailed information on these items can be found in Robert P. Newman and Dale R. Newman, *Evidence* (Boston: Houghton Mifflin Co., 1969), 74–87.
11. From Marvin Karlins and Herbert Abelson, *Persuasion: How Opinions and Attitudes Are Changed*, p. 35. Copyright © 1970 by Springer Publishing Company, Inc., New York. Used by permission.
12. Beardsley, pp. 283–291.
13. Beardsley, p. 287.
14. I. Janis and S. Feshbach, "Effects of Fear-Arousing Communication," *Journal of Abnormal and Social Psychology* 48 (1953): 78–92.

15. Fredric A. Powell, "The Effects of Anxiety-Arousing Messages When Related to Personal, Familial, and Impersonal Referents," *Speech Monographs* 32(1965): 102–6.
16. Powell, pp. 102–106.
17. Frances Cope and Don Richardson, "The Effects of Reassuring Recommendations in a Fear-Arousing Speech," *Speech Monographs* 39 (1972): 148–50.
18. C. I. Hovland, A. A. Lumsdaine, and F. D. Sheffield, *Experiments in Mass Communication* (Princeton: Princeton University Press, 1949), pp. 201–27.
19. A. Lumsdaine and I. Janis, "Resistance to 'Counter-Propaganda' Produced by a One-Sided versus a Two-Sided 'Propaganda' Presentation," *Public Opinion Quarterly* 17 (1953): 311–18.
20. Jack L. Whitehead, Jr., "Effects of Authority-Based Assertion on Attitude and Credibility," *Speech Monographs* 38(1971): 311–15.
21. Beardsley, p. 29.
22. C. Hovland and H. Pritzker, "Extent of Opinion Change as a Function of the Amount of Change Advocated," *Journal of Abnormal and Social Psychology* 54(1957): 257–61.
23. Karlins and Abelson, pp. 11–14. See also W. Weiss and S. Steenbock, "The Influence on Communication Effectiveness of Explicitly Urging Action and Policy Consequences," *Journal of Experimental Social Psychology* 1(1965): 396–406.

Chapter 11

Outline

Introduction: The role of listening in the public speaking classroom.
  I. Three false assumptions about listening.
      A. Do you assume that you listen well?
      B. Do you assume that you cannot be taught to listen better?
      C. Do you assume that listening and hearing are the same thing?
  II. Barriers to effective listening.
      A. Prejudging the speaker.
      B. Prejudging the speech.
      C. Yielding to distractions.
  III. Informative listening.
      A. Suspend judgments about the speaker.
      B. Focus on the speaker as a source of information.
      C. Concentrate your attention on the speaker.
      D. Give the speaker a full hearing.
      E. Focus on the values or experiences that you share with the speaker.
      F. Focus on the main ideas the speaker is presenting.
      G. Recall the arbitrary nature of words.
      H. Focus on the intent, as well as the content, of the message.
      I. Remove or ignore physical distractions.
  IV. Evaluative listening.
      A. Establish standards of appraisal.
      B. Consider the positive as well as the negative aspects of the speech.
      C. View the speech as a whole entity rather than as a composite of isolated parts.
Conclusion: A review of listening to public speeches.

Objectives

After completing chapter 11, you should be able to answer the following questions:
  1. What are three common false assumptions concerning listening?
  2. What three sets of factors provide barriers to effective listening?
  3. How does informative listening differ from evaluative listening?
  4. What practices help you to become a more effective informative and evaluative listener?

When you have completed chapter 11, you should have practiced skills in
  1. Informative listening to student speeches;
  2. Evaluative listening to student speeches; and
  3. Establishing criteria by which to appraise a student's speech.

Application Exercises

  1. Identifying your barriers to effective listening.
  2. Determining your ability to listen for information.
  3. Establishing standards of appraisal for evaluating speeches.
  4. Writing speech criticism.

258

Informative and Evaluative Listening

It is the province of knowledge to speak and it is the privilege of wisdom to listen.

Oliver Wendell Holmes

When you enrolled in the public speaking course, you probably wondered how many speeches you would give, how long each would be, and whether you had to submit an outline with your speeches. In other words, you focused on the speaking function of the course. Ironically, most of your time in public speaking class is spent listening to and evaluating speeches. If you have twenty-five classmates, you spend *twenty-five times* as much time listening to speeches as you do delivering them!   **Introduction**

"I KNOW IT HURTS, JOEY, BUT THERE'S NO USE BAWLIN' 'WAY UP HERE WHERE NOBODY CAN HEAR YOU."

The public speaking classroom provides an opportunity for you to become a better informative and evaluative listener. Your skill as an informative listener brings many benefits. You will learn a great deal about a variety of subjects in the one to two hundred speeches you hear, and you will learn more about public speaking techniques as your classmates and instructor present models of effective and ineffective public speaking skills. As an evaluative speech listener, you will learn standards for appraising public speeches that can be applied outside the classroom; you will learn appropriate skills helpful to your own public speaking; and you will help your fellow students improve their ability as effective public speakers. In order to improve as a listener, you should understand the subject of listening and grow in confidence as an informative and evaluative listener by practicing the component skills. Your effort to understand this subject begins with some of the inaccurate assumptions that people hold about listening.

Three False Assumptions about Listening

Perhaps you are already questioning the value of this chapter. You may believe you are already a good listener, that listening, unlike speaking, is something that cannot be taught, or that your most recent hearing test demonstrates you can listen well. If any of these thoughts have occurred to you, you have one or more of the three most common mistaken notions about listening. These mistaken ideas or false assumptions are worth considering in more detail.

Reprinted by permission. © 1980 NEA, Inc.

If you ask a classmate if he or she listens well, the likely answer is yes. Virtually everyone from the beginning kindergarten student to the college sophomore to the graduate professor believes that he or she listens effectively to other people. This assumption is not borne out by research. Ralph Nichols and his associates conducted considerable research at the University of Minnesota on thousands of students and hundreds of business and professional people. They found that people remember only half of what they hear immediately after a message and only twenty-five percent of what they hear when tested two months later.[1] You may be comforted by these statistics the next time you do poorly on a final exam. After all, the average person remembers only twenty-five percent of what he or she heard early in the term. Nichols' research and your own experience in recalling information demonstrate that the assumption that you listen well is probably inaccurate.

Do You Assume that You Listen Well?

If you feel that you are already an effective listener, you probably do not attempt to identify ways you can improve your listening. If you feel that you are not an effective listener, you may have resigned yourself to being inadequate in this area. One of the reasons you may fail to seek out ways to improve your listening is that there are few alternatives available. Studies show that most of your communication time is spent listening, followed, in order, by speaking, reading, and writing.[2] Curiously, you probably spend an inverse proportion of time in required classes studying these other subjects. You probably spent much of your time in grade school, junior high, and high school studying the two communication skills that we actually use the least: reading and writing. But you have probably never taken a course at any grade level on the communication skill you use the most: listening. Because of the lack of course work and study in listening, we incorrectly assume that listening is a communication skill that cannot be learned.

Do You Assume that You Cannot Be Taught to Listen Better?

Informative and Evaluative Listening

Do You Assume that Listening and Hearing Are the Same Thing?

How many times have you said or had someone say to you, "What do you mean you don't know? I told you!"? People assume that if they say something to someone, the person is listening. For instance, you know how frequently you daydream while hearing a lecturer, how often you are distracted by the person next to you as you hear a student speaker, and how regularly you spend time planning your afternoon while sitting in morning classes. In each case, you can hear the speaker, but you may not do well on an examination of the material. Passing a hearing test is not a sufficient guarantee that you are an effective listener.

Hearing and listening are separate activities. **Hearing** is a physical function you are able to perform unless you suffer from physiological damage or cerebral dysfunction. **Listening,** on the other hand, is a selective activity that involves the reception and interpretation of aural stimuli. You can probably hear if your ears are normal, but you can listen only if you recognize the barriers to effective listening and actively do something to overcome them.

Barriers to Effective Listening

After reading the previous section, you may no longer believe that you just naturally listen well, that you cannot learn listening skills, and that your hearing is the same as your listening ability. What are some of the factors that interfere with your ability to listen? Have you ever sat in a lecture and smiled when the lecturer made a joke, nodded when he or she sought affirmation, established eye contact with the lecturer, and still not remembered a single thing that the lecturer said? As students, it is easy to learn how to fake attention. This is the strategy you use in situations where the most acceptable social behavior is paying attention. It is the strategy you may use in classes, at social gatherings, and in "listening" to fellow students' speeches. You undoubtedly use this strategy when you are bombarded with more messages than you want to hear. Consequently, you may learn the appropriate nonverbal behavior—eye contact, attentive appearance, and apparent note taking—when you are actually wondering if the speaker is as tired as you are as you scribble pictures in your notebook. Faking attention is both a result and cause of poor listening.

Three additional barriers to effective listening are prejudging the speaker, prejudging the speech, and yielding to distractions. Each of these barriers in turn has subtypes that concern you if you wish to improve your listening skills.

Barriers to Effective Listening

1. Faking attention
2. Prejudging the speaker
3. Prejudging the speech
4. Yielding to distractions

We all make judgments about a speaker before he or she says a word. In chapter 5 you learned about trait errors—the tendency to overrate or underrate a speaker because of personal bias. You might dismiss a speaker because of attire, posture, stance or unattractiveness.

Prejudging the Speaker

Researchers have found that the speaker's sex appears to be an important variable in our judgment. For instance, when male and female speakers are given the same grade, the male speakers receive fewer positive comments than do the female speakers.[3] Female evaluators give men higher evaluations than women,[4] and male evaluators tend to grade women higher than men.[5] In addition, one of the authors found that sexist teachers grade speeches differently: they do not write as many comments as do nonsexist teachers.[6]

Status and stereotypes are two additional preconceived attitudes which affect our ability to listen to another person. If the speaker has high status, you may tend to accept what he or she says more easily without listening critically to the message. You may not exercise careful judgment if the speaker is a visiting dignitary, a physician, an attorney, or a distinguished professor. If you perceive the speaker to be low in status—a beginning student, a maintenance worker in the dormitory, or a student who flunked the mid-term—you tend not to listen to his or her message at all, and you are unlikely to remember what the speaker said. Perceived status seems to determine whether you are likely to listen critically or at all.

Stereotypes also affect our ability to listen. If the other person announces that she is a Republican, is opposed to women's rights, or believes a woman's place is in the home, you may prematurely judge her as a reactionary and ignore her speech. When speakers seem to belong to groups for whom you have little regard—rich, poor, jocks, brains, or flirts—you may reject their messages.

Do you dismiss seniors as too pretentious, or people who slouch as uninteresting? If you draw such conclusions about a speaker before he or she begins a speech, and then ignore the message as a result of this prejudgment, you are handicapped by a factor that interferes with your listening.

Prejudging the Speech

A second set of factors which may interfere with your ability to listen to a speaker is your tendency to prejudge the speech. The same human tendency that causes you to judge the speaker before he or she speaks causes you to judge the speech before you understand it. The most common conclusions we prematurely draw about a speech is that it is boring, too difficult to understand, irrelevant, or inconsistent with our own beliefs.

You may judge a speech to be boring because you feel you already know the information the speaker is presenting, you have already experienced what the speaker is describing, or the speaker is trying to persuade you to do something that you already do. In other words, your own feelings of superiority—informational, experiential, or attitudinal—interfere with your ability to listen.

You may decide a speech is too difficult to understand and dismiss it because, "I wouldn't understand it anyway." You may have the tendency to dismiss many topics as too difficult, or you may selectively identify topics that deal with thermonuclear power, quantum mechanics, or Keynesian economics as too complex for your understanding, even though the speaker's purpose is to simplify the concept or to inform you of the basic terminology.

Occasionally you may decide that a speech is irrelevant. For some people nearly all topics may seem to be irrelevant. For others, a few topics are dismissed as soon as they are announced. A business major in the audience may feel that American Indian literature does not affect him, a college sophomore may conclude that a speech on retirement is irrelevant, or a black student may show no interest in a description of life in an all-white community.

One of the reasons people dismiss another person's topic as irrelevant is because of simple egocentrism. **Egocentrism** is the tendency to view ourselves as the center of any exchange or activity. A person who is egocentric is only concerned with him- or herself and pays little or no attention to others. Egocentrism may cause a listener to dismiss any speech but his or her own as irrelevant. Whether you dismiss most speeches as irrelevant or ignore certain topics, you are blocking your ability to become an effective listener. If you listen attentively to the speech beyond the statement of the topic or purpose, you may find information that clearly shows the relevance of the topic for you.

Finally, you may dismiss the speech because you decide that you disagree with the topic or purpose. You may feel that a speaker should not inform you about paraphernalia for smoking marijuana, provide information on birth control, show examples of pornography, or persuade you to limit salt or sugar consumption. Your opposition to smoking marijuana, practicing birth control, seeing nudity, or learning about nutritional findings may block your ability to listen to the speaker. You may conclude that the speaker is "on the other side" of the issue and that your seemingly different attitudes prohibit open communication.

Defensiveness commonly occurs when a speaker's topic or position on an issue is different from your own. You may be threatened by the speaker's position and feel that you must defend your own. You may believe you are being attacked because you champion a specific cause—like women's rights, energy conservation, or the anti-tax movement—that the speaker opposes. You may be standing ready for anyone who dares provoke you on your favorite cause. You may be only too eager to find fault with another person's speech. Try to recognize possible blocks to effective listening that defensiveness and dismissal of the speech through disagreement provide in the speaking-listening process.

The listener's four most common distractions are factual, semantic, mental, and physical. Yielding to **factual distractions** means listening only for the facts instead of the main ideas or general purpose of the speech. The formal educational experiences you have had in which you were required to listen to teachers in order to successfully pass objective exams may contribute to this tendency. Rather than looking at the entire speech, you may be focusing on some small, isolated facts. You jeopardize your understanding of the speaker's main idea or purpose when you jump from fact to fact rather than attempting to weave the major points into an integrated pattern.

Yielding to Distractions

Semantic distractions are specific words or phrases that we allow to affect us emotionally. You may react this way if someone uses a word or phrase in an unusual manner, or you find a particular concept distasteful or inappropriate, or you do not understand the meaning of a term. Regionalisms—words that are used in a way unique to a particular geographical area—provide one example of words used in a different way. If a speaker talks about the harmful qualities of "pop," and you refer to soft drinks as "soda," you may react negatively to "pop." If you feel that "girl" should not be used to designate an adult woman, then you may be distracted in your listening. Finally, unfamiliar words may cause a reaction that interferes with listening to the speaker's message.

Mental distractions include daydreaming, counterarguments, recollections, or future planning in which you engage while listening to a speaker. These mental distractions may originate from something the speaker has stated or from your own preoccupation with other thoughts. Perhaps mental distractions occur because of the difference between the speed at which we can listen and the speed at which we can speak. The average American talks at a rate of 125 words per

". . . And the history of the Primitive Boobungoo people
shows, beyond a doubt that . . ."

minute, but can receive about 800 words per minute. This discrepancy allows us
to engage in many mental side trips that may be more relevant to us. Unfortunately, we may become lost on a side trip and fail to return to the original path.

Physical distractions include any physical stimuli that interfere with our attention to the speaker. Stimuli that may affect our listening are sounds such as
a speaker's lisp, a buzzing neon light, or an air hammer; sights such as a speaker's
white socks, a message on the chalkboard, or bright sunlight; smells such as a
familiar perfume, baking bread, or freshly popped corn.

In this section we surveyed three sets of barriers to effective listening: prejudging the speaker on the basis of sex, status, or stereotypes; prejudging the
subject and dismissing it as boring, too complex, irrelevant, or opposed to our
own point of view; and yielding to factual, semantic, mental, or physical distractions. Consider how you can overcome these barriers and become more effective as an informative and evaluative listener.

What kind of a listener are you? After listening to a speech in class, complete the following:

Questions	Examples	Barriers
What characteristics could have caused you to prejudge the speaker?	Tapped the podium as he talked; used no gestures.	_____ _____ _____ _____
What factors could have caused you to prejudge the speech?	Topic selected was economics—too difficult for me to understand.	_____ _____ _____
What distracted you?	Speaker used the word "Keynesian," which sounds like "Ephesians" and reminded me of Bible study.	_____ _____ _____ _____ _____

Did you prejudge the speaker or the speech? Did you yield to any of the distractions? How were you able to overcome the barriers to effective communication?

Application Exercise 1: Identifying Your Barriers to Effective Listening

We have considered three false assumptions about listening and some barriers to effective listening. We will now examine the two types of listening that occur most frequently in the public speaking situation: informative listening and evaluative listening.

Informative Listening

Informative listening refers to the kind of listening you engage in when you attend class and listen to an instructor, attend baseball practice and listen to the coach, or attend a lecture and listen to a visiting speaker. Your purpose in informative listening is to understand the information the speaker is presenting. You may try to understand relevant information about the speaker and factors that led to the speech, as well as the central idea of the speech itself. Informative listening requires a high level of involvement in the communication process. What are some of the other factors that contribute to effective informational listening? What can you do to overcome many of the barriers discussed in the previous section?

In order to be successful at informative listening, you can engage in at least nine practices. These practices include (1) suspend judgments about the speaker, (2) focus on the speaker as a source of information, (3) concentrate your attention on the speaker, (4) give the speaker a full hearing, (5) focus on the values or experiences that you share with the speaker, (6) focus on the main ideas the speaker is presenting, (7) recall the arbitrary nature of words, (8) focus on the intent, as well as the content, of the message, and (9) remove or ignore physical distractions. Let us consider each of these in more detail.

Practices for Effective Listening

1. Suspend judgments about the speaker
2. Focus on the speaker as a source of information
3. Concentrate your attention on the speaker
4. Give the speaker a full hearing
5. Focus on the values or experiences that you share with the speaker
6. Focus on the main ideas the speaker is presenting
7. Recall the arbitrary nature of words
8. Focus on the intent, as well as the content, of the message
9. Remove or ignore physical distractions

Suspend Judgments about the Speaker

You should suspend your premature judgments about the speaker so that you can listen for information. Instead of concluding that the speaker is, or is not, worthy of your attention before you have heard him or her, wait until you have heard the speaker out.

If you make decisions about people because of their membership in a particular group, you risk serious error. Beer drinkers may be thin, members of fraternities may not be conformists, and artists may be disciplined.

If you categorize people, it is easy to dismiss them. When you focus on the speaker as a valuable human resource who can share information, ideas, thoughts, and feelings, you are better able to listen to him or her with interest and respect. Every speaker you hear is likely to have some information you do not already know. Try to focus on these opportunities to learn something new.

Focus on the Speaker as a Source of Information

If you find yourself dismissing many of the speeches you hear as boring, consider whether you are overly egocentric. Perhaps your inclination to find your classmates' speeches boring is due to your inability to focus on other people. Egocentrism is a trait that is difficult to overcome. The wisest suggestion, in this case, is to keep in mind one of the direct benefits of concentrating your attention on the speaker: if you focus on the other person while he or she speaks, the person will probably focus on you when you are speaking. Even more important, you will come across better if the speaker perceives you to be a careful listener. Nothing else you can do—including dieting, using makeup, wearing new clothing, or making other improvements—will make you as attractive to others as the ability to listen to someone else.

Concentrate Your Attention on the Speaker

Do not dismiss the speech after you have heard the topic. More than likely the speaker will add new information, insights, or experiences which will shed additional light on the subject. One professor teaches an upper-division argumentation course to twenty students each quarter. Four speeches are assigned, but every speech is given on the same topic. In a ten-week period, students hear eighty speeches on the same topic, but every speech contains some new information. The class would be dismal if the students dismissed the speeches after hearing that they would all cover the same topic. Instead of considering the speeches boring, the students find them interesting, exciting, and highly creative.

Give the Speaker a Full Hearing

If you find that you are responding emotionally to the speaker's position on a topic and that you directly oppose what he or she is recommending, try to concentrate your attention on those attitudes, beliefs, or values you have in common. Try to identify specific statements the speaker is making with which you can agree. The speaker might seem to be attacking one of your pet beliefs or attitudes, but, if you listen carefully, you may find that he or she is actually defending it from a different perspective. Maximizing our shared ideas and minimizing our differences result in improved listening and better communication. In addition, if we are able to control our defensiveness against other people's perspectives, we may find ourselves gaining in credibility with them. As a consequence, we may become more persuasive and able to cause a change in their attitudes.

Focus on the Values or Experiences that You Share with the Speaker

Focus on the Main Ideas the Speaker Is Presenting

Keep in mind that you do not have to memorize specific facts that the speaker is presenting. Rarely will you be given an objective examination on the material in a student speech. If you want the specific information that is being presented, ask the speaker after class for a copy of the outline, bibliography, or other pertinent documentation. Asking the speaker for specific information is flattering. Stating in class that you can recall the specific population figures cited but that you have no idea of the speaker's purpose may seem offensive.

Recall the Arbitrary Nature of Words

If you find that you sometimes react emotionally to four-letter words or to specific usages of some words, you may be forgetting that words are simply arbitrary symbols people have chosen to represent certain things. Words do not have an inherent, intrinsic, "real" meaning. When a speaker uses a word in an unusual way, or when you are unfamiliar with a certain word, do not hesitate to ask how the word is being used. Asking for such information makes the speaker feel good because you are showing some interest in the speech, and the inquiry will contribute to your own knowledge. If you cannot overcome a negative reaction to the speaker's choice of words, recognize that the emotional reaction is yours and not necessarily a feeling shared by the rest of the class or the speaker. Keep in mind that this emotional reaction may affect your evaluation of the speech and that you may have lost your objectivity as a competent evaluator.

Focus on the Intent, as well as the Content, of the Message

Use the time between your listening to the speech and the speaker's rate of speaking to increase your understanding of the speech. Instead of embarking on mental excursions about other topics, focus on all aspects of the topic the speaker has selected. Consider the speaker's background and his or her motivation for selecting a particular topic. Try to relate the major points the speaker has made to his or her stated intentions. By refusing to consider other unrelated matters, you will greatly increase your understanding of the speaker and the speech.

Frequently, you can deal with physical distractions like an unusual odor, bright lights, or a distracting noise by moving the stimulus or yourself. In other words, do not choose a seat near the doorway that allows you to observe people passing by in the hall; do not sit so that the sunlight is in your eyes; and do not sit far away from the speaker and close to maintenance noises in the building. If you cannot remove the distraction by moving your seat or removing the distracting object, try to ignore it. You probably can study with the radio or television on, sleep without having complete darkness, and eat even while other people are milling around you. Similarly, you can focus your attention on the speaker when other physical stimuli are in your environment. Consider whether you would be able to concentrate on the speech if it were, instead, a movie you have been wanting to see or a musical group you enjoy or a play that has received a rave review. A friend said that when he had difficulty staying up late to study in graduate school, he would consider whether he would have the same difficulty if he were on a date. If the answer was no, he could then convince himself that the fatigue he felt was a function of the task, not of his sleepiness. The same principle can work for you. Consider whether the distractions are merely an excuse for your lack of desire to listen to the speaker. Generally you will find you can ignore the other physical stimuli in your environment if you wish to do so.

Remove or Ignore Physical Distractions

**Application
Exercise 2:
Determining
Your Ability
to Listen for
Information**

Are you an effective informative listener? After you have listened to a number of speeches in class, select one and complete the following.

Speaker's name _____

Topic _____

Statement of purpose _____

Main points:

1. _____

2. _____

3. _____

4. _____

What did the speaker say to describe his or her qualifications to speak on the subject?

_____

_____

What response was the speaker seeking from the audience?

_____

_____

If you have difficulty in completing this exercise, then consider the barriers to effective listening that were described earlier in this chapter. Which sets of factors contributed to your inability to listen for information?

As we observed earlier, two kinds of listening are most common in public speaking situations. We have concluded our discussion of informative listening and turn now to evaluative listening.

**Evaluative
Listening**

Evaluative listening is the kind you engage in when you listen to two opposing political speakers; judge the speaking ability of an author, attorney, or instructor; or listen to students speaking in public speaking class. Your purpose in evaluative listening is to judge the speaker's ability to give an effective speech. Evaluative listening is an essential skill in and out of the classroom. What can you do to become a better evaluative listener?

272

You can be more effective by following three guidelines. First, establish standards of appraisal. Second, consider the positive, as well as the negative, aspects of the speech. Third, view the speech as a whole entity, rather than as a composite of isolated parts. Let us consider each of these guidelines in more depth.

Ways to be an Evaluative Listener

1. Establish standards of appraisal
2. Consider the positive as well as the negative aspects of the speech
3. View the speech as a whole entity rather than as a composite of isolated parts

In order to evaluate another person's public speaking ability, you must establish criteria by which you make your judgments. The criteria you establish should reflect your beliefs and attitudes about public speaking. Your instructor may suggest a set of criteria by which to judge your classmates' speeches. Many different sets of standards can be used to provide equally valid evaluations of public speaking. Most will include some consideration of the topic choice, purpose, arguments, organization, vocal and bodily aspects of delivery, audience analysis and adaptation. The criticism form shown in figure 11.1 is based on the authors' perception of a successful public speech and follows the suggestions offered in this text.

Establish Standards of Appraisal

Too often people use the word *evaluation* to mean negative criticism. In other words, if they are to evaluate a speech, a newspaper article, or a television program, they feel they must state every aspect of it that could be improved or did not meet their standards. Evaluation should include both positive and negative judgments of what is being evaluated. As a matter of fact, many speech instructors feel you should begin and end your criticism of a speech with positive comments, and "sandwich" your negative remarks in between. Research shows that students perceive positive comments to be more helpful than negative comments.[7]

Consider the Positive, as well as the Negative, Aspects of the Speech

It is very easy to focus on delivery aspects of the speech, to look only for a recognized organizational plan, or to consider only whether the research is current. Viewing small bits of the speech in isolation, you may be able to justify a low evaluation you give to a classmate. Considering all of the parts that went into the speech may not allow such a judgment.

View the Speech as a Whole Entity Rather Than as a Composite of Isolated Parts

Evaluation Form for a Public Speech

Speaker _____

Critic _____

Use this scale to evaluate each of the following:

1	2	3	4	5
Excellent	Good	Average	Fair	Weak

Introduction
_____The introduction gained and maintained attention.

_____The introduction related the topic to the audience.

_____The introduction related the speaker to the topic.

_____The introduction revealed the organization and development of the speech.

Topic selection and statement of purpose
_____The topic selected was appropriate for the speaker.

_____The topic selected was appropriate for the audience.

_____The topic selected was appropriate for the occasion.

_____The statement of purpose was clear and appropriate for the speaker, audience, and occasion.

_____The stated purpose was achieved.

Content
_____The speaker consulted available sources including personal experience, interviews, and printed materials for information.

_____The speaker supplied a sufficient amount of evidence and supporting materials.

_____The speech was organized in a manner that did not distract from the speech.

_____The main points were clearly identified.

_____Sufficient transitions were provided.

Source
_____The speaker described his or her competence.

_____The speaker demonstrated trustworthiness.

_____The speaker exhibited dynamism.

_____The speaker established coorientation.

Delivery

_____The vocal aspects of delivery—pitch, rate, pause, volume, enunciation, fluency, and vocal variety—added to the message and did not distract from it.

_____The bodily aspects of delivery—gestures, facial expressions, eye contact, and movement—added to the message and did not distract from it.

_____Visual aids were used appropriately to clarify the message.

Audience analysis

_____The speaker demonstrated his or her sensitivity to the interests of the audience.

_____The speaker adapted the message to the knowledge level of the audience on the particular topic.

_____The speaker adapted the message to the demographic variables of the audience.

_____The speaker adapted the message to the attitudes of the audience.

Conclusion

_____The conclusion forewarned the audience that the speaker was about to stop.

_____The conclusion reminded the audience of the central idea or the main points of the speech.

_____The conclusion specified precisely what the audience was to think or do in response to the speech.

_____The conclusion ended the speech in an upbeat manner that caused the audience members to think or do as the speaker intended.

Figure 11.1
Evaluation form for a public speech.

Speeches are like the people who give them. They are composites of many complex, and sometimes conflicting, messages. They must be examined along a variety of considerations in order to be evaluated completely and fairly. Do not be distracted by a topic that represents one of your pet peeves, or allow the speaker's language choices to overshadow her creativity, or accept the arguments of a speaker who demonstrates a smooth delivery. In short, consider the entire speech in your evaluation.

Reprinted by permission:
Tribune Company
Syndicate, Inc.

Application Exercise 3: Establishing Standards of Appraisal for Evaluating Speeches

In order to make valid judgments about your classmates' speeches, you need to have standards by which to evaluate them. Based on your understanding of public speaking, create a criticism form which would include all of the essential elements of effective public speeches. Would you weigh all aspects of your criticism equally or would delivery, say, be worth more than the arguments, or organization worth more than audience adaptation? Note exactly what you would include in your evaluation and how you would weigh each aspect.

Conclusion

We have considered informative and evaluative listening in this chapter. You learned the role of listening in the public speaking classroom. You learned to identify three false assumptions about listening: most people assume that they listen well, that they cannot be taught how to be better listeners, and that hearing and listening are the same phenomenon. After we dispelled these misconceptions, you learned three sets of barriers to effective listening: prejudging the speaker on the basis of sex, status, stereotypes, or other factors; prejudging the subject and dismissing it as boring, too complex, irrelevant, or opposed to your own point of view; and yielding to factual, semantic, mental, or physical distractions. You then considered twelve practices in which you should engage when you listen for informative and evaluative purposes. These practices are (1) suspend judgments about the speaker, (2) focus on the speaker as a source of information, (3) concentrate your attention on the speaker, (4) give the speaker a full hearing, (5) focus on the values or experiences that you share with the speaker, (6) focus on the main ideas the speaker is presenting, (7) recall the arbitrary nature of words, (8) focus on the intent, as well as the content, of the message, (9) remove or ignore physical distractions, (10) establish standards of appraisal, (11) consider the positive, as well as the negative, aspects of the speech, and (12) view the speech as a whole rather than as a composite of isolated parts.

Using the criticism form that you created in Exercise 3, evaluate three speeches other students delivered in class. After you have completed your criticism, give each finished form to the speaker. Together discuss how accurately you have assessed the speech. Are you satisfied with the form? Do you believe your form would be useful for others? Does the speaker feel that the form included all relevant factors? Can he or she suggest items that could or should be included? Is he or she satisfied with your use of the form? What differences of opinion exist between the two of you? Why? Can you resolve these differences? What has the experience demonstrated?

Using the evaluation form shown in figure 11.1, evaluate one or more speeches delivered by classmates. The form asks you to evaluate the introduction, topic selection, statement of purpose, content, source, delivery, audience analysis, and conclusion. Which aspects of the speech do you find easiest to evaluate? Which aspects do you find more difficult to evaluate? What can you do to strengthen your ability to evaluate those aspects?

egocentrism The tendency to view oneself as the center of any exchange or activity; overconcern with the presentation of oneself to others; a barrier to listening.

evaluative listening Listening to a speaker for the purpose of evaluating his or her ability to present an effective speech.

factual distractions Factual information that detracts from our attention to primary ideas; a barrier to listening.

hearing The physiological process by which sound is received by the ear.

informative listening Listening to a speaker in order to understand the information that he or she is presenting.

listening The selective process of receiving and interpreting sounds.

mental distractions Communication with ourselves while we are engaged in communication with others; a barrier to listening.

physical distractions Environmental stimuli that interfere with our focus on another person and a message; a barrier to effective listening.

semantic distractions Bits or units of information in the message that interfere with our understanding of the main ideas or total meaning of the message; a barrier to effective listening.

Endnotes

1. Ralph Nichols and Leonard Stevens, "Listening to People," *Harvard Business Review* 35 (1957): 85–92.
2. See, for example, P. T. Rankin, "The Measurement of the Ability to Understand Spoken Language," *Dissertation Abstracts* 12 (1926): 847; D. Bird, "Teaching Listening Comprehension," *Journal of Communication* 3 (1953): 127–30; Mariam E. Wilt, "A Study of Teacher Awareness of Listening as a Factor in Elementary Education," *Journal of Educational Research* 43 (1950): 626; D. Bird, "Have You Tried Listening?" *Journal of the American Dietetic Association* 30 (1954): 225–30; and B. Markgraf, "An Observational Study Determining the Amount of Time That Students in the Tenth and Twelfth Grades Are Expected to Listen in the Classroom" (Master's thesis, University of Wisconsin, 1957).
3. Judy C. Pearson, "The Influence of Sex and Sexism on the Criticism of Classroom Speeches" (Paper presented at the International Communication Association, Philadelphia, Pennsylvania, May 1979); and Jo A. Sprague, "An Investigation of the Written Critique Behavior of College Communication Instructors," (Ph.D. dissertation, Purdue University, 1971) pp. 44–46.
4. Emil R. Pfister, "A Study of the Influence of Certain Selected Factors on the Ratings of Speech Performances" (Ed.D. dissertation, Michigan State University, 1955) p. 88.
5. Pfister, 92.
6. Pearson, 14.
7. Stephen Lee Young, "Student Perceptions of Helpfulness in Classroom Speech Criticism," *Speech Teacher* 23 (1974): 222–34.

Appendix A
Introducing Another Person

This appendix includes two student speeches as assigned in chapter 2, in which the speaker was instructed to interview a classmate that he or she did not know; to gather facts, stories, and observations; and to communicate this information to the class. The purpose of the speech was to help people in the class get to know each other better because they would constitute the audience for the speeches that were to follow. These two students proceeded to the front of the room and wrote their names on the board. Their speeches follow:

> My name is Michelle Hutzell.* I would like to introduce you to Mike Leaders. Mike grew up on a farm in Council Bluffs, Iowa. He is the middle child of a large family which includes five brothers and three sisters. Mike is a junior here at Iowa State University majoring in Industrial Education. When he has completed college, he hopes to teach high school shop and coach football.
> Speaking of football, Mike has made some outstanding contributions to this sport at Iowa State. Mike is a linebacker on the football team,

*From a speech delivered by Michelle J. Hutzell in Fundamentals of Public Speaking, Iowa State University.

and he was selected for the second team in the Big Eight Conference. Mike was also chosen recently as the ABC "Player of the Week," and Chevrolet donated a $1,000.00 scholarship to this university in his name. The money will be awarded to a student in need of financial aid.

Mike was married this past June. After a honeymoon in the Bahamas, he and his new wife moved into University Village. Studying and football practice keep Mike pretty busy, but in his spare time he enjoys snow skiing, water skiing, camping, and many other outdoor activities.

I found Mike to be a friendly, outgoing person, who likes to meet new people. He was really easy to talk to, and he seemed to have a good outlook on life.

As you may guess, Mike's main interest is football, so his future speeches may cover this and other sports-related topics.

The outstanding feature of this introduction was the focus on a central theme, sports, which helped the audience to remember that Mike was active in athletics. The speech was conversational and personal. It helped the audience to see Mike as a qualified speaker on subjects related to athletics. The second example of a speech introducing another moves easily from the facts of the person's life to some disclosures that reveal his humanity.

This is Michael Alan Carnahan.* Mike was born in Ottumwa, Iowa, and since that time he has moved often within three states—Maryland, New Jersey, and Virginia—and one country—Belgium.

As you might have guessed, Mike's dad is in the Army!

When Mike was in the sixth grade, he was a boy scout patrol leader. In high school he and his trumpet were quite involved in the band, a band which he tells me was *outstanding.* Mike concentrated his sports ability in baseball where he played first base and pitcher. He was also a member of the Honors Society.

*From a speech by Jan Havener delivered in Fundamentals of Public Speaking, Iowa State University.

Mike is currently a junior with an Industrial Administration major in accounting. He lives in the university residence halls.

As a sophomore, Mike served as vice president on the cabinet of his dormitory floor. Now ROTC is what keeps his time occupied along with being Captain of the Army Rifle Team and active in the Pershing Rifle Team, an Army ROTC honorary. That's right, Mike likes rifle shooting.

Mike has a younger brother, Doug, who is a senior in high school, and a sister, Susan, a sophomore here at Iowa State.

It just so happens that Susan, Mike's sister, is engaged to Mike's roommate, and Mike is dating Susan's roommate! A funny and interesting situation.

Becky and Mike enjoy walking in the state park, wading in the streams, and walking in the rain without an umbrella. Walking in the rain without an umbrella is mainly Becky's idea, but Mike is learning what fun it is too.

Mike was an easy person to get to know. He has a very warm personality and seems like a real sensible person. I present you with Mike Carnahan.

Appendix B
The Outline

This appendix provides an illustration of a sentence outline in correct form as described in chapter 5. Notice that the immediate purpose of the speech is stated behaviorally: The audience is expected to write on the critique sheet two pieces of information that are revealed in the speech. The student followed the principle of subordination by indicating in form and content whether each sentence was more or less important than another. This subordination was indicated by the correct use of symbols (I, A, 1) and by the indentions which moved to the right to indicate less important points. The student also observed the principle of division by always dividing a point into two or more subordinate parts. In no case does an A or a 1 stand alone. Finally, the student followed the principle of parallelism by making every entry a complete sentence.

RESERVE OFFICERS TRAINING CORPS*

Immediate purpose: to inform the audience about some of the benefits of the ROTC. The audience should be able to write on the critique form at least two ways the ROTC program can benefit a college student.

Introduction

    I. Students who associate with ROTC students often know little about the program.

   II. My purpose today is to have you remember at least two of the benefits of the ROTC program that I mention in my speech.

*From an outline submitted by Michael Carnahan, Fundamentals of Public Speaking, Iowa State University.

III. A student can obtain up to twenty-seven credit
hours in the ROTC program.
   A. The twenty-seven credits can be used to
      meet a minor in your college.
   B. The twenty-seven credits can also be used
      as elective credits.
IV. Students can earn money as a member of the ROTC
program.
   A. Two thousand tax-free dollars are paid
      during the student's last two years as an
      undergraduate.
   B. Scholarship money is available for
      qualified students for various time
      periods and for various expenditures.
      1. Scholarships are available for one,
         two, three, and four years.
      2. Scholarships can provide money for
         tuition, laboratory fees, and
         textbooks.
V. ROTC courses emphasize leadership and
management training through classes and
application.
   A. The classes provide the principles needed
      to help a student work with people.
   B. The laboratory sessions provide an
      opportunity to practice those principles.
VI. A student can be commissioned as a second
lieutenant upon completion of the Military
Science IV class and graduation.
   A. The student has the option of entering the
      regular army.
   B. The student may choose to enter the
      National Guard.
   C. The student may join the Army Reserve.
VII. We now know how you can earn credits, money,
leadership and management skills, and a
commission in the military.
VIII. To demonstrate that you learned from my
speech, I would like you to write on your
evaluation two of the specific benefits that
you remember.

Bibliography

Army ROTC Scholarships. Washington, D.C.: U.S.
   Government Printing Office, November 1977. RPI
   677.
Army ROTC Basic Facts. Washington, D.C.: U.S.
   Government Printing Office, August 1977. RPI 664.
For Your Life After College. Washington, D.C.: U.S.
   Government Printing Office, 1978. 798-096.

Appendix C
Introducing Your Speech

Chapter 6 discusses four functions of an introduction. They are: (1) gaining and maintaining audience attention; (2) relating the topic to the audience; (3) relating the speaker to the topic; and (4) forecasting organization and development of the speech. Notice in the following student speech how the speaker uses the four functions.

ARE VIDEO GAMES A MENACE TO OUR SOCIETY?*

It is 3:00 in the morning. The house is dark and silent except for the rhythmic explosions of nuclear bombs destroying small cities. Frank is determined to beat his record score of 9,000 before going to bed. He pushes the reset button and begins again.

Gain and Maintain Attention

Frank is one of America's many victims of the home video game epidemic. The highly competitive and greatly expanding video game industry is attracting millions of addicts. Most of the addicts are under thirty years of age; many are still in high school. The best are becoming

Arouse Audience Interest

*From a speech introduction composed by Chris Stiller in Fundamentals of Speech Communication, School of Interpersonal Communication, Ohio University.

millionaires. Not since the days of rock'n roll
could a recent high school graduate walk into a
recording studio with a guitar and emerge with a
$50,000 contract. Young adults can become
involved with this lucrative industry by
establishing their own video game corporation.

Origin of Speaker's
Credibility

My interest in the video game syndrome was
aroused by my brother, Steven, who is obsessed
with video games. His obsession inspired me to
explore the topic further. The fact is that many
individuals like you and me enjoy playing and
conquering video games in homes or arcades. The
problem arises when the video game phenomenon
becomes a fanatical habit, a top priority that
interferes with everyday life. Then we have to
ask: "Are video games a menace to our society?"

Forecast of Organization
and Development

Today I would like to spend five minutes
discussing with you the role of video games for
America's youth. The three main points that I
intend to cover are how the video game phenomenon
began, the types of video games that are most
popular at the moment, and a few of the effects that
the games have on individuals today.

286   Appendix C

Appendix D
The Speech of Definition

Chapter 7 on language examines the use of comparison, contrast, synonyms, antonyms, etymology, differentiation, operationalization, and experience to define a concept. The student speech in this appendix illustrates the speech of definition described at the end of chapter 7. Because the speech is intended as a brief example of defining skills, it has no formal introduction or conclusion. The speaker was expected to use at least three means of defining a concept. Those means are labeled in the marginal notes.

GEORGE*

George in its adjective form is a word which is unlikely to be found in any dictionary. It is a term which is known only to a limited group of people, but because the term signifies something to those individuals, it can be called a word.

George belongs to a group of adjectives which   Denotations
deal in colloquial use with social acceptability, or, more specifically, with what is fashionable. These adjectives fall into two categories: positive adjectives such as *chic*—meaning cleverly   Synonyms

*From a speech of definition delivered by Jana Milford in Fundamentals of Public Speaking, Iowa State University.

stylish or currently in fashion—and *cool,* and negative adjectives such as *gauche*—defined as lacking social experience or grace. A generalization which extends to words in both categories is that they are often misused. Most of the time one must rely on the situation and the tone of the speaker's voice to determine the intended meaning. *George,* correctly used, belongs to the latter set of adjectives, those suggesting negative characteristics.

Something which is "george" is not only currently out of style, but is also regarded as tasteless to the extent that it never should have been in style, that anyone espousing it would have been crazy. Most persons using the term *george* are aware that differences in taste are results of varied backgrounds and therefore they use *george* as an emphatic declaration of their opinion, not an objective evaluation.

An illustration would probably define the word best. I was shopping with my aunt one fine summer day when a woman in a lime green outfit strolled past. The woman was lime green from head to toe with a silky scarf, a polyester double-knit pantsuit, and vinyl pumps, all of different shades of that vivacious color. Admittedly, lime green might have been an acceptable color in the Paris of the sixties, and I have seen it used in frog costumes recently, but somehow it seemed out of place in the conservative Midwest during the subdued eighties. My aunt, without a trace of sarcasm in her voice said: "That is george."

Antonym

Connotation

Differentiation

Connotation

Experiential Definition

Appendix E
The Speech of Description

Chapter 7 suggests an application assignment in which the speaker describes a person, place, object, or experience using specific, concrete language, a diverse vocabulary, connotative and denotative meanings, comparisons, and a familiar item described in an unfamiliar way. The student who delivered the speech used in this appendix told about his hometown of Phoenix, Arizona, describing the transition from desert daytime heat to desert night. This application assignment is a brief demonstration of the student's powers of description and, therefore, has no formal introduction or conclusion. The marginal notes indicate the means he used in his description.

TRANSITION*

The heat cannot be escaped. As the sun beats mercilessly on the endless lines of automobiles, waves of shimmering heat drift from the blistering, black pavement, creating an *atmosphere of an oven* and making the minutes drag into eternity. The wide avenues only increase the sense of oppression and crowding as lane after lane clogs with rumbling cars and trucks. Drivers

Comparison with Oven

*From a speech of description delivered by Mark Dupont in Fundamentals of Public Speaking, Iowa State University.

who have escaped the heat of the sun in their air-conditioned cars fall prey to the heat of frustration as they *do battle* with stoplights and autos which have *expired* in the August sun. Valiant pedestrians *wade through the heat,* pausing only to wipe from their foreheads the sweat that stings their eyes and blurs their vision. It is the afternoon rush hour at its peak, Phoenix, Arizona, at its fiercest. The crawl of automobiles seems without end as thousands of people seek out their homes in the sweltering desert city.

Gradually, almost imperceptibly, the *river of traffic* begins its descent past the 100-degree mark; the streets become quieter and more spacious. The mountains enveloping the city begin to glow as their grays and browns awaken into brilliant reds and oranges. The haze which has blanketed the valley throughout the day begins to clear. The lines of buildings become sharper, their colors newer and brighter. The shadows of peaceful palm trees lengthen, inviting the city to rest. The fiery reds and oranges of the mountains give way to serene blues and purples. The water of hundreds of backyard swimming pools, which have been turbulent with the afternoon frolicking of overheated children and adults alike, calms and mirrors the pink and lavender dusk sky. The fading sunlight yields to the lights of homes and streets as the Valley of the Sun becomes a lake of twinkling lanterns reflecting the *sea of stars* above. The *inferno* is gone, forgotten. The rising swell of crickets and cicadas lulls the desert inhabitants into relaxation and contentment. The desert floor gives up its heat, cooling the feet of those who walk on it. The heat of anger and hatred for the valley dissipates, and in the hearts of the people who have braved another summer day in Arizona, there is only the warmth of love for their desert home.

Comparison with War
Comparison with Death

Unfamiliar Description

Comparison with River

Comparison with Sky and Sea and Hell

Appendix F
The Speech of Explanation

Chapter 9 on informative speaking contains an application assignment in which the speaker is directed to explain how something works, why something occurred, or how something should be evaluated. In the speech of explanation below, the student speaker explains diabetes, reveals what it is, how it affects a person, and what one can do about it.

A SWEET KILLING*

Everyone with a brother or sister is an expert on sibling warfare. My little blonde brother and I are no different. We have our share of fights. One of us always ended up crying—usually him. My mother prayed that we would both outgrow it, but my brother and I are still fighting. Only now what we are fighting is my brother's disease—juvenile diabetes.

According to the American Diabetic Association, another diabetic is diagnosed every sixty seconds.[1] Diabetes with all of its complications is regarded as the third leading cause of death in the

*From a speech composed by Lura Kaval in Communication and Persuasion, School of Interpersonal Communication, Ohio University.

United States. It claims over 300,000 lives annually. Diabetes can strike at any age: my brother is sixteen. Although incurable, diabetes can be controlled with early diagnosis.[2] Diabetes is a major health problem, but you can protect yourself with some precautionary measures such as regular visits to your physician.

Diabetes is an inability of the body to turn food into glucose, a simple sugar solution, which is responsible for producing energy. The hormone insulin is what makes this process possible. Insulin is produced in the pancreas. When the pancreas fails to produce the proper amount of insulin, the body is unable to process the food. The unprocessed sugar-energy is then released from the body through urination, for it can't be used.[3] Donnell Elizweter of the University of Minnesota and president of the American Diabetic Association states, "Early diagnosis and proper control under the supervision of a qualified medical team generally mean a diabetic will be able to live an active and productive life. The trouble is that two out of five diabetics either don't know they have it or choose to ignore it and don't receive proper medical attention."[4]

There are two different types of diabetes. If a person has juvenile diabetes, as my brother has, where the body creates no insulin supply, there are seven warning signs or symptoms. They include: (1) constant urination; (2) abnormal thirst; (3) unusual hunger; (4) rapid weight loss; (5) weakness/fatigue; (6) nausea/vomiting; and (7) craving for sweets. Juvenile diabetes is treated with direct insulin shots, a planned diet, proper exercise, and regular medical examinations.[5]

The second type of diabetes is maturity-onset diabetes. This is where the pancreas produces insulin, but (a) doesn't create enough insulin or (b) the body doesn't use what is made properly. The warning signals are: (1) slow to heal skin; (2) cramps in the legs and feet; (3) blurred vision; (4) genital rash; (5) men's impotence; (6) drowsiness; and (7) excessive weight.

Maturity-onset is treated by proper diet, exercise, and occasionally, by oral medication. Many diabetics never have any warning signs or symptoms and are diagnosed during an annual medical examination.[6]

There are several different kinds of tests that you can perform in your own home to help you monitor yours and your family's blood sugar. The first is a urine test. This test is performed by placing two drops of urine in ten drops of water and one Clentest tablet into a container and then shake. By matching the color of the solution to the colors on the side of the package, the amount of blood sugar can be determined. The normal reading is 120. There are also other test tapes, which just need to be dipped in a urine sample and then read.

The second test is a blood test, which is taken by placing a small drop of blood on the end of a test tape. The reading can be taken after the tape dries.[7] These tests are easy and safe and only take a minimal amount of time. These tests are rather inexpensive and are available at most drug stores. It is a small price when it comes to your family's well being.

These steps to monitor diabetes should be taken by every family to protect their loved ones. If these early detection measures aren't taken, someone you love could become another statistic before you know it. Half of juvenile diabetics face the possibility of death due to kidney failure. Diabetics are two-to-three times more likely to develop hardening of the arteries, stroke, and heart attack than are non-diabetics; and diabetics are fifty times as likely to develop blood vessel problems.[8]

Actress Mary Tyler Moore, comedian Dan Rowen, baseball player Jackie Robinson, and inventor Thomas Edison were diagnosed as diabetic[9]—and so was my little brother. But because we watch his diet, regulate his insulin, make sure he gets enough exercise and sees his doctor regularly, we are winning our fight. I encourage and strongly urge you to become aware of the warning signs of diabetes and to purchase and use the urine or blood tests regularly to monitor your family's blood sugar. It is also important that your family see a doctor regularly because some symptoms of diabetes can only be detected through a medical examination.

Diabetes causes too many deaths a year and robs too many people of the sight and the touch of their loved ones for you not to take these simple early detection measures. If more people took these precautions, we might not only win the fight but the battle too.

Endnotes

1. Wentworth and Hoover, "Students with Diabetes," *Today's Education* (March 1981), p. 42.
2. *Ibid.*
3. Covelli, Peter J. "New Hope for Diabetics," *Time* (March 8, 1981), p. 63.
4. Wentworth and Hoover, *Today's Education*, p. 43.
5. *Ibid.*
6. *Ibid.*, p. 44.
7. Wilkins and Odayle, "Sugar Sensor, Measuring Glucose Concentrations in the Body," *Science News* (September 5, 1981), p. 154.
8. Covelli, *Time*, p. 62.
9. *Ibid.*, p. 64.

Appendix G
The Speech of Demonstration

In Chapter 9 you read the instructions for the demonstration speech, one of five different kinds of informative speeches. Notice in the speech in this appendix that the speaker has to spend less time and effort describing the origins of her credibility because she shows the audience her credibility throughout the speech. The photos are provided to help you visualize what Donna was doing as the speech progressed.

BACK WALKOVERS IN GYMNASTICS*

How many of you have heard of Nadia Comaneci? How many of you have heard of Kurt Thomas? How many of you have seen gymnastics on television? How many of you have been to a gymnastics meet or exhibition? What you see in elite-level gymnastics are usually very different moves such as double-back somersaults or back-layout somersaults on the balance beam, among other things. Well, it takes a gymnast a long time to learn moves such as those. A gymnast has to learn strength, flexibility, coordination, and courage

*From a speech delivered by Donna Griffith in Public Speaking, School of Interpersonal Communication, Ohio University.

before she could even attempt a move such as a back-layout on the balance beam. I would like to show you some of the work that goes into learning gymnastics. It looks easy, but even the simplest skills require a lot of work. For example, I will use a back walkover, which is a basic skill, and show you how it is learned. I will show you what muscles need to be stretched, what flexibility is required, the preliminary moves, the back walkover itself, related moves, and then I will tell you how these skills are used in gymnastics.

Before you attempt anything in gymnastics, you must warm up. Make sure your clothes don't inhibit movement; leotards, shorts, tee shirts, and sweats are some of the best things to wear. In gymnastics, you use almost every set of muscles in your body, so it's important to stretch all of them. I always begin by stretching my arms and shoulders. Try arm circles backward and forward, up and down, and side to side. Then swing your arms around, pivoting at the waist; these are called windmills. To stretch your shoulders, grasp your hands behind you, turn your wrists out, and pull up. As you pull upward, lean forward and let the weight of your arms stretch your shoulders while you begin stretching your legs. Toe touches are really important, but it's also important that you pull gently to each leg; don't bounce because that isn't stretching at all. Next are butterflies. Sit on the floor with your feet together and your knees apart. Grab your ankles, push your knees down with your elbows, and pull down to the ground. Straddle stretches are important for flexibility. Straddle as far as you can, but make sure your knees and toes are pointing up and out. Pull down to each leg, then to the center, making sure to pull slowly. This next stretch is what I call hamstring stretches. Keep one leg straight on the floor while lying down and pull the other leg straight up and toward your head as far as you can. Do this for both legs. You can stretch your back by walking your hands down a wall or by lying on the floor and pushing up into a bridge.

There are some preliminary moves that you must be able to do before you even attempt a back walkover. You should be able to do the splits in at least one direction: right, left, or center. Flexibility is important to this move. Bridges are important. When you "bridge up," be sure to push simultaneously with your hands and feet. Some people don't, and they can't get up. You should try lifting one leg at a time, and then one hand at a time, off the ground. After a bridge, you should be able to do a backbend. A lot of people say they can do a backbend, and they'll go down, but they can't come up. Well, it's not a backbend unless you can begin and end standing. So begin standing with your arms overhead. Keep your weight on your feet while you're arching backwards and gradually shift some weight to your hands. Push off the floor with your hands and come back to a stand. Cartwheels are important because they teach you what it feels like to be upside down and supporting yourself on your hands. After cartwheels and backbends, you should master the front limber. It's a lot like a backbend, but it also involves a handstand. Begin standing, arms overhead, and kick into a handstand. Arch over, but don't throw your weight over, or you'll fall. Push up and end standing.

Now we're ready to do back walkovers. I consider form very important. Arms and legs should be straight, toes pointed whenever they're not on the floor, and legs split as much as possible. Begin standing, arms overhead. Keep your head up and look for the floor as you arch backwards. Extend one leg out (I'm left handed, so I use my left leg) with the toe pointed. Arch over, keeping your weight on your supporting leg while your lead leg moves higher. Look for the floor. As your hands touch the floor and your lead leg rises, kick off the floor with your supporting leg. Keep your arms straight so you don't smash your face. Step out and end standing. A more difficult back walkover begins with the lead leg off the floor.

There are other moves you can learn that are similar to back walkovers. A front walkover is a lot like a limber, except you step out of it. A front tensica combines a cartwheel with a front walkover, and it goes hand-hand-foot-foot. A back limber begins like a back walkover, but you bring your legs together in the air and down on the floor together. There are also back tensicas, which are back walkovers with one hand going down at a time, and back handsprings, which involve an arching jump backwards to your hands and a spring off to your feet.

Back walkovers are used in lower-level gymnastics as a part of a tumbling pass. You can see them in high school and lower-level meets. In higher levels, back walkovers are used as an artistic element in floor exercise and as connecting elements in beam routines. While a back walkover on the beam may be a major element in a high school routine, many elite gymnasts use it to begin a tumbling pass on the beam. A gymnast such as Nadia may begin with a back walkover, do two back handsprings, then dismount with a double twist from the beam.

I hope you now understand some of the work that goes into gymnastics. I showed you some of the flexibility required, some different moves and how they are done, and what back walkovers are used for in gymnastics. Gymnastics is meant to look easy, but it, in many ways, requires more strength and coordination than sports such as basketball and football. The gymnasts you see on television are probably stronger in proportion to their weight and size than any other athlete. So, the next time you watch gymnastics, instead of just being amazed, you hopefully can appreciate the work it takes to be a gymnast, and you may also recognize some of the moves I've shown you.

Appendix H
The Speech of
Investigation

In Chapter 9 you learned about the speech of investigation in which the speaker digs deeper than personal experience for information about an issue or an idea. The particular speech of investigation in this appendix was based on a personal experience that gave the speaker the incentive for discovering more about the issue and for sharing it with her audience.

RAISING THE DRINKING AGE NATIONALLY
TO TWENTY-ONE*

Legislators and concerned citizens have recently turned their attention to the issue of raising the national legal age for alcohol consumption to twenty-one. The reasoning behind this move is to lower alcohol-related traffic fatalities and reduce alcohol abuse among the youth of America. This speech will reveal why I am concerned with this issue and with what I was able to discover about it through my own investigation.

*From a speech composed by Diane Rettos in Communication and Persuasion, School of Interpersonal Communication, Ohio University.

My interest in the issue of the legal drinking age was first aroused when I was in high school. Our local bar had a Sunday night event which attracted nearly everyone in the eighteen-to-twenty-five-year-old set and anyone else who could find a fake ID. Customers paid $3.00 at the door and then drank as much 3.2% draft beer as they wanted.

On the Sunday night of the 4th of July weekend the summer I graduated from high school, my best friend died after the car in which she was riding plunged twenty-five feet over a cliff and landed on its top. Stacey's neck was broken; she died in the arms of the police officer who pulled her from the wrecked car. The twenty-year-old driver was going 65 miles per hour on a 35-mile-per-hour curve in the road. His perception had been distorted by $3.00 worth of 3.2% beer. My friend was dead at age seventeen.

This experience devastated me. I had nightmares about the accident for many months; I still cannot forget the senselessness responsible for her death. When the recent interest in the drinking age surfaced, I decided to do some research on alcohol-related traffic accidents among the eighteen-to-twenty-year-olds in states with different legal drinking ages. The facts are startling.

First let me provide some background information. The legal drinking age issue became widely publicized in the early 1970s. In 1971 the legal voting age was lowered from twenty-one to eighteen and at least eighteen states subsequently lowered their legal drinking age to eighteen. Two states in particular—Michigan and Massachusetts—then became very concerned when they experienced an alarming increase in alcohol-related accidents involving eighteen-to-twenty-year-olds.

After Michigan lowered its legal drinking age in 1972, a study conducted by the University of Michigan's Highway Safety Research Institute found a 17% increase in traffic accidents involving eighteen-to-twenty-year-olds and alcohol. According to the Michigan Department of

State Police, within six months after the law was passed on January 1, 1972, there was a 100% increase in alcohol-related accidents involving eighteen-to-twenty-year-olds compared to the same period in 1971.[1] Massachusetts reported that alcohol-related traffic fatalities involving teenagers nearly tripled after the drinking age was lowered in 1973.[2]

As a result of these types of studies, states began raising their drinking ages. Their statistics show the positive results. A followup study in Michigan after the drinking age was raised from eighteen to twenty-one showed a significant drop in accidents involving alcohol and eighteen-to-twenty-year-old drivers. Officials in Maine reported that after their drinking age was raised from eighteen to twenty in 1977, there was a ". . . 30% drop in arrests of 17- and 18-year-olds for drunken driving. . . ."[3] One fact that helps validate these studies is that there was no change in accidents involving twenty-one to forty-five-year-old drivers which suggests a direct correlation between the raised drinking age and the reduction of accidents with eighteen-to-twenty-year-old drivers.

Another reason behind raising the legal drinking age nationally is an effort to combat growing alcohol abuse among young people. Under present law in many states an eighteen-year-old high school senior can buy alcohol; too often that person will share the alcohol with younger friends. According to Ron Baily, Superintendant of Schools in Farmington, Maine, after the legal age for drinking was raised in 1977 from eighteen to twenty, the "drinking in schools isn't as flagrant as it was."[4] He says the illegality of drinking makes it easier to curtail the problem and that many students refuse to drink when it is illegal.

A national law raising the drinking age to twenty-one would eliminate the problem of young people driving to another state where the drinking age is lower. Some states have already developed regional cooperation on the drinking age issue. In

New England, for example, Maine and Massachusetts raised their drinking age to twenty, and the governors of neighboring states are beginning to express interest in the idea.

My research on the issue of the legal drinking age included the search for evidence on keeping the drinking age at eighteen. However, the evidence on this side of the issue is less compelling. Vermont, for instance, reported no significant increase in alcohol-related accidents when they lowered the drinking age to eighteen. However, Dr. Richard Douglass, who conducted a study for the University of Michigan's Highway Safety Research Institute, produced a graph that showed an increase of twenty deaths the year after Vermont lowered its drinking age.[5] It is possible that the state of Vermont found twenty deaths statistically insignificant, but probably the family and friends of the twenty dead persons would feel otherwise.

A frequently cited argument concerning the legal drinking age is the one that says if a person is old enough to vote, marry, and defend our country at eighteen, then that person is old enough to decide what and how much to drink. But facts and statistics indicate that substantial numbers of eighteen-to-twenty-year-olds have not made responsible decisions about drinking in the past. As Bertram H. Holland, Executive Secretary-Treasurer of the Massachusetts Secondary School Administrators Association, stated in an interview in *U.S. News & World Report*, ". . . is drinking before the age of 19, 20, or 21 a constitutionally protected right, or is it a privilege? . . . What we're dealing with here is a practical problem."[6]

My investigation into the issue of legal drinking age leads me to believe that college-age students should take a serious interest in this problem that affects us more than any other group. We should be the ones who find the facts and publicize them to others. The resulting changes in the laws could save our lives.

Endnotes

1. Richard L. Douglass, "The Legal Drinking Age and Traffic Casualties: A Special Case of Changing Alcohol Availability in a Public Health Context," *Drinking and Traffic Accidents—U.S.*, ed. Henry Weschler (Lexington, Mass.: D.C. Heath and Co., 1980), p. 93.

2. M. Beck and P. Malamud, *Newsweek* (April 2, 1979), p. 38.

3. Beck and Malamud.

4. Beck and Malamud.

5. Douglass, p. 104.

6. B. Holland and B. T. Cheney, *U.S. News & World Report* (April 16, 1979), pp. 61-62.

Appendix I
The Speech of Reasons

The speech of reasons is explained in chapter 10. The speech of reasons attempts to shape an audience's responses by presenting arguments and evidence—reasoning—to induce change in the audience. The student speech presented here assumes that many college students talk themselves out of an exercise program and tries to overcome that problem by examining the students' rationale and by providing reasons for change.

AEROBICS*

"The way I look at it, my heart is only going to beat a certain number of times, and I'm not going to waste some of my valuable heartbeats on aerobics."

"Well, I just can't afford aerobic exercise. I mean, it just takes too long. I've got to study and go to work, and I have an eight o'clock every morning. I just don't have the time."

"Hey, I'm only eighteen. My heart and lungs are in great shape. I don't need aerobics; that's for old people, and I'm nowhere near thirty yet."

*From a speech delivered by Mark Dupont in Fundamentals of Public Speaking, Iowa State University.

Why should we care about aerobic exercise? We're either too young, can't afford it, or don't want to "waste those valuable heartbeats." Too young? Autopsies done on American soldiers killed in the Vietnam War, young men whose average age was 22.1 years, revealed that 55% of them showed evidence of arteriosclerosis, a hardening of the arteries. Maybe we're not so young. Can't afford aerobics? Well, a program of aerobics does demand that we make time in our busy schedules to exercise regularly, but the time we devote to our bodies is an inexpensive alternative to spiraling medical costs we might have to face because of an unhealthy heart, circulatory system, and lungs. Insurance companies are now recognizing this fact in the form of discounts to policyholders who participate in exercise programs like aerobics. Maybe we can afford it after all. But what about those heartbeats? Well, there is no evidence that the number of times our hearts will beat is limited. What there is evidence of is that by strengthening the heart and improving the lungs and blood vessels, aerobic exercise can improve your health and perhaps increase your life span. Maybe it's time we learn something more about aerobics.

In 1968, when Dr. Kenneth Cooper published his book, *Aerobics,* he introduced to America an exercise program which has become so popular that aerobics is well on its way to becoming a household word. And as America becomes more interested in physical fitness and preventive medicine, more of us are being urged to participate in aerobic exercise. Ultimately, the decision on whether to do so is up to each of us. But to make such a decision, we need to have a general knowledge of what aerobics is.

Today, I'd like to acquaint you with what I call the three Ps of aerobics—its purpose, its program, and its profit, which I have learned through research on exercise. What you do with this knowledge is up to you, but knowing the purpose, the program, and the profit of aerobics will enable you to make a well-informed judgment of it and make you familiar with a program millions of Americans have made a part of their lives.

But first, a definition of *aerobics*. The word aerobic means "requiring air or oxygen." Aerobic exercises, or aerobics, are those that demand a long-term, relatively moderate use of oxygen. Unlike such anaerobic exercises as weightlifting which rely on oxygen stored in the muscles and create sporadic high/low demands on the heart and lungs, aerobic exercises increase heart and breathing rates to a steady, moderate level. Herein lies the purpose of aerobics: to strengthen the cardiovascular-pulmonary system—the heart, blood vessels, and lungs—through exercise which demands long-term, moderate use of oxygen.

The program to accomplish this end is basically simple. The choice of what exercise you will perform is up to you. A wide range of exercise or sports, from walking to baseball, rope-skipping to stair-climbing, are considered aerobic because of their long-term, moderate oxygen requirements. But their benefits differ. As you can see from this chart [student shows visual aid], running ranks higher than tennis in improving flexibility. Based on their overall effects on the cardiovascular-pulmonary system, running, swimming, bicycling, and walking (in that order) rank highest among the aerobic exercises.

For people over thirty-five, the first step in a program of aerobics should be a consultation with a doctor who can administer a stress test. Following this is the twelve-minute test which everyone should take. This test simply determines how far you can run, walk, swim, or cycle in twelve minutes, giving you a gauge of your overall fitness. The results are categorized from very poor to superior, depending on age and sex. From this point you begin to exercise from three-to-six times per week by following a program of progress given in charts in Dr. Cooper's latest book, *The Aerobics Way*. Under Dr. Cooper's system, points are given for the amount of weekly exercise. You begin by seeking a certain number of points per week gradually by—in the case of running—running farther, longer, or more times per week. Once into the program full swing, men should be earning thirty points per week; women should be earning twenty-four points per week. At this level of activity, steady progress will be made toward more efficient heart, blood vessels, and lungs.

This brings us to the profit of aerobics. While not all of the benefits are known, the book *Rating the Exercises* summarizes the benefits nicely: "your lungs will process more air with less effort; your heart will grow stronger and pump more blood with each beat; the number and size of the blood vessels carrying blood to the body tissues will be increased; tone of the blood vessels and muscles will be improved; and your total blood volume will increase."

Thus, a simple program of aerobics, made a permanent part of your lifestyle, will strengthen the cardiovascular-pulmonary system through regular exercise which requires long-term, moderate use of oxygen. And because your heart, lungs, and blood vessels are at work whether you're awake or asleep, running or sitting, giving a speech or listening to one, every aspect of your life is affected. So not only do you create a better body through aerobics, but a better life as well, and perhaps a longer one.

Bibliography

Cooper, Kenneth H. *The Aerobics Way.* New York: M. Evans and Company, 1977.

Fixx, James F. *The Complete Book of Running.* New York: Random House, 1977.

Kuntzleman, Charles T. *Rating the Exercises.* New York: William Morrow, 1978.

Appendix J
The Speech of
Opposition

Chapter 10 describes the speech of opposition in which the speaker uses argument and evidence to oppose a commonly held idea or an idea presented by another speaker. Notice how the speech in this appendix begins by arousing the interest both of men and women and then proceeds to forecast the topic and to relate the speaker to the topic. The speech attempts to shape the audience's attitudes by arguing for a change in the way men behave in our society.

LET'S LET MEN CRY*

Throughout all time, there have been many distinct differences between males and females. Some of these are more obvious than others. One difference that is very evident is the fact that males do not display emotion as women do. For some reason, in the beginning of time, someone decided that women should be free to express sadness, fear, anxiety, and concern. Men, although experiencing these very same emotions, were told that they must be suppressed. Except under extreme

*From a speech delivered by Dorothy M. Takacs in Communication and Persuasion, School of Interpersonal Communication, Ohio University.

circumstances, men are not supposed to cry, show fear, or feel sadness, even though they experience these emotions just as women do.

Our society has made it difficult for men. Forcing men, or anyone for that matter, to suppress feelings and emotions leads to several problems and concerns. Society, making men feel that they must act and be "macho," has done all of us a great wrong. From the time of birth, males are taught to act a certain way. The time has now come for this to stop. Society must allow men to become and express whatever they wish. Men, like women, should be given the freedom to express their emotions whenever they deem it necessary.

I have been interested in this topic for a long time and have done extensive reading on it. I believe now that I have enough evidence to convince you of the need for change. In the next few minutes, I would like to present some reasons why I think men have been treated unfairly by society. I will tell you how rewards and punishments have shaped their behaviors and of the negative outcomes of their behaviors, such as greater amounts of stress and lack of certain interpersonal skills. I will give you some facts and opinions to make each of you aware of this problem and encourage you to take the proper steps to insure that this male "myth" is not perpetuated.

To begin, we must first address the problem itself. An article in *McCall's* magazine pinpoints the problem by stating that although biology has something to do with it, we now have evidence that most of the differences between male and female behavior are learned. They are the product of how we are raised and socialized. One of the most important and evident of these learned differences is the way in which men and women deal with their feelings.[1] The typical boy is encouraged from early childhood to "act like a man." Research has revealed that boy babies are picked up less promptly and are held less often when they cry when compared to girl babies. Male children are often spoken to more harshly than their female

counterparts when exhibiting similar behavior. A
boy who is treated in this manner learns early to
suppress feelings of anxiety, fear, or pain. That
very suppression may discourage the expression of
other feelings as the boy matures, such as love,
joy, and excitement.[2] As you can see, the
suppression process begins at a very early age and
can lead to serious effects in later life.

While women are often rewarded for behavior such
as crying, men are almost always punished in some
way. This punishment can be physical or emotional.
For example, when a man and a woman have an argument
and the woman begins to cry, the man usually gives
in. The very act of his giving in to her behavior is
a reward to her because it either ends or postpones
the fight. When a man shows his emotions, he is
usually punished by a significant other who shows
disapproval of the action. When the man displays
behavior identical to that of the woman, the
responses and rewards are very different.

This difference between males and females is so
ingrained in our society and in our minds that,
despite all of the intentions, desires, and
efforts to do away with it, men who do venture out
to give free rein to their feelings may be met with
rejection from women and from other men who see
this behavior as a lack of masculinity.[3] Although
females claim that they want their men to be more
sensitive and emotional, they tend to avoid males
who exhibit those behaviors, seeing them as too
feminine.

McCall's magazine reported a recent study in
which males and females of similar age groups were
asked to rank their values in order from greatest
to least importance. Among the highest ranking
were companionship, love, satisfying work,
rewarding sexual and emotional relationships,
spiritual sustenance, financial security, and the
right to make personal decisions. Comparing men
and women, these values were ranked equally.
Authors Lasswell and Lobsenz conclude, "If men so
clearly share the same goals as women, it seems
likely that they will ultimately refuse to be
trapped by the myths that perpetuate men as

strong, silent types, untouched by fear, sadness, or uncertainty."[4] If males exhibit the same feelings as females, and research shows that they do, why are they not given the same choice and opportunity as females to let their emotions show?

Females have another advantage over males because they are free to allow themselves to exhibit emotion. Females are more able to discern the emotions of others because they have full use of both hemispheres of the brain, according to research. Males, on the other hand, use primarily the right half of their brains. The left half of the brain is responsible for the "verbal codes" we experience, such as anger, happiness, and sadness. The right half is responsible for the "imagery codes" such as vocal tones and visual images. In discerning the emotions of others, females have the advantage over males because of their ability to utilize both halves of their brains.[5] According to *Psychology Today,* "Since emotions are largely a part of the right hemisphere and men are discouraged from acknowledging their emotions, they may not build connections between hemispheres as women do."[6] Hence, because males are taught not to show emotions, they may be limiting themselves when it comes to relationships and understanding others.

Probably *the* most important reason for men to modify their behavior concerning expression of their emotions is stress. Many feel that there is a strong correlation between suppression of emotions and stress. The mere "bottling-up" of one's feelings can bring on the symptoms of stress. Although stress is a part of everyone's life, great amounts of stress can lead to exhaustion, illness, accidents, nervous breakdowns, and even heart attacks.[7] It seems obvious that if one has the opportunity to let out emotions, less stress will occur, and the individual will feel better.

Males have come a long way since earlier "macho" image days. According to an article in *Newsweek,* "Men are becoming more and more aware of how pointless and painful it can be to keep their emotions veiled."[8] Since this myth is beginning to change in our own lifetime, it is up to us to perpetuate the trend that it is okay for men to show their feelings. It is okay for men to cry. We all need to be aware of this as we bring up our own children, as we confront those males who are trying to break custom and show their emotions, and as we try to help those males who cannot cope with this drastic change. We need to teach our males proper skills and rewards rather than to punish their emotional behavior. This appeal goes out to both males and females. We all must strive for accomplishment of this goal.

To sum up what has been said: males are only hurting themselves when they continue to participate in the "macho" myth. Men can hurt their relationships with others, their perceptions of others, and can hurt themselves physically and psychologically. There is no good argument which supports the cultural "given" that males are not to show emotion; there are only arguments against it. We all have an obligation to the males in our lives and to the children of the future. Let us all be aware of the male myth, and let us all do our best to stop it from continuing.

Thank you.

Endnotes

1. Marcia Lasswell and Norman Lobsenz, "Why Men Can't Talk about Their Feelings," *McCall's* 105 (September 1978), p. 60-62.
2. Lasswell and Lobsenz, pp. 60-62.
3. Lasswell and Lobsenz, pp. 60-62.
4. Lasswell and Lobsenz, pp. 60-62.
5. Jack C. Horn, "Women's Ambidextrous Brains," *Psychology Today* 16 (March 1982), p. 23.
6. Horn, p. 23.
7. Hans Selye, M.D., "How to Master Stress," *Parents Magazine* 52 (November 1977), pp. 25-27.
8. David Gelman, "How Men are Changing," *Newsweek* (January 1978), p. 52.

Bibliography

Gelman, David. "How Men are Changing," *Newsweek* (January 1978), pp. 52-61.

Horn, Jack C. "Women's Ambidextrous Brains," *Psychology Today* 16 (March 1982), p. 23.

Lasswell, Marcia and Lobsenz, Norman. "Why Men Can't Talk about Their Feelings," *McCall's* (September 1978), pp. 60-62.

Selye, Hans, M.D. "How to Master Stress," *Parents* Magazine (November 1977), pp. 25-27.

Appendix K
The Speech of Action

Chapter 10 describes the speech of action in which the speaker seeks some overt behavioral evidence of effect from the speech. In the student speech in this appendix, notice how the speaker opens with a narrative approach to capture audience attention and how the speech addresses the advantages of being an organ donor, involves the commitment of the speaker, meets the objections of the audience, and seeks audience compliance.

GIVING YOURSELF: THE ORGAN DONOR*

In 1978 Robert McFall had a fatal blood and bone marrow disease. His only chance, his only hope for survival, was a marrow transplant. Robert's cousin, David Shimp, was that hope. Shimp was a perfectly matched marrow donor. However, Shimp refused the operation that would save his cousin's life even though the bone marrow would regenerate after giving it to McFall. Shimp never consented to be a donor for his cousin. Three weeks later, McFall died.[1]

*From a speech delivered by Lisa Schaffner in Communication and Persuasion, School of Interpersonal Communication, Ohio University.

Several months ago, a young girl was very close to dying. She needed a kidney transplant from a donor close to her own age if she were to survive. Unfortunately, no donors were available. Her only hope for survival was that someone would come along quickly to be her donor. Four-year-old Michael became that strand of hope. Michael was killed in a car accident. Upon his death, his parents donated his kidney to the young girl. The organ transplant was successful, and the young girl celebrated her fourth birthday two weeks ago.

These two stories demonstrate how organ transplants can determine the life or death of another person. In the first story, Robert McFall died for lack of a willing donor. In the second story, based on an actual case, an organ transplant saved another human being's life.

Increasing numbers of people are donating their body organs to individuals or to research institutions.[2] People are joining this movement as they become increasingly aware of the desperate need of donated organs. During the last ten years, millions of Americans have unselfishly pledged their organs for transplant when they die.[3] The movement to donate body organs gained favor a decade ago when Dr. Christian Barnard performed the first heart transplant. However, even with steady support, some persons harbor misconceptions about organ donation that have resulted in a shortage of organ donors.

I believe in doing something constructive about the shortage of organ donors. About a year ago I signed a Uniform Donor Card that wills, upon my death, any of my needed organs to a person who needs them. Why did I do this? The reasons why one should become an organ donor are very clear.

First of all, medical scientists are seriously short of organ donations to save the lives of those doomed by disease or accident. The National Kidney Foundation recorded 4,600 successful transplants in 1978.[4] Unfortunately, more than 15,000 persons needed kidney transplants.[5] The result: over 10,000 individuals were doomed to die for lack of available transplants. Those 10,000 would have had a chance to live if all of the people killed in car accidents that year had been organ donors.

A second reason for becoming a donor involves your family's need for comfort. According to Dr. Currier, director of transplantation at Georgetown University Hospital, relatives are comforted with the thought that the death of their loved one represents the beginning of life for someone else.[6] Dr. VanHook of the University of Minnesota Organ Donor Program adds that the donor's family has a chance to receive something positive from a loved one's death.[7] Becoming an organ donor, then, not only allows you to save the life of another individual, but also permits your family to find some meaning and comfort in your death.

In addition to the shortage of organs for transplants and the comfort of your family, a third reason for being a donor is that upon dying you have no further need for your body parts. Therefore, the donation of your organs to someone who is living and has a need for them seems both reasonable and natural. The dying person's need for your body organs far outweigh your need for those organs upon your death.

These three reasons strongly support the idea of becoming an organ donor and for signing a donor card. However, I can see that many of you have reservations regarding the donor transplant process. You probably have valid reasons why you think you cannot be a donor. Well, let me admit that originally I had many reservations about the donor process. However, I found that my reasoning was faulty and that my reasons for refusing to become an organ donor were based on misconceptions.

For example, one misconception is that donating an organ will result in a closed-casket funeral. This notion is simply untrue. Vernon Gambill, administrator of the Tissue Bank of the Naval Medicine Research Center in Bethesda, Maryland, says that painstaking efforts take place to avoid altering the donor's appearance.[8] Gambill adds that if the appearance of the donor's body is altered, meticulous reconstructive procedures restore the donor's appearance.

A second misconception is that donating your organs after your death violates religious beliefs. Christian Science is the only American religious group that opposes the practice of organ donation.[9] In fact, according to Moses Tendler, Ph.D., an orthodox rabbi who chairs the biology department of New York's Yeshiva University, if an individual is in a position to donate an organ to save another person's life, it is obligatory to do so, even if the donor never knows the beneficiary.[10] The Lutheran Church-Missouri Synod indicated its position with a recent resolution encouraging its members to sign organ donor cards.[11]

A third misconception about organ donation centers on the idea that donors must be in perfect health. This idea is not necessarily true. All organs for transplant must be healthy; however, the entire body of the donor does not have to be in perfect physical condition. For example, a paralyzed person could donate glands, blood vessels, cartilage, parts of the inner ear, and corneas. A blind person can donate a cornea if the cornea was not the cause of blindness. An accident victim can donate any body organ that was not injured in the accident that took his or her life. Clearly, the body does not have to be in perfect health for a donation that can save someone else.

A fourth and very common misconception involving organ donation is the idea that your decision to donate body organs is irreversible. Not true. Any individual who decides not to be an organ donor can simply destroy the donor card and notify the proper officials. The decision to become an organ donor is an important one. However, once made, the decision is not permanent. The decision can be changed at any time by the person who made it in the first place.

How do you become a donor? The steps involved are simple. You merely need to fill out and carry a Uniform Donor Card. The card is available from the American Medical Association, independent donor groups, organ associations, and many hospitals. In addition, forty-seven of the fifty states now provide space on or with the driver's license that declares you as an organ donor. Ours is one of those states. An individual can easily register with the Department of Motor Vehicles upon renewing his or her license. Signatures of two witnesses are all that is required to legalize the donor card on the back side of the driver's license.

Most of you appear to be over the age limit of eighteen; but if you are not, parents may sign the consent for minor children. As a donor, you can bequeath specific organs or donate all needed organs or parts for persons who need them. You are encouraged to inform relatives and the nearest of kin regarding your decision to donate. You should make your donation known in writing to your attorney and to relatives, so that your request can be honored.

Your decision to become an organ donor is a serious one. By becoming a donor, you can help alleviate the serious organ shortage, while providing life for a person who might otherwise die. Furthermore, by donating your organs upon your death, you can help your family adjust to your death and create in them some positive feelings about your death. The decision to become an organ donor is completely up to you. Make the choice for the life of others; make the decision and the commitment to become an organ donor.

Endnotes

1. "Do You Own Your Body?" *The Futurist* 15 (December 1981), p. 73.
2. "How Can You 'Will' Parts of Your Body?" *U.S. News & World Report* 85 (December 18, 1978), p. 72.
3. *Ibid.*
4. *Ibid.*
5. *Ibid.*
6. *Ibid.*
7. "Easing Shortage of Organs," *USA Today* 110 (October 1981), p. 16.
8. "Can You Be A Donor?" *Health* 14 (April 1982), p. 43.
9. *Ibid.*, p. 56.
10. *Ibid.*
11. *Ibid.*

Credits

Photographs

Chapter 1
Jim Shaffer: 5(top left); Jean-Claude Lejeune: 5(bottom left); Michael Hayman/Corn's Photo Service: 5(right); Bob Coyle: 8, 16.

Chapter 2
Mimi Forsythe/Monkmeyer Press Photo Service: 22; Jean-Claude Lejeune: 25; Dwight Cendrowski: 28; Louis Cremonie: 29; Robert Eckert/EKM-Nepenthe: 32.

Chapter 3
Jim Shaffer: 38, 42; United Press International: 40; Robert A. Walsh: 41; Jean-Claude Lejeune: 48; Emil Fray: 53.

Chapter 4
Jay Black: 62; Vivienne della Grotto: 65(left); John Messineo: 65(right); Rick Smolan: 74.

Chapter 5
Jean-Claude Lejeune: 78; H. Rogers/Monkmeyer Press Photo Service: 80; Frank Siteman/EKM-Nepenthe: 83; Jim Shaffer: 84; William Hensel: 99.

Chapter 6
Chris Grajczyk: 117; Jim Shaffer: 120, 123.

Chapter 7
Steve Meltzer/West Stock, Inc.: 142; United Press International: 146; Jean-Claude Lejeune: 149, 152.

Chapter 8
Jim Shaffer: 165; Cathy Cheney/EKM-Nepenthe: 167; Jill Cannefax/EKM-Nepenthe: 170; Dwight Cendrowski: 176; Michael Hayman/Corn's Photo Service: 181, 195.

Chapter 9
Jim Shaffer: 195; Jean-Claude Lejeune: 199; Rick Smolan: 204.

Chapter 10
United Press International: 225; Rick Smolan: 235; Robert Eckert/EKM-Nepenthe: 239; Jim Shaffer: 243.

Chapter 11	Jean-Claude Lejeune: 262, 271; Jim Ballard: 267.
Appendix G	Mark Rightmire: 296 and 297 (all).

Line Art

Chapter 3	Don Hedeman: 47, 49.
Chapter 4	Don Hedeman: 67.
Chapter 5	Don Hedeman: 100.
Chapter 6	Don Hedeman: 127.
Chapter 7	Don Hedeman: 141, 156.
Chapter 10	Don Hedeman: 228.
Chapter 11	Don Hedeman: 266.

Text

Chapter 8	Poetry on pp. 173–75 from *Smoke and Steel* by Carl Sandburg, copyright 1920 by Harcourt Brace Jovanovich, Inc.; copyright 1948 by Carl Sandburg. Reprinted by permission of the publisher.

Index